NAKED CITY

NAKED CITY

Sharon Zukin

THE DEATH AND LIFE

OF AUTHENTIC

URBAN PLACES

OXFORD

UNIVERSITY PRESS

OXFORD

UNIVERSITY PRESS

Oxford University Press, Inc., publishes works that further
Oxford University's objective of excellence
in research, scholarship, and education.

Oxford   New York
Auckland   Cape Town   Dar es Salaam   Hong Kong   Karachi
Kuala Lumpur   Madrid   Melbourne   Mexico City   Nairobi
New Delhi   Shanghai   Taipei   Toronto

With offices in
Argentina   Austria   Brazil   Chile   Czech Republic   France   Greece
Guatemala   Hungary   Italy   Japan   Poland   Portugal   Singapore
South Korea   Switzerland   Thailand   Turkey   Ukraine   Vietnam

Published by Oxford University Press, Inc.
198 Madison Avenue, New York, New York 10016
www.oup.com

First issued as an Oxford University Press paperback, 2011

Oxford is a registered trademark of Oxford University Press.

Library of Congress Cataloging-in-Publication Data
Zukin, Sharon.
Naked city : the death and life of authentic urban places / Sharon Zukin.
p. cm.
Includes bibliographical references and index.
ISBN 978-0-19-538285-3 (cl.); 978-0-19-979446-1 (pbk.)
1. City and town life—New York (State)—New York.
2. Urbanization—New York (State)—New York.
3. Community development, Urban—New York (State)—New York.   I. Title.
HN80.N5Z85   2009
307.1'4164097471—dc22   2009038248

9 8 7 6 5 4 3 2 1

Printed in the United States of America
on acid-free paper

Trish

For my students and for students of cities everywhere

Is the beginning of a given work its real beginning, or is there some other, secret point that more authentically starts the work off?
—Edward Said, *Beginnings*

CONTENTS

PREFACE

This is a good moment to take stock of recent changes in cities that we think we know well, changes that both surprise us in the daily routine of walking through our neighborhoods and contradict the images in television replays and earlier films noirs that we see in popular culture. *Naked City* is one of those films noirs, a black-and-white police thriller made in 1948 on the streets of New York, a film that tracks a murder suspect from Park Avenue to the Lower East Side and finally to an end with no escape in sight, high over the East River, on the Williamsburg Bridge. Realistic in its time, especially because it was filmed on location, *Naked City* contrasts the brute power of New York's skyscrapers with the cultural vitality of its streets and the everyday lives of the men and women who work in small shops and diners, drive taxis, clean offices, and solve crimes. "There are eight million stories in the naked city," the voice-over narrator famously declares. But he might just as well have said: It is these stories, these buildings, and these streets that create the authentic city of our lifetime.

Today this black-and-white city seems less permanent and less authentic than it did in 1948. During the past few years, cities have become sites of massive redevelopment, with bulldozers tearing down old buildings, giant shovels digging holes in the ground so other big machines can lay new foundations, and cranes popping up like push pins from the ground. Since 2008, though, a worldwide economic crisis has stilled the financial weapons of mass construction. More than a periodic bust in the real estate boom that fueled a global economic expansion, this crisis halted the ebb and flow of origins and new beginnings that continually wash over the city's shores—the ebb and flow of economic growth, immigration, and, most recently, gentrification.

Just before the crisis broke, New Yorkers were complaining about their disenchantment with the city. Too many favorite landmarks had disappeared, replaced by faceless towers. One neighborhood after another had lost its small scale and local identity. People who had been in place for what seemed like forever—tenement dwellers, mom and pop store owners, whole populations of artists and workers and people of color—were suddenly gone. In their place we found gentrifiers, cocktail bars, Starbucks, and H&M. Though realists dismissed these complaints as blatant nostalgia and pointed out that cities are constantly changing, cynics, who are often the most idealistic city lovers, insisted that New York was no longer "authentic." The city, they said, had lost its soul.

I am one of those New Yorkers. If I am not yet disenchanted, I too have been dismayed by the way the city has morphed from a lumbering modern giant to a smooth, sleek, more expensive replica of its former self. I have seen this not just as a gradual or even inevitable process of revitalization but as a determined, concentrated process of destruction, beginning in the 1980s and speeding up since then. I don't call my dismay nostalgia. I don't miss the street crime or heroin trade or graffiti-covered subway cars. I don't think that poor tenants should be condemned to live forever in old-fashioned apartments with bathtubs in the kitchen because the landlord won't build a bathroom. I do miss the look and feel of neighborhoods whose diversity was tangible in the smells and sounds of ethnic cooking, experimental art galleries and performance spaces, and faces and voices of men and women who came from everywhere to create the distinctive character of the streets.

I can still find these neighborhoods in Brooklyn, the Bronx, and Queens, where formerly Irish, Jewish, and Italian shopping streets are now multi-ethnic patchworks of Chinese, Russians, Latinos, and Pakistanis. The artists' district of SoHo, the East Village countercultural scene, and the indie rock area of Williamsburg have only moved to cheaper neighborhoods farther from Manhattan. Harlem has been upgraded and racially integrated. But the city's historic diversity of uses, local specializations, small stores, and cheek-by-jowl checkerboard of rich people, poor people, and people broadly in the middle has been submerged by a tidal wave of new luxury apartments and chain stores. Global investment firms have bought thousands of low-cost apartment houses and prepare to raise the rent or sell them as condos, driving out older and poorer tenants. The fertile urban *terroir* of cultural creation is being destroyed by the conspicuous displays of wealth and power typical of private developers and public officials who build for the rich and hope benefits will trickle down to the poor, by the promotions of the media who translate neighborhood identity into a brand, and by the tastes of new urban middle classes who are initially attracted to this identity but ultimately destroy it. These forces of redevelopment have smoothed the uneven layers of grit and glamour, swept away traces of contentious history, cast doubt on the idea that poor people have a right to live and work here too—all that had made the city authentic.

The rebuilding of public spaces since the 1980s shows signs of the same homogenizing forces of redevelopment. Like the World Trade Center site, which is partly a place of mourning and partly a spectacle for mass consumption, these spaces are funded by private money and focus on the two issues that became our preoccupations after 2001: shopping and security. Public parks that are now managed by private conservancies and shopping areas that are governed by Business Improvement Districts do enjoy cleaner streets and greater public safety. But we pay a steep price for these comforts, for they depend on forces that we cannot control—private business associations, the police bureaucracy, and security guard companies—signaling that we are ready to give up on our unruly democracy. This is another way the city loses its soul.

Walking around New York, I see people, streets, neighborhoods, and public spaces being upscaled, redeveloped, and homogenized to the point of losing their distinctive identity. Not all of them are historic places, for one of the city's main distinctions is that it nurtures a constant dialogue between the two faces of authenticity: between features that every generation views as "original" because they have been there throughout their lifetimes, and features that each new generation creates on their own. The tension between origins and new beginnings produces the desire to preserve the "authentic" city, which has been, since the 1960s, the goal of historic preservationists, and to develop centers of cultural innovation, which has become, since the 1980s, the goal of many who wish to find a magic motor of rapid commercial redevelopment. This tension has made New York more modern, more interesting, and also more vulnerable than it seemed when *Naked City* was filmed. It has also convinced me that the debate is far from ended between Robert Moses, New York's extraordinary public sector developer of parks, bridges, public housing projects, and highways from the 1930s to the 1960s, and the great urban writer and community organizer Jane Jacobs, who, with her neighbors and allies, fought Moses and won in the late 1950s. While Moses pushed to build the corporate city, Jacobs struggled to preserve the urban village.

Though Jacobs and her fellow community activists were able to stop Moses's plans to destroy significant parts of Lower Manhattan and replace them with highways and high-rise housing projects, the struggle between the corporate city and the urban village continues in our time. It is fought not only in terms of the bricks and mortar of new construction projects, but also in terms of which groups have the right to inhabit both old and new city forms. Who benefits from the city's revitalization? Does anyone have a right to be protected from displacement? These stakes, which the French social theorist Henri Lefebvre calls the right to the city, make it important to determine how the city's authenticity is produced, interpreted, and deployed.

Neither Jane Jacobs nor Robert Moses used the term "authenticity." Each would have thought it unnecessary or even misguided in the 1950s to apply it to their work. But the term has crept into popular language in the past few years, appearing in shop signs—right there on Fourteenth Street: "Red Mango: The Authentic Yogurt"—as well as in marketing strategies and cultural critiques. Claiming authenticity becomes prevalent at a time when identities are unstable and people are judged by their performance rather than by their history or innate character. Under these conditions, authenticity differentiates a person, a product, or a group from its competitors; it confers an aura of moral superiority, a strategic advantage that each can use to its own benefit. In reality, few groups can be authentic in the contradictory ways that we use the term: on the one hand, being primal, historically first or true to a traditional vision, and on the other hand, being unique, historically new, innovative, and creative. In modern times, though, it may not be necessary for a group to *be* authentic; it may be enough to claim to *see* authenticity in order to control its advantages.

If authenticity has a schizoid quality, it can also be deliberately made up of bits and pieces of cultural references: artfully painted graffiti on a shop window, sawdust on the floor of a music bar, an address in a gritty but not too thoroughly crime-ridden part of town. These fictional qualities of authenticity are not "real," but they have a real effect on our imagination of the city, and a real effect as well on the new cafés, stores, and gentrified places where we like to live and shop. Because the emergence of the term reflects the importance of our roles as cultural consumers who consume the city's art, food, and images and also its real estate, authenticity becomes a tool, along with economic and political power, to control not just the look but the use of real urban places: neighborhoods, parks, community gardens, shopping streets. Authenticity, then, is a cultural form of power over space that puts pressure on the city's old working class and lower middle class, who can no longer afford to live or work there.

But authenticity could become a potent tool to combat the recent negative effects of upscale growth if we redefine it as a cultural right to make a permanent home in the city for all people to live and work. This does not mean the end of struggles over who controls urban spaces, struggles between gentrifiers and long-time residents, between Business Improvement Districts and community organizations, or between a mayor who wants to build big, in the style of Robert Moses, and historic preservationists and community activists who protest this kind of development, in Jane Jacobs's way. Yet the right to produce authentic places in both senses, historically old and creatively new, offers an alternative to the kind of growth that pushes many groups out. Claiming authenticity can be a means of gaining ownership for *any* group.

This view updates the examination of culture and capital in New York City that I began in my earlier books, *Loft Living* and *The Cultures of Cities*. Today I have a longer perspective for looking at the changes those books describe, especially the emergence of culture as both a strategy and a theme of urban redevelopment and the rise of the symbolic economy of art, finance, food, and fashion that has done so much both to nourish and to destroy the city's distinctive cultures. Some readers may feel uncomfortable with the growing prominence of culture in this view along with my focus on the apparently elitist concept of authenticity. But a concern with authenticity need not neglect the forces of power. I argue that we cannot consider power to control urban spaces, usually seen as the economic power of capital investors and the legal power of the state, without considering the cultural power of the media, including new media such as wikis and blogs, and that of consumers' tastes. All of these factors now shape the struggle to control the city's future.

For the past five years my students and family have had to live with *Naked City* as both an organizing vision and a topic of conversation. My students have probably done better with it—or maybe I just want to think so, for after all, they had less choice. This book could not have been written, though, without the valuable help of Valerie Trujillo, my research assistant at the City University Graduate School for the first few years, who followed up methodically on my every wild inspiration and kept our work on track; of the informal research group of graduate students who worked faithfully with me on boutiques and gentrification in Harlem and Williamsburg, including, besides Valerie, Peter Frase, Danielle Jackson, Tim Recuber, and Abraham Walker; and of Kathleen Dunn, who carried out insightful interviews with the Red Hook food vendors and did additional research on the neighborhood. Andrew McKinney collected information on food programs in community gardens. Peter Frase and Colin Ashley made field trips to Williamsburg and Red Hook at odd hours of the day (and night). As a senior at Brooklyn College, Dmitri Chitov wrote a wonderful honors essay on different types of social capital in community gardens that helped to clarify my thoughts. As a graduate student, my colleague Tamara Mose-Brown did independent research on a shopping street in a gentrifying neighborhood that also helped me to think through the cultural power of urban middle-class consumers. I would not have been able to expand those thoughts without the opportunity to teach, and learn from, all of these students. I am grateful to them, and hope I have not disappointed them. I also want to thank the PSC-CUNY Award Program, whose small, annual research fellowships kept our work going.

I am grateful to David McBride, my editor and friend, who has been persuaded by this book's argument from the beginning. Dave brought his broad knowledge of politics and culture, and his specific experience of some Brooklyn neighborhoods, to his editorial duties, teaching me as much as I have tried to teach him. Niko Pfund, my publisher, has shown the graciousness and love of books that I thought disappeared with the great publishers of the past. Production editor Jessica Ryan has been a voice of sanity at trying times. I am glad that *Naked City* found a place in this family.

Within my own family I continue to rely on the photographer's eye of Richard Rosen and the critic's eye of Elisabeth Zukin Rosen. I have tried to press them into service more times than I would like to admit, though they would be the first to point out that I don't always follow their advice. I should tell those readers who last met Elisabeth in *The Cultures of Cities* that, now a college student, she no longer "plays museum." But when she walks with me through the Lower East Side, noting new boutiques and luxury apartments, or travels with me to the Red Hook ball fields to eat empanadas, she shows a true appreciation of the city.

I was able to try out parts of my argument in articles published during the past few years. Sections of chapters 1 and 8 appeared in "Reading *The Urban Villagers* as a Cultural Document: Ethnicity, Modernity, and Capital," *City and Community* 6, no. 1 (March 2007): 39–48; "Consuming Authenticity: From Outposts of Difference to Means of Exclusion," *Cultural Studies* 22, no. 5 (September 2008): 724–48; and "Changing Landscapes of Power: Opulence and the Crisis of Authenticity," *International Journal of Urban and Regional Research* 33, no. 2 (June 2009): 543–53; part of chapter 4 was published in an article written with Ervin Kosta, "Bourdieu Off-Broadway: Managing Distinction on a Shopping Block in the East Village," *City and Community* 3, no. 2 (June 2004): 101–14. Any errors that remain despite this exposure are, of course, my own.

NAKED CITY

Introduction

The City That Lost Its Soul

It was a story of origins—a creation story, in fact—a tale about the modern rage for perpetually new beginnings, fresh starts and makeovers; in short, a story about the genesis of genesis.
—Herbert Muschamp, *New York Times,* February 28, 2007

In the early years of the twenty-first century, New York City lost its soul. Some people doubt that the city ever had a soul, because New York has always grown by shedding its past, tearing down old neighborhoods and erecting new ones in their place, usually in a bare-faced struggle for financial gain. Others just shrug because, today, all big cities are erasing their gritty, bricks-and-mortar history to build a shiny vision of the future. Beijing, Shanghai, and other Chinese cities are clearing out the narrow, rundown alleys in their center, removing longtime residents to the distant edges of town, and replacing small, old houses with expensive apartments and new skyscrapers of spectacular design. Liverpool and Bilbao have torn down their abandoned waterfronts and turned aging docks and warehouses into modern art museums. In London, Paris, and New York artists and gentrifiers move into old immigrant areas, praising the working-class bars and take-out joints but overwhelming them with new cafés and boutiques,

The "timeless" urban village: Elizabeth Street, NoLIta, 2001. Photograph by
Richard Rosen.

which are soon followed by brand-name chain stores. A universal rhetoric
of upscale growth, based on both the economic power of capital and the
state and the cultural power of the media and consumer tastes, is driving these changes and exposing a conflict between city dwellers' desire for
authentic origins—a traditional, mythical desire for roots—and their new
beginnings: the continuous reinvention of communities.[1]

To speak of a city being authentic at all may seem absurd. Especially in
a global capital like New York, neither people nor buildings have a chance
to accumulate the patina of age. Most residents are not born there, neither
do they live in the same house for generations, and the physical fabric of
the city is constantly changing around them. In fact, all over the world,
"Manhattanization" signifies everything in a city that is *not* thought to be
authentic: high-rise buildings that grow taller every year, dense crowds
where no one knows your name, high prices for inferior living conditions,
and intense competition to be in style. Lately, though, authenticity has

taken on a different meaning that has little to do with origins and a lot
to do with style. The concept has migrated from a quality of people to
a quality of things, and most recently to a quality of experiences. *Time*
magazine named authenticity one of the ten most important ideas of 2007,
partly because of the promotional campaign of two marketing gurus,
James H. Gilmore and B. Joseph Pine II, whose work emphasizes this journey from things to experience, and partly because of the anxiety fueled
by social theorists such as Walter Benjamin and Jean Baudrillard, who
say that, through technology, imitation of novelty, and the normal hype
of consumer culture, experience is increasingly seduced by appearances.
Viewed through either of these lenses, a city is authentic if it can create
the *experience* of origins. This is done by preserving historic buildings and
districts, encouraging the development of small-scale boutiques and cafés,
and branding neighborhoods in terms of distinctive cultural identities.[2]

Whether it's real or not, then, authenticity becomes a tool of power.
Any group that insists on the authenticity of its own tastes in contrast
to others' can claim moral superiority. But a group that imposes its own
tastes on urban space—on the look of a street, say, or the feeling of a

neighborhood—can make a claim to that space that displaces longtime residents. To be sure, a group that can afford to pay higher rents can also be reasonably sure their claim will win: artists displace manufacturers in live-work lofts, and are displaced in turn by lawyers and media moguls who buy these lofts as luxury condos; a gourmet cheese store or quirky coffee bar replaces a check-cashing service or take-out food shop, and is in turn displaced by a chain store that pays many thousands of dollars each month for the location. But this power over space is not just financial. Even more important, it's *cultural* power. New tastes displace those of longtime residents because they reinforce the images in politicians' rhetoric of growth, making the city a 24/7 entertainment zone with safe, clean, predictable space and modern, upscale neighborhoods. The sociologist John Hannigan says that the more spectacular new urban cultural spaces—a Disneyfied Times Square or a hipster district of art galleries, performance spaces, and vegan cafés—promise the safe excitement of "riskless risk." I prefer to think about a more ordinary domestication by cappuccino, with wilder places getting an aesthetic upgrading by the opening of a Starbucks or another new coffee bar. The tastes behind these new spaces of consumption are powerful because they move longtime residents outside their comfort zone, gradually shifting the places that support their way of life to life supports for a different cultural community. Bistros replace bodegas, cocktail bars morph out of old-style saloons, and the neighborhood as a whole creates a different kind of sociability. Against the longtimers' sense of origins newcomers pose their own new beginnings.[3]

Who can say, though, that these new spaces are not authentic? New stores and new people produce new urban *terroirs,* localities with a specific cultural product and character that can be marketed around the world, drawing tourists and investors and making the city safe, though not cheap, for the middle class. It wasn't always this way. Life in the original "urban village" of ethnic and working-class neighborhoods before the 1960s was a re-creation of tradition. In the gentrified and hipster neighborhoods that have become models of urban experience since then, authenticity is a consciously chosen lifestyle and a performance, and a means of displacement as well.[4]

The desire for an authentic urban experience began as a reaction to the urban crisis of the 1960s, when American cities were routinely described as hopeless victims of a fatal disease. They were losing their more affluent and ethnically whiter families to the suburbs. Public schools, parks, and streets were shoddy and uncontrollable. Elected officials worried about a growing budget gap between the services they were required to provide and the taxes they could collect from a poorer population, and a disastrous perception gap between the central city's image of glamour and sophistication and neighborhoods that were being abandoned by landlords, residents, and businesses.

In truth, cities were losing their competitive advantage. Government policies after World War II helped suburbanites more than city residents, and white middle-class families who could afford it, often with U.S. government–backed mortgage loans, moved outside cities to larger homes, backyards, and better schools. Corporate headquarters also deserted the city for the suburbs, where they spread out along the highways to create sprawling new business districts surrounded by parking lots. Bankers invested in new steel and auto plants in Italy, Korea, and Brazil, and airplane, clothing, and electronics factories sought large shop floors and cheaper labor first in the suburbs and then overseas. Working-class neighborhoods in Detroit, Chicago, Philadelphia, and Boston, as well as in New York, were caught between postwar optimism about social progress and an inability either to understand or to confront their postindustrial fate.

With public officials beginning to believe that cities suffered from an image crisis, they reached out to business executives to forge a new strategy for growth. Cities would target investors and visitors—people with money—by rebuilding the center and making themselves look as attractive as suburbs. Beginning in the 1970s, developers of downtown shopping centers turned derelict industrial and waterfront land into profitable attractions to compete with suburban malls. Culture—the theaters and museums that display a city's unique creative product—pursued a wider audience outside the urban center. In the 1980s, with financial firms and the real estate industry playing leading roles in reshaping the local economy, especially in global cities like New York, cultural districts, ethnic tourist zones, and artists' lofts presented a clean image of diversity for mass consumption. By the 1990s the commercial success and global media prominence of some of New York's neighborhoods, notably SoHo and Times Square, seemed to justify the rhetorical promise of their new beginnings.[5]

But city officials forgot about the city's origins. "Origins" refers not to which group settled in a neighborhood earliest; that would be difficult if

not ridiculous to prove, since every city is built up of layers of historical migrations. "Origins" suggests instead a moral right to the city that enables people to put down roots. This is the right to inhabit a space, not just to consume it as an experience. Authenticity in this sense is not a stage set of historic buildings as in SoHo or a performance of bright lights as at Times Square; it's a continuous process of living and working, a gradual buildup of everyday experience, the expectation that neighbors and buildings that are here today will be here tomorrow.[6]

A city loses its soul when this continuity is broken. It begins with little changes you suddenly notice in your own neighborhood. The local hardware store or shoe repair shop closes down overnight; steel gates shutter the window where cans of Rustoleum and wrenches lay in the sun; a "For

Rent" sign replaces the tattered Cat's Paw logo for leather lifts and the ancient, hand-lettered sign "Not Responsible for Shoes Left Over 30 Days." Laundromats disappear, for the neighborhood's new residents are buying two small apartments or an entire four-story house, knocking down the walls to make bigger rooms and installing their own washers and dryers. The sports bar where the Italian owner always had the TV tuned to a soccer match yields first to a video store and then to a Starbucks. The serial repetition of small stores that defined the city's neighborhoods for so long is gradually broken up, imploded by new investment, new people, and "the relentless bulldozer of homogenization."[7]

These changes are not only visible, they reshape our everyday routines. Some are welcome, like savoring a latte instead of a scorched black caffeine brew, though they may be costly, like paying double the old price for the latte or triple the old price for a pair of rubber lifts because the new shoe repair shop several blocks away has to pay a higher rent. Some changes make you feel like a stranger in the neighborhood where you have lived for years, when the local drugstore where the pharmacist knows your medications is replaced by a Duane Reade or CVS and you never see the same cashier twice. "So complete is each neighborhood," E. B. White wrote in 1949, "and so strong the sense of neighborhood, that many a New Yorker spends a lifetime within the confines of an area smaller than a country village. Let him walk two blocks from his corner and he is in a strange land and will feel uneasy till he gets back."[8]

It isn't only the stores; the people are different too. In some neighborhoods artists, actors, computer software writers, and musicians—the hipperati—are hanging out in sidewalk cafés, eating brunch at 2 P.M., and heading off at midnight to performance spaces in warehouses and music bars. In other areas of the city, editors, professors, lawyers, and writers are wheeling baby strollers, talking on cell phones, and window-shopping in small design shops; these "bourgeois bohemians" prefer to lead a comfortable life, especially after they have children, but don't want to live like their parents do—especially not in the suburbs—and don't mind a little dirt on the streets as long as they feel safe. In the areas where hipsters and gentrifiers live there's a new cosmopolitanism in the air: tolerant, hip, casual. And that isn't bad. But little by little the old ethnic neighborhoods they have moved into are dying, along with the factories where longtime residents plied their trades and the Irish bars, Latino bodegas, and black soul food restaurants where they made their homes away from

New luxury construction on the Bowery, 2008. Photograph by Richard Rosen.

home. The people who seemed so rooted in these neighborhoods are disappearing.

As recently as the 1980s many of these areas still looked shabby; houses were abandoned, vacant lots were covered with garbage and worse. "There goes the neighborhood" pointed to a downward slide from modest shops and homes to poor tenants, high crime rates, and gritty streets. Now it's the Bowery transformed from Skid Row to a boulevard of boutique hotels, Harlem with cafés, Williamsburg with condos on the waterfront. We often call these changes gentrification because of the movement of rich, well-educated folks, the gentry, into lower-class neighborhoods, and the higher property values that follow them, transforming a "declining" district into an expensive neighborhood with historic or hipster charm.

At first these changes are limited to the oldest *ur*-neighborhoods close to the center of the city, where gracious brownstone or redbrick houses have fallen on hard times and where artists and writers, and occasionally lawyers and professors or museum curators, indie band members, and graphic artists, come to live, looking for the good life at a moderate price, as the sociologist Pierre Bourdieu says about the aspirational consumption of people who work in cultural jobs. This could be Greenwich Village in the 1920s, Brooklyn Heights after World War II, Park Slope in the 1960s, SoHo after 1970. Some years later, though, depending on how generously financial markets have rewarded big investors and their advisors, property values rise all over the city, and the new beginnings gradually spread from the center to other neighborhoods. In gentrified areas the merely affluent upper middle class sell their nicely restored houses and apartments to the superrich. The British geographer Loretta Lees calls this process "super-gentrification." But when one neighborhood after another goes upscale and new residents are not just fixing up old houses and lofts but also moving into newly built luxury condos and mom-and-pop stores are replaced by bank branches, trendy restaurants, and brand-name chains, we're looking at more than a single trend of gentrification. Neil Smith calls this "gentrification generalized." I think that it is really a broad process of re-urbanization, with changes that loosen the grip of old industries and their ways of life and expand the space taken up by white-collar men and women and their preoccupation with shopping and other kinds of consumption; bringing new residents, their tastes, and their concerns into the city's mix; and creating not just an economic division but a cultural barrier between rich and poor, young and old. This is what happens when a city loses its soul.[9]

Ours is not the first generation of city dwellers to mourn a loss of origins. In *Gotham* Edwin Burrows and Mike Wallace point out that New Yorkers have had to deal with the erosion of the city's physical fabric at least since the great building boom of the mid-nineteenth century. Manhattan is a "modern city of ruins," the *New-York Mirror* wrote in 1853. "No sooner is a fine building put up than it is torn down." *Harper's Monthly* declared, "A man born in New York forty years ago finds nothing, absolutely nothing, of the New York he knew." In the early 1900s, sailing into New York Harbor from the old world of Europe, the novelist Henry James added his voice to these laments. He deplored the tall buildings—at that time, ten stories high—towering over the spire of Trinity Church near Wall Street. Despite the solid steel and granite of their construction, the baby skyscrapers looked to his eyes like temporary place-holders on the crowded "pincushion" of Lower Manhattan. They badly need a sense of history, James wrote. Unlike "towers or temples or fortresses or palaces"—all powerful reminders of a city's ancient origins—New York's tall buildings lacked "the authority of things of permanence or even of things of long duration."[10]

With these words Henry James sounded themes that resonate to this day: hostility to overbuilding, desire to hold back rapid change, and distaste for an aesthetic of standardization—distaste for a city, and a neighborhood, that looks like any other. Like the mid-nineteenth-century Parisians who mourned the way Baron Haussmann rebuilt that city over its medieval origins, James drew an aura of regret around the landscape of memory and feeling that was being destroyed by a surge of new construction fueled by economic growth and the flexing of muscle by entrepreneurs who ran the steel industry, railroads, and banks. Less consciously he also bore witness to the arrogance of an entire era of modernization and to the arrogance of state power when politicians help real estate developers to change the use of prime parcels of urban land in order to make money.

Henry James's critical themes were submerged first by prosperity and easy credit for construction, and then by the Great Depression and the Second World War. The need to divert capital to other needs imposed a thirty-year lull on the tearing down and building up of all U.S. cities. After World War II ended, however, peacetime conversion of the economy brought new investment in highways and suburban housing and, with pressure from local public officials and developers, in rebuilding the centers of cities, which by now looked tired and worn in contrast to the new ranch houses and shopping malls of Levittown and the San Fernando Valley and failed to project an impressive image of the United States as a global power. During the Great Depression business leaders and national lobbying groups for the real estate industry had continually called for government investment to remove the "blight" of cheap tenements, entertainment streets, and single-room-occupancy hotels that clustered on a derelict Skid Row around the big cities' central marketplace of city hall, bus station, and department stores. Unlike President Franklin D. Roosevelt, they didn't call for adequate housing for the urban poor. But after the war local business leaders and elected officials were willing to take federal money to build new public housing and government centers, as long as they could also tear down neighborhoods where the urban poor and working class lived to build corporate office towers, luxury housing, cultural centers, and hotels. Title I of the federal Housing Act passed by Congress in 1949 included a provision for funding these projects, as well as the expansion of urban universities, and it enabled developers and public sector entrepreneurs to make the city grow as they desired.[11]

This vision of the city provoked opposition and even outrage. Henry James's critical themes reemerged, but from a far more populist point of view. He had never liked the immigrants, namely Jews, who in his time thronged the streets of the tenement districts of the Lower East Side. Critics of urban renewal, though, added what we would now call positive goals of affordability and diversity to James's hostility to overbuilding.

In Boston the sociologist and urban planning researcher Herbert Gans wrote a stunning indictment of how local elites needlessly destroyed the Italian working-class district of the West End, coining the term "urban village" to depict the close-knit, family-based, ethnic community that was displaced in the name of slum clearance. Even more famously, in New York the journalist and community activist Jane Jacobs published a call to arms against the fatal machinery of modern urban planning, which brought in the bulldozers and "cataclysmic money" of urban renewal projects to destroy old, but still vibrant, neighborhoods. By the early 1960s, with urban renewal moving forcefully ahead, its opponents developed a modest, street-level defense of urban authenticity to confront the arrogance of both modernization and state power, which threatened to sweep away people as well as buildings.[12]

The men and women who spoke up for authenticity in the 1960s were a mixed group socially, culturally, and politically, and they argued for somewhat different visions of the city. They included three different groups: historic preservationists, often, like Henry James, members of the upper class who deplored the destruction of old buildings that embodied urban memory; community preservationists, political activists and socially conscious intellectuals such as Jacobs and Gans, who defended the right of all poor people not to be displaced by new building projects, and especially opposed "Negro removal," the targeting of those who, because of racial discrimination, were least able to move to new homes in the suburbs; and gentrifiers, who since the 1940s had begun to move into poor neighborhoods, buying and restoring late nineteenth-century houses with "great symbolic value" to nurture an urban lifestyle untainted by modernity. As democratic reformers, gentrifiers came into conflict with the white ethnic groups on whom old-style Machine politicians relied, while fearing, and being feared by, their poorer black and Latino neighbors.[13]

Membership in these three groups—historic preservationists, community preservationists, and gentrifiers—often overlapped. This gave them not only a critical mass but also a critical position in the interconnected networks of politics, media, and design. Their successful campaigns led to a series of important public policy changes that made Jane Jacobs's vision of urban authenticity more prominent. First, New York, followed by other cities around the world, passed local historic preservation laws; these established official landmarks preservation agencies and a system of public hearings to oversee, and sometimes prevent, the tearing down of old buildings and

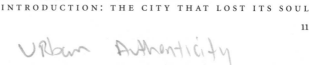

districts. During the 1970s historic landmark designations enabled both the majestic Beaux Arts Grand Central Terminal and the rundown, industrial loft buildings of SoHo to survive developers' plans to demolish them. Second, planners of high-rise public housing projects gradually shifted to designs for low-rise buildings that were less visibly warehouses for the urban poor. By the early 1970s liberal opposition to the aesthetics of "the projects" and their social concentration of poverty joined a conservative movement to eliminate state spending for public housing, which effectively ended large-scale efforts to keep the urban poor in the central city. Eliminating plans for the tall towers and sprawling campuses of public housing projects minimized their potential as both physical and symbolic barriers to upscaling, while reducing the potential power of the poor—in terms of numbers—to oppose gentrification. A third change concerned gentrifiers such as Jane Jacobs herself. While they increased in numbers, they developed into an influential political force and, less expected but even more important, into an image-maker for the city. Neighborhoods like the West Village, Brooklyn Heights, and Park Slope created a model of aesthetically interesting, inner-city living that by the 1980s would attract and retain a post-postwar middle class of professionals, artists, and intellectuals—a "creative class" before the name was invented. These significant changes nonetheless left a gap between celebrating the authenticity of historic houses and acknowledging the authenticity of the lower-class families who lived in them.[14]

Jane Jacobs seemed to bridge this gap by praising both the city's social diversity and its physical fabric. Arguing against modern planning strategies that favored tall towers surrounded by empty parks, wide streets built for auto traffic rather than pedestrians, and large-scale development by demolition and new construction, Jacobs emphasized the authentic human contacts made possible by the city's old and unplanned messiness. She praised crowded sidewalks for keeping people safe, shabby buildings with low rents for incubating small new businesses, and mixed uses—housing alongside stores, offices, and manufacturing—for exerting greater aesthetic appeal than the "dullness" that was so palpable in homogeneous corporate office districts, public housing projects, and residential suburbs. The much-quoted set piece in the first section of Jacobs's best-selling 1961 book, *The Death and Life of Great American Cities*—an hour-by-hour description of the "intricate sidewalk ballet" on Hudson Street, outside her window—dramatizes the neighborly interdependence of local shopkeepers, housewives, schoolchildren, and customers at the corner bar, all patron

saints of social order in the city's neighborhoods who were either scorned
or ignored by the powerful forces that controlled urban renewal.

Jacobs also argued for authenticity as a democratic expression of origins, for a neighborhood's right, against the decisions of the state, to determine the conditions of its own survival. *Death and Life* raised an alarm
against the arrogance of state power, especially as it was personified by
Robert Moses, the larger-than-life administrator who headed the most
important state and city redevelopment agencies in New York City from
the 1930s to the 1960s. In these positions, supported by political leaders
on all levels of government, Moses oversaw the planning and building
of a huge number of public works, from public beaches and swimming
pools to bridges, highways, and parks, as well as public housing projects.
These projects modernized New York City in many ways: linking it to the
national highway system so that cars and trucks could move goods and
workers around the region, replacing shoddy tenements with new apartment houses, and creating green space and playgrounds amid thousands of
acres of asphalt. As residents of many neighborhoods discovered, though,
public works could exact a heavy price from those who lived near them.
Moses insisted on placing new highways in the middle of active neighborhoods, destroying homes and parks if they stood in the way, and refused to
pay attention to community residents' pleas or complaints. Though other
public sector administrators were equally intolerant of opposition and also
controlled massive amounts of government funding, Moses had a bigger
public image and a willingness to directly antagonize anyone who dared
to criticize his decisions. He became the supreme villain who threatened
both the neighborhoods' small-scale social networks and the city's diverse
historical character—a twentieth-century Baron Haussmann who would
destroy all reminders of New York's uneven origins in his pursuit of sanitized, efficient new beginnings.[15]

Jacobs, her neighbors, and her allies managed to bring down Robert
Moses by defeating three of his projects that would have changed the physical fabric of Lower Manhattan. These conflicts began in the early 1950s,
when Greenwich Village residents protested Moses's plan to build a road
through Washington Square Park, a fairly small green space in the heart
of the Village, not far from where Jane Jacobs lived. Led by Shirley Hayes,
whose children played in the park, and joined by Jacobs and her family and
by other writers and critics who lived in the community, a grassroots movement challenged Moses by collecting names on petitions, writing editorials

addressed to local government officials, and loudly disrupting city planning meetings. Moses tried to insult the activists, especially the women, by calling them mere "mothers" who had neither experience nor expertise in city planning. But when the mothers won the support of the city's Democratic Party political boss Carmine De Sapio, who also lived in the Village, the road plan was voted down by the citywide Board of Estimate, and Moses suffered a stunning loss. A few years later, faced with similar grassroots opposition to his plan to build an expressway across Broome Street, which would have destroyed a large number of nineteenth-century loft buildings across a wide swath of the neighborhood that soon became known as SoHo, Moses suffered another big defeat at the hands of artists, historic preservationists, and the same Greenwich Village residents, including Jacobs, who had fought him on Washington Square Park. In the third battle, a plan to tear down old houses and warehouses near Jacobs's home in order to build high-rise, low-income public housing, Moses lost again.[16]

Robert Moses enraged people not just because of his arrogant manner or the architectural designs he chose; his use of Modernist urban planning principles struck deep into the heart of a traumatized liberal community. The Allies' bombing of Dresden, Berlin, Hiroshima, and Nagasaki and the German air attacks on London during World War II had shown how easy it was to destroy the historic heart of cities. Though postwar governments in the United States did not try to murder thousands of urban dwellers, they did aim to annihilate the material landscape of the past, and the same gut feeling of terror caused by the threat of the atomic bomb could be aroused by the rubble of districts razed for urban renewal. Even E. B. White, celebrating postwar New York as "both changeless and changing," wrote, "The intimation of mortality is part of New York now: in the sound of jets overhead, in the black headlines of the latest edition." And it wasn't only New York: "All dwellers in cities must live with the stubborn fact of annihilation."[17]

Less morbidly, but with no less sincerity, distaste for Modernism grew because the stark designs were cheapened and standardized after they were adopted on a massive scale as the dominant postwar architecture for buildings ranging from corporate headquarters and government offices to public housing projects. When every new building looked like the same big glass box, old redbrick buildings and cobblestone streets gained cultural distinction. Those who chose to put down roots in the old city identified with origins rather than with new beginnings; their choice signified

identifying w/ origins vs. new beginnings

rejection of the homogeneous mass culture of both the corporate city and suburbia. While this view looks backward to Henry James's aristocratic disdain of mass culture, it also looks forward to the downtown artists of the 1970s and 1980s, who celebrated the city's grit and grunge. But it speaks with special relevance to the political stalemate of the 1950s: rejecting the dominant Modernist landscape at that time struck a blow against political conformity. Middle-class liberals who had been silenced by McCarthyism found a voice and a place to protest by reclaiming the city's streets. Claiming to speak for urban authenticity was, in their case, a cry for democracy.

Defeating Robert Moses's plans did more than end his career; it changed the way new development was planned. Between the late 1950s and the early 1970s New York City voters transformed the approval processes for big development projects to require more public input. Both public sector and private sector plans now had to pass through a series of public hearings, beginning with land-use hearings at local community boards that were established in the 1970s as a result of the grassroots activism that challenged Moses's power, and moving up by stages to the City Planning Commission, City Council, and Mayor's Office. At least in theory the voice of the authentic city—a voice that speaks of origins rather than of new beginnings—would be heard.

During the next decade another cry for the "great symbolic value" of authenticity arose in a different form and in a younger generation. No less a product of its time than the conflict between Jane Jacobs and Robert Moses, the counterculture would also have a huge, though less direct impact on the shape and character of cities. By the beginning of the 1970s broad political protest expressed by radical youth movements against the Vietnam War, consumer society, and mainstream concern with social status had simmered down to an individual concern with lifestyle goals of liberation and personal authenticity, or what the sociologist Sam Binkley calls "getting loose."[18] While many advocates of a looser lifestyle abandoned cities to live off the land in rural communes, others moved into low-key urban neighborhoods where college students, artists, and workers, including Latinos and blacks, would tolerate, exploit, or grudgingly coexist with their bohemian ways. Some ex-hippies became entrepreneurs, selling drugs, psychedelic posters, and used clothing, and gradually the consumer products and spaces that went along with the hippies' looser lifestyle became visible symbols not just of a more interesting *way* to live, but of a more interesting *place* to live. Haight-Ashbury in San Francisco and the

East Village in New York marked spaces of social diversity and cultural experimentation; they also indicated how the counterculture's conflict with modernization could create excitement around a city's old neighborhoods. In a curious and unexpected way, the counterculture's pursuit of origins—by loosening the authentic self and bonding with the poor and underprivileged—opened a new beginning for urban redevelopment in the 1970s, alongside gentrification and gay and lesbian communities.[19]

The allure of newly hip neighborhoods spread through the power of alternative media. Years before "edgy" became another word for "hip" and the Internet was invented, independent weekly newspapers like the *Village Voice*, followed by the *East Village Other*, *SoHo Weekly News*, and *East Village Eye*, put gritty downtown streets on the must-see itinerary for anyone who wanted to be in the know about new cultural trends. At the same time, new urban lifestyle media for the middle class, led on the East Coast by *New York* magazine, created a buzz around the remaining small shops selling ethnic foods in old neighborhoods—a traditional Italian cheese store in Little Italy, a pickle maker on the Lower East Side—and taught readers how to buy "the best for less" in the city's new wine shops, boutiques, and ethnic restaurants. The way *New York* depicted the sensual variety of urban life glamorized the old neighborhoods, showing them as great places for consuming authenticity—the authenticity that modernizers and suburbanites had lost.[20]

By the 1980s new communities of artists stretched through the old districts of Lower Manhattan, and by the 1990s they extended across the East River to Brooklyn and Queens. The concentration of artists in SoHo, the East Village, and Williamsburg confirmed these areas' distinctive appeal and emphasized their otherness to the enforced homogeneity of both the suburbs and the city's corporate center. These neighborhoods were intensely cool, identifiably local, and ethnically diverse. Their physical and social distinctiveness connected residents to the city's origins, embodied by the tenements and loft buildings of *ur*-neighborhoods downtown, and engaged their yearning for a looser self. The cultural process of distilling value from the city's origins created the sense of authenticity nurtured by *New York* magazine and increasingly also by the *New York Times*, as these media developed the new form of writing called lifestyle journalism.

Jane Jacobs expressed the appeal of this new sense of urban authenticity better than anyone. It's not surprising that she was a journalist by profession, but in writing about the social uses of authenticity she became a theorist of the streets, neighborhoods, and districts that make up a city's complex system of interrelated parts. *Death and Life* celebrated the human capacity for regulating social life by the simple routines of walking to school, shopping in mom-and-pop stores, watching through the window to make sure neighbors and passersby get through the day and night. Jacobs discovered that the social life of common spaces depends on variety, the density of crowds, and the liberty to devise unanticipated uses. Working with her neighbors, she showed that a bottom-up activist movement can force powerful government agencies to back down. Strangely, though—and here is the great problem with her work—Jacobs failed to look at how people use capital and culture to view, and to shape, the urban spaces they inhabit. She did not see that the authenticity she admired is itself a social product. In a review of *Death and Life* published when the book came out, Herbert Gans criticized Jacobs for falling victim to the "fallacy of physical determinism." She hones in on the physical characteristics of buildings, he said, "ignor[ing] the social, cultural, and economic factors that contribute to vitality or dullness." Neighborhoods that Jacobs admires, Gans pointed out, such as the North End of Boston and New York's West Village, are *white ethnic* neighborhoods with a *working-class* culture.[21]

This culture shapes the ballet of the street that Jacobs describes. She delights in telling us about Mr. Halpert and his laundry, the Cornacchia family's deli, Mr. Goldstein's hardware store, the Dorgene restaurant (where the poet Ezra Pound once dined with the editor of the *Hudson Review*), Mr. Slube's cigar store, Mr. Koochagian's tailor shop, and Mr. Lofaro the green-grocer, as well as the barbershop, drugstore, dry cleaner, locksmith, pizzeria, and café. Rereading her description now, we see that Jacobs is painting an idyllic picture of small town life in the midst of the big city. It's an urban imaginary like Disneyland's Main Street, also dating from the 1950s, with an equally rosy postwar view of local shops, their European immigrant owners, and residents living above and around them. Jacobs's view perpetuates the image of the New York City block as a microcosm of social diversity. This is the block we know from films, from the tenements in 1930s movies like *Dead End* to the brownstone houses in Alfred Hitchcock's *Rear Window,* filmed in Greenwich Village in the 1950s, and Spike Lee's *Do the Right Thing,* filmed on a brownstone block in Brooklyn in the 1980s.

Jacobs's image of her block is just as much a social construction as the movie image of a New York City street. It is a product of its time, the end of the second generation of the great wave of Southern and Eastern European immigration, and of its location in New York's postwar political economy, with rent control enabling many of the tenants to stay in their apartments and a lack of new investment keeping the small-scale houses that Jacobs likes from being replaced. Jacobs's block is a modernized, sanitized version of the urban village; it's the West End of Boston without Italian Americans and with residents who have better jobs. It could be a remake of *The Honeymooners,* the 1950s television comedy in which Jackie Gleason and Art Carney play a bus driver and a sewer worker in Bensonhurst, Brooklyn, but now they are sharing their neighborhood with journalists, artists, and architects. Jacobs fails to recognize the growing influence of her own perspective, to see that families like hers are gradually moving to the West Village's nineteenth-century houses because they appreciate the charm of the area's little shops and cobblestone streets. She doesn't seem to realize that she expresses a gentrifier's aesthetic appreciation of urban authenticity.

What is also missing from Jacobs's image of Hudson Street is an awareness of the importance of capital in the broadest sense: the economic capital that for a hundred years bypassed this part of the Village, leaving small shops and short blocks in place; the social capital of local immigrant entrepreneurs, who open restaurants, dry cleaners, and hardware stores in our time as well as in hers; and the cultural capital of gentrifiers like Jacobs herself, and of many urban dwellers today, who find their subjective identity in this particular image of urban authenticity.

I should say that I am one of those urban dwellers. I would like "origins" to speak for the politics of the underprivileged, to offer an objective standard of authenticity that defends their right to the city. I am all too aware, though, that I belong to the city's "new beginnings." I define my identity in terms of the same subjective kind of authenticity that Jane Jacobs admires, while seeing that it displaces the poor by constructing the habitus, latte by latte, of the new urban middle class. This self-awareness doesn't deny that tastes reinforce social distinctions. I like traditional, small food shops with moderate prices, but I don't shop at dollar stores or bodegas. Yet the means of consumption on which the new urban middle class depends are destroying the city of the working class. Our pursuit of authenticity—our accumulation of this kind of cultural capital—fuels rising real estate values; our rhetoric of authenticity implicitly endorses the new, post-Jacobs rhetoric of upscale growth.

"I'm not even going to start playing the authenticity game," the novelist Hari Kunzru writes about his role in the upscaling of Broadway Market, a shopping street in Hackney, his gentrifying neighborhood in the East End of London. Like Elizabeth Street in NoLIta or Smith Street in Cobble Hill, Broadway Market has recently changed from being a working-class shopping street with an inexpensive butcher, baker, and other local stores to a high-price location for niche-market shops. "I came to Hackney," Kunzru says, "for reasons that I guess are not dissimilar to a lot of the bike-riders, creative slackers, live-workers and thrift-store princesses I nod to on the street: because it is full of weird places and eccentric people and has a grubby glamour to it that has not yet been stamped out and flattened into the same cloned corporate hell-hole as the rest of Britain." "But the thing is," he admits, "I am partial to a nice piece of raclette."[22]

How many shopping streets have been transformed by cafés, bars, and gourmet cheese stores for people who want to consume differently from the mainstream culture? Who go for better coffee not to Dunkin' Donuts but to Starbucks, which tries to live down the fact that it's a chain, or, even better, to an anti-Starbucks, a dark little café where the tattooed barista knows how to foam the milk just right, the beans are organically grown on bird-friendly trees and purchased through fair trade, and you can connect to Wi-Fi along with other customers who share your tastes? This is the authenticity that Kunzru is talking about. It is produced not only by new residents, but by new retail entrepreneurs who speak to these new residents' social and cultural needs. They have gradually replaced Jane Jacobs's neighbors and changed the city's streets.

New retail entrepreneurs often move into a neighborhood as residents and can't find a place to buy a good latte or a magazine store that carries *Wired* or the *New York Times*. "I realized early on that the neighborhood was on the brink of change," says a store owner who came to Williamsburg to live in the 1990s, "and I knew one thing we were lacking was a good wine store." Another says, "There were a lot of people interested in film, but the neighborhood lacked a good video store." Retail store owners who belong to a neighborhood's new population and share their needs represent the interests of a *cultural* community that contrasts with that of longtime residents.[23]

Other new retail entrepreneurs come to a neighborhood for the *economic* opportunity, because they see that the population is beginning to change to men and women with a higher social profile and more disposable income and they want to start a business that caters to their tastes. This is especially true of the second wave of new store owners, who don't live in the neighborhood themselves; they often see a changing neighborhood as a good place to open a branch of a small boutique they have already started in another gentrifying locale.

New retail entrepreneurs are also, in a sense, *social* entrepreneurs. By opening places of sociability where new residents feel comfortable—and longtime residents do not—they help to create a neighborhood's new beginnings. Polish residents of Williamsburg don't go to bars that feature indie rock bands or indoor miniature golf. But hipsters and gentrifiers don't wire money to Warsaw or Pueblo or stand around all night at an all-male, working-class bar. The new consumption spaces that they patronize—music bars, cafés, boutiques, vintage clothing stores—reinvent the urban community.[24]

New retail entrepreneurs don't have to be elitist. You find the same mix of cultural, social, and economic motivations among new immigrant entrepreneurs: the men from northern India who open sari shops on Seventy-fourth Street in Jackson Heights in Queens; the Salvadoran women who cook and sell pupusas from carts at the Red Hook ball fields in Brooklyn; the West African restaurateurs who create a Little Senegal in Harlem. All these new beginnings mark emerging spaces of urban authenticity.

We can see "authentic" spaces only from outside them. Mobility gives us the distance to view a neighborhood as connoisseurs, to compare it to an absolute standard of urban experience, to judge its character apart from our personal history or intimate social relationships. If we are connected to a neighborhood's longtime social life, especially if we grew up there, we are likely to recall how it was back in the day; we are less likely, though, to call it *authentic.* Just thinking of authenticity in this way recalls its usual meaning, according to which an expert objectively evaluates the origins of a piece of art, an antique rug, or any other object we can isolate like a specimen, examine, and compare with other examples of its category. In contrast to the subjectivity that comes from really living in a neighborhood, walking its streets, shopping in local stores, and sending children to local schools, the other kind of authenticity allows us to see an inhabited space in aesthetic terms. Especially when we look at a rundown neighborhood we ask, Is it interesting? Is it gritty? Is it "real"? Like the criteria we use while shopping for consumer products, these standards objectify the authenticity that we desire. We are often seduced by appearances and assumptions. How many times do we think, the cheaper the beer, the more authentic the bar? Or, the grittier the streets, the more authentic the neighborhood? How we think about these questions makes an ethical as well as a social statement about the way we want to live, and so our stand on urban authenticity is ultimately subjective because it refers to us. Are we Levis (West Village) or True Religion (Meatpacking District) jeans? Are we organic food co-op (Park Slope) or mass-consumption Costco (Bay Ridge)? Pathmark (East Harlem) or Whole Foods (East Village)? Which is the authentic space for our authentic self?[25]

These are peculiarly modern questions. In Western culture the idea of authenticity arose between the ages of Shakespeare and Rousseau, when men and women began to think about an authentic self as an honest or a true character, in contrast to an individual's dishonesty, on the one hand, and to society's false morality, on the other. As a social theorist Rousseau developed a structural understanding of the authenticity of individual character. Men and women are authentic if they are closer to nature—or to the way intellectuals imagine a state of nature to be—than to the institutional disciplines of power. While this view continues to inspire people to abandon the false lifestyle of modern society and form a commune, it also offers psychic consolation to social groups who have neither wealth nor power. German intellectuals, who in the eighteenth century were less integrated into courtly life than their French counterparts, were reconciled to the difference between themselves, rich in cultural capital, and the princes who controlled state power and patronage as a difference of authenticity. Unlike the frivolous, Frenchified "civilization" of the courts, the intellectuals' "culture" was serious, virtuous, *authentic*. It gave them a sense of moral superiority. Though these intellectuals did not hold power, their claim to authenticity foreshadowed the way more ambitious groups would eventually use the term as a means of excluding others.[26]

The habit of identifying authenticity with the downwardly mobile gradually spread from Germany to France and from university towns to cities, where major art collections, theaters, and publishers thrived and artists and intellectuals could sell their work. Most artists who produced paintings or novels or journalism for these urban markets were not well paid. They lived from contract to contract, earning money, like factory workers of the time, by the number of pieces or column inches they produced.

These artisans of words and images, the first "creative class," lived in working-class quarters not just because they were rebelling against the conformity of the bourgeoisie; they couldn't afford to live in better neighborhoods. Like earlier German intellectuals who scorned the princely courts, and like French writers who left Paris for the garrets of London before the French Revolution, poets and novelists living *la vie de bohème* in mid-nineteenth-century Paris contrasted authentic, lower-class urban life, especially the tenuous lives of the most marginalized groups, criminals and gypsies, with what they saw as the overly comfortable, totally conformist lives of the rich. Writers romanticized the shabby and sordid, and often diseased, outcast lower class, and this romantic image became a source of their artistic inspiration.[27]

Despite all the social and economic improvements since that time, nineteenth-century bohemians' attitudes live on in new hipster districts and gentrified neighborhoods. From Baudelaire's prose poems to the musical drama *Rent,* the slums so feared by the righteous middle classes continue to appeal to artists and writers because of their reservoir of danger and decay as well as their tolerance of, or unwillingness to police, cultural diversity. By the same token, rundown nineteenth-century houses and small shops are appealing to many people with middle-class cultural tastes because they embody the aesthetic distinction of objects that are, on the one hand, simple, handmade tokens of craftsmanship and, on the other, living history. As Thorstein Veblen said more than a hundred years ago, these quirky marks of distinction are cast into relief by the sameness of mass production. And as the journalist David Brooks says today, the "gentry" don't want "opulent, luxurious,…magnificent and extravagant," they want "*authentic, natural, warm,*…*honest, organic,*…*unique.*" To the use-values of longtime residents and the exchange-values of real estate developers, bohemians and gentrifiers add aesthetic values.[28]

Although gentrification was just beginning in the United States and England when Jacobs wrote *Death and Life* and still lacked an American name, Herbert Gans had some idea of what the next stage of modernity would bring. In the preface to *The Urban Villagers* he tells us that the first residents of the luxury apartment houses that replaced the West End's tenements are just moving in. If they are like the middle-class people of Gans's generation, the second generation of the Great European Immigration, "their tastes are no longer ethnic, but not yet esoteric." They don't want to live in a neighborhood like the West Village; they want to move to the suburbs. They won't patronize the old-fashioned corner store that Jacobs loves, even if it still exists; they prefer modern supermarkets and shopping malls. One day, though, when they realize that their choices result in a homogenized, and even an inauthentic experience, they will return to the old ethnic foods and at least a simulation of the old ethnic neighborhoods. They will rediscover the charms of the Italian Market in South Philadelphia, the North End of Boston, and Manhattan's Lower East Side. Like future loft dwellers and brownstone townhouse owners, the new West Enders will lay claim to the bricks and mortar of the historic city, indulging in a collective amnesia about the earlier eras of factory work and mass migration that made these neighborhoods come alive. The urban authenticity to which they will aspire won't be inborn or inherited; it will be achieved.[29]

These desires were given wings by an inflow of investment capital from globalization and deregulation. During the 1980s, when governments loosened restrictions on overseas investment, foreign money flowed like Perrier into New York real estate markets, coming mainly from Western Europe, Japan, and Canada. Despite sharp setbacks in the following years due to stock market crises, changing domestic conditions in other countries, and, exceptionally, the terrorist attack on the World Trade Center and the Pentagon in 2001, the influx of foreign investment has continued to grow, even during the financial crisis that began in 2008. Trophy buildings in Midtown Manhattan were captured by foreign investors, first by the Japanese, then by Middle Easterners with a surplus of petrodollars, and most recently by dollar-rich Russian business barons and Chinese firms. Foreign investors pay high prices for luxury condos and mansions on the Upper East Side but they also buy rent-controlled apartment houses in socially marginal areas of the city, such as the Bronx, the city's poorest borough, where they empty the apartments and raise the rents or demolish the buildings and replace them with taller, sleeker towers when the city government gets around to rezoning the areas.[30]

Rezoning has become the city government's preferred tool of redevelopment. Since the first years of the twenty-first century it has opened the door to the type of development that private investors think will be most profitable while giving a nod of approval to Jane Jacobs's kind of authenticity: upzoning to taller buildings on the wide avenues and waterfront, downzoning to three-, four-, and five-story houses on the narrower, gentrified side streets. In reality these restrictions privilege both developers and supergentrifiers. They broaden the sweep of demolition and new construction while making the historic districts and small-scale neighborhoods that represent the city's origins rarer, more precious—and more authentic.

Hudson Street turned toward a more precious kind of authenticity in the 1990s, three decades after Jacobs and her family had moved to Toronto. Foreign investment in New York City property was running high, Wall Street salaries and bonuses were climbing into the stratosphere, and media moguls were buying brownstone houses in the West Village and SoHo lofts as East Village artists were packing their bags for cheaper lofts in Williamsburg. Near Jacobs's old home the rough and casual character of the old ethnic neighborhood, a reflection of the working docks that ended their useful commercial life by 1960, had vanished. That working life was still active around Fourteenth Street, in the old meat market, where wholesale butchers and meatpackers unloaded animal carcasses from one set of trucks and loaded porterhouse steaks and ground chuck onto other trucks from late night till the next afternoon. But by 1990 the meat market was on its way out. Since the 1970s raunchy gay bars followed by trendy restaurants had attracted a different crowd, and the pressure from this new nighttime economy, as well as from all the nearby Greenwich Village attractions, and the growing desire on the part of city officials and well-heeled residents to "reclaim" waterfront districts had turned the area from prime meat to prime real estate. During the 1990s the Meatpacking District became a visibly chic, and remarkably expensive, place to live, which also reshaped Jacobs's old neighborhood a few blocks to the south.

Hudson Street is different today from what it was in Jacobs's time. Although the two short blocks on either side of her old home are still filled with small stores, most of the old merchants are gone. Local customers now are likely to be Hollywood actors and editors of fashion magazines. Gone too are many of the specialized, local services the old stores offered. Now there are eight restaurants, two bars, a café, a convenience store, and a nail salon, as well as a shoe store, a children's boutique, and three empty storefronts. Today Mr. Goldstein's hardware store is the New York branch of Belly Dance Maternity, a small Chicago chain selling "hip maternity clothes for stylish moms to be." Dorgene is still a restaurant, but now it's the Hudson Corner Café. Mr. Halpert's laundry disappeared around 1980, the storefront hosting an endless series of restaurants. The butcher shop changed names and probably owners in the 1960s, and by 1990 the nail salon took its place. The drugstore lasted until the mid-1980s; now customers who need to fill a prescription walk one block uptown to the nearest branch of the Duane Reade chain or one block downtown to Rite Aid. Only a few establishments remain from Jacobs's time: two schools, though the archdiocese sold St. Veronica's to an independent private school in 1970, after most of the old Irish and Italian families who sent their children to the Catholic school had died or moved away and new, affluent residents swelled the demand for secular private school education; and the White Horse Tavern, a well-known watering hole recommended by many guidebooks. In 2005 the ground floor of Jacobs's former house was occupied by a fancy cookware store; three years later City Cricket had moved in, selling "one-of-a-kind, hand-made, antique treasures for children," a precious, though quickly changing kind of authenticity. Now the store is empty.

Bricks and mortar remain in place only as long as real estate developers aren't interested in building something new there. Unlike Herb Gans, though, who blamed an unholy alliance between developers and white ethnic politicians for destroying the West End, Jane Jacobs blamed the death of lively blocks on urban planners, a relatively powerless group who only work for developers and government agencies. It is true that in the first half of the twentieth century Le Corbusier and other architects popularized designs for superblocks and disdained narrow, crowded streets. But developers and state agencies built these designs, and, with her intelligence and progressive political activism, Jacobs should not have ignored the power of capital that they wielded. Yet for one reason or another, perhaps because she was funded by the Rockefeller Foundation and was associated with the media empire *Time-Life*, or because of the lingering aftershocks of McCarthyism, she chose not to criticize the interests of capitalist developers who profit from displacing others. "Private investment shapes cities," she wrote, "but social ideas (and laws) shape private investment."[31]

Today city planners swear loyalty to Jane Jacobs's vision. Her goal of preserving the city's physical fabric by maintaining the small scale and interactive social life of the streets has been translated into laws for preserving much of the built environment. But these laws go only part of the way toward creating the vibrant city that Jacobs loved. They encourage mixed uses, but not a mixed population. They never speak of maintaining low rents on commercial properties, so they cannot combat the most common means of uprooting the small shop owners who inspired Jacobs's ideas about social order and the vitality of the street. More and more of the owners, in any case, are chains; there are few traditional shopkeepers left. The city government has overturned communities' plans for low-key, mixed development that place a priority on maintaining existing tenants and uses, and responds with "affordable" units only if a community rises up in protest, as Harlem recently did, when longtime residents and store owners challenged the rezoning of 125th Street for high-rise office buildings and apartment houses. Despite the mandated public hearings, both local and citywide, on changes in land use, city government agencies most often endorse the prior decisions of the City Planning Commission, which tends to approve big new development projects supported by the mayor. In one of the most important contemporary projects in New York, the rebuilding of the World Trade Center site, a state agency, the Lower Manhattan Development Corporation, controls the process without a public vote or even a deciding voice for the local community board. The largest contemporary redevelopment project in Brooklyn, Atlantic Yards, on a site Robert Moses picked for urban renewal many years earlier, stirred a lot of public protest but was derailed only by the collapse of financial markets in the subprime mortgage crisis.[32]

The major difference between Moses's time and ours lies in a shift from the ideal of the modern city to that of the authentic city. To the extent that the city planning commissioners honor Jane Jacobs's vision, they say, "If you allow the character of a neighborhood to be eroded, the people who live in that neighborhood will leave the city."[33] Whose character, though, is most authentic? If authenticity is a state of mind, it's historic, local, and cool. But if authenticity is a social right, it's also poor, ethnic, and democratic. Authenticity speaks for the right of a city, and a neighborhood, to offer residents, workers, store owners, and street vendors the opportunity to put down roots—to represent, paradoxically, both origins and new beginnings.

Neither the West Village nor New York as a whole is typical of all cities. What happens there, though, offers both a big vision and an advance warning of changes to come. Because New York is a media center, images of its neighborhoods, shops, and streets are broadcast globally in films, television series, and videos posted on the Internet. Because New York was also one of the first cities to undergo an extensive branding process, beginning with the Big Apple slogan and the "I ♥ New York" public relations campaign of the 1970s, what happens there is a road map for other cities eager for a makeover. But if all of New York's neighborhoods are made over with generic chain stores, expensive houses, and ever taller towers, it will be too late to bring back the "authentic" urban experience of Mr. Goldstein's hardware store, the residents of modest means, including artists, and the men and women who work with their hands for a living. If we don't confront the question of what we have already lost, how we lost it, and what alternative forms of ownership might keep them in place, we risk destroying the authentic urban places that remain.

New York's growth in recent years has both created and depended on new consumption spaces that respond to changing lifestyles and make the city more desirable. Our tastes as consumers—tastes for lattes and organic food, as well as for green spaces, boutiques, and farmers' markets—now define the city, as they also define us. These tastes are reflected in the media's language and images, from lifestyle magazines to local wikis and food blogs; this discourse, which has become more participatory through the Internet, forms our social imaginary of the "authentic city," including the kinds of spaces and social groups that belong there. Filtered through the actions of developers and city officials, our rhetoric of authenticity becomes their rhetoric of growth. We need tools to talk about these changes.

media influence on authentic city

Looking at wikis and blogs acknowledges that media discourse, along with economic power, state power, and consumer culture, shapes the contemporary urban experience. It's not just that old media keep running articles about how important web-based media have become, and that we know in our own lives how true this is, but that the circulation of images about the city, and about who has the right to be in specific places in the city, from neighborhoods to public spaces, is fueled to a great extent by the self-referential online conversations in local blogs. Posts are not always positive or politically correct. But they are spontaneous (or seemingly spontaneous) attempts to express common feelings of loss, quest, and anxiety about the city, and they show an urgency to convince unseen readers. Though I do not think that online communities have replaced face-to-face interaction, I do think it is important to understand the way web-based media contribute to our urban imaginary. The interactive nature of the dialogue, how each post feeds on the preceding ones and elicits more, these are expressions of both difference and consensus, and they represent partial steps toward an open public sphere in troubling times.

Lately there has been a rumble of interest among urban writers about how to analyze the social impact of these new media. Nobody knows. The usual methodological problems are compounded by the Web's anonymity, the predominance still of more affluent and highly educated users, the difficulty of judging accuracy and objectivity or, on the other hand, of interpreting subjectivity and, in the case of locally based blogs, not knowing where posts are really made. But they do express the writers' immediate experience of the city in all their apparent sincerity and naïveté. Look at one of the first posts, on Chowhound.com, to draw widespread public attention to the Latino food vendors in the Red Hook ball fields: "As usual, I pointed and bought, but [I] don't have much of an idea exactly what each item was." There is no better way to suggest the cultural confusion between native-born and immigrant New Yorkers, the willingness on both sides to find common ground, and the limitations of that exchange to items for consumption. Yet this exchange and the post about it are also a means of working out who has a right to a specific urban space—determining, in the narrow case, the food vendors' right to sell food at the ball fields and, in a broader sense, their right to the city.

Though it is clear to anyone who has spent even a day in any big city that urban spaces have been reshaped in recent years by consumer culture, those who write about cities haven't focused on how these changes occur, how they are experienced on the ground, and what their social consequences are for both specific areas and the city as a whole. When I look at New York's changing neighborhoods, in the three chapters on "uncommon spaces," I am struck by the instrumental role places of consumption, and media coverage of them, play. Everyone knows that art galleries and performance spaces fueled SoHo's transformation in the 1970s and 1980s, but retail chain stores made another big change in the 1990s, and not an altogether good one. Indie music bars and ethnic restaurants brought attention to Williamsburg, a terrific farmers' market and restaurants stabilized the East Village, new boutiques and chain stores (including the omnipresent Starbucks and H&M) helped to create Harlem's new identity. All of these changes also raised real estate prices, and, as beneficial as each store may be to certain groups of consumers, many acted as a wedge of displacement against traditional, locally owned stores before, in some cases, being displaced themselves. Yet each form of commercial culture constructs a new form of authenticity that anchors the claim of new groups to live and work in that space. Consumers' tastes, backed by other resources, become a form of power.

During the past thirty years, food has emerged as the new "art" in the urban cultural experience, with places to sample many different tastes. The three chapters on "common" spaces show how central an urban attraction food has become: the farmers' market at Union Square (okay, so I'm a supporter), the pupusas at the Red Hook ball fields (I don't even eat most fried food), and the growing of organic vegetables and herbs at many community gardens (this is not something I do myself). In each case the sale, preparation, or growing of food traces struggles that are at this book's heart: between different social groups and the city government, between different social groups in the same physical space, and between each group's initial identity as marginalized and its later identity as "authentic." These struggles also express a right to the city. I could not make up the post on Mark Bittman's blog by the guy who guiltily admits that he likes the Swedish meatballs sold at IKEA as much as the Salvadoran pupusas sold at the ball fields. Yet this single posting makes my point (initially made, in a different way, by the sociologist Pierre Bourdieu): tastes for different kinds of food are a means of consolidating, if not always taking, power.

This brings me to a final virtue of using authenticity to talk about the city: it forces us to think about time as well as space. Authenticity involves time, though, in three different ways. First, the appeal of authenticity suggests that we cling to the ideal of a timeless city that never changes, and we use this ideal, represented by cultural images of a specific historical period, as an absolute standard for judging urban experience. But second, our mental images of authenticity do reflect change, for each generation has an experience of the city in its own time that shapes what its members think about the houses, stores, and people that "belong" on a block, in a neighborhood, and in the city as a whole. Third, thinking about authenticity shows the importance of time in the broadest sense because city dwellers are increasingly concerned with making their way between the promise of creation and the threat of annihilation, whether by urban renewal or gentrification, by warfare or ecological disaster.

In the following chapters I show how origins and new beginnings create a sense of authenticity in both "uncommon" spaces, neighborhoods with distinctive histories and traditions, and "common" spaces, such as parks and community gardens that are meant for broad public use. I focus on these spaces not just because they have played a prominent role in the reshaping of New York City during the past thirty years, but because each illustrates a different aspect of what we mean when we say that an urban experience is "authentic." Each chapter moves from place to place and season to season on the streets, like the unfolding of the narrative of the 1948 film *Naked City*. Instead of pursuing a murderer, though, this book pursues the idea of authenticity.

Each chapter focuses on a different dimension of authenticity the way it is understood today. Chapter 1 begins with Brooklyn and shows how this borough's longtime reputation for authenticity changed during the 1990s from rough and gritty to hip and cool. Chapter 2 takes up the theme of race, looking at Harlem, which in the past few years has been gentri-fied, rezoned, and redeveloped by new market-rate apartments and stores. Harlem is a large area with a varied population, but the recent increase in white residents makes it fair to ask if this urban ghetto can keep its authen-tic character as both poor and black. From Harlem we move downtown to the East Village, and chapter 3 shows how new restaurants and shops have shifted the neighborhood's strong sense of local authenticity from political and cultural rebellion ("Die Yuppie scum") to trendy consump-tion (organic produce, cocktail bars).

These uncommon spaces lead us in turn to the city's "common" spaces of public parks, streets, and community gardens, where a timeless ideal of authentic public space that is free, democratic, and open to all is rein-terpreted by different modes of private stewardship. I begin in chapter 4 at Union Square, which has been managed since the 1980s by a privately controlled Business Improvement District. Paradoxically, despite the BID's reliance on private security guards and revenue-producing activities, Union Square has become a more "authentic" public space than the pub-licly controlled World Trade Center site, two miles away. In chapter 5 I go to Red Hook, an old industrial area on the Brooklyn waterfront, and see how the "authenticity" of a small group of Latino vendors who have been selling food in the ball fields since the 1970s has created another kind of private stewardship of public space in contrast to a nearby IKEA store. In chapter 6, I visit a community garden in East New York, one of the poorest areas of the city, and observe how the "authenticity" of the citywide com-munity garden movement has changed since its origins during the 1970s from political protest to urban food production. Taken together, these three public spaces offer models for authentic urban places that provide a permanent right to the city, though not without conflicts and inequalities.

In the conclusion, I look at what has been gained and lost with the creation of the city of "destination culture": a social as well as a physical transformation by the combined powers of private investors, the state, the media, and consumer tastes. Returning to the work of Jane Jacobs and Robert Moses, I conclude that there is not so great a difference as we often assume between the cultural values that they pursued. Though Jacobs fought strenuously to preserve an ideal vision of the urban village, and Moses just as strenuously fought to replace it with the ideal of the corporate city, their ideas have been joined to create the hybrid city that we consider authentic today: both hipster districts *and* luxury housing, immigrant food vendors *and* big box stores, community gardens *and* gentrification. Though this city pays its respects to both origins and new beginnings, it does not do enough to protect the right of residents, workers, and shops—the small scale, the poor, and the middle class—to remain in place. It is this social diversity, and not just the diversity of buildings and uses, that gives the city its soul.

Uncommon Spaces

How Brooklyn Became Cool

Travel guidebook publisher Lonely Planet named Brooklyn as one of the top destinations in its 2007 "Blue List," its annual worldwide best-of guide. "Brooklyn's booming," the two-page spread begins. "Any New Yorker worth their street cred knows the new downtown lies just across the East River...." So adventurers seeking wild fauna in their natural habitat should go to Honduras for howler monkeys, Gabon for elephants and Brooklyn for tattooed bloggers in $50 T-shirts?
—New York *Daily News,* January 8, 2007

It's one o'clock in the morning on a warm October night, and the streets of northern Brooklyn are eerily deserted. The hulks of warehouses and the chimney of the old Domino sugar refinery stand guard along the water-front, while grim industrial buildings hunker down in the shadow of the Brooklyn-Queens Expressway. Steel gates hide the windows of small plastics and metalworking shops. Nearby tenements are silent and dark.

You're wide awake, though, driving through the darkness on Kent Avenue, bumping over warped asphalt and steering around potholes. You're circling Williamsburg, looking for the neighborhood that made Brooklyn cool.

First you pass the Northside, the original center of Brooklyn's hipster culture, a cluster of art galleries, cafés, bars, and boutiques around the subway station at North Seventh Street and Bedford Avenue.

Then you pass the Southside, where French bistros and Japanese hair salons have recently joined yeshivas and bodegas, and artists and graduate students are a noticeable presence on the streets. Ahead of you stretch neighborhoods that have been predominantly black since after World War II but are now rapidly gentrifying and becoming socially and ethnically more diverse—that is, richer and whiter: Bedford-Stuyvesant, Fort Greene, Clinton Hill. The old Brooklyn Navy Yard sits vast and uninhabited just one block to the west. A few blocks beyond that, brownstone townhouses sell for a million dollars and up.

Navigating solo through this dark landscape, you don't see any sign of life. But when you turn onto the wider roadway of Flushing Avenue, you meet up with men and women walking in couples and groups of four. They are Hasidic Jews, women with heads covered in wigs and scarves, skirts below their knees, and black-hatted men wearing long black overcoats. Sabbath began at sundown. Because driving is prohibited then, any believers who are out on the street at this hour must find their way home on foot.

After you pass the Hasidim, you find a few more people walking on the street; these men are wearing tight jeans and the women are in short skirts. But one of the young men wears a cowboy outfit, and one of the young women is dressed as a witch. Music begins to rumble in the distance.

You park the car and continue on your way on foot. Soon you discover a group of young men and women standing and talking outside the beat-up garage door of a two-story factory building. Their faces gleam in the light coming from the windows of the top-floor loft. Loud rock music thuds through the air.

You knock, a reinforced steel door swings open, and suddenly you're face to face with a robot, a Black Panther, and an Arabian sheik. Two large men stand guard, outfitted as bouncers, clearly for real: shaved heads, neatly trimmed goatees, long black leather coats, and earpieces. They usher you up a staircase lined with plastic skulls and Christmas lights. When you reach the second floor you hand the doorman a crisp ten-dollar bill, and he waves you into the crowded front room where a band is playing and dozens of revelers drink and dance. Flashing colored lights are strung across the ceiling on bare sprinkler pipes. People stand around a table at the far end of the room picking through piles of paper, feathers, wire, and glue, showing each other the masks they are making.

It's Halloween, and you have found the underground party called Rubulad.

Rubulad is one of those new neighborhood institutions that inspired Lonely Planet's 2007 *Blue List* to name Brooklyn "the hippest part of New York City." It's on a circuit of illegal and semilegal music shows, occasional parties open to the public and one-time-only events like raves that are held in the deserted warehouses, lofts, and Polish bars of Williamsburg, Poles being the gradually disappearing ethnic group in this part of the city. You find out about these events on Internet websites, email newsletters, and individual blogs, and also by word of mouth.

Knowing about Rubulad is one marker that you are cool. Another is actually finding the party, though when the party promoter Todd P was written up in the *Village Voice,* some people said the publicity killed the underground vibe. They also said that another party promoter's landlord canceled his lease because of the attention drawn to what was, after all, an illegal use of the space. ("Legal or illegal is really an imprecise subject," Todd P says. "It's a matter of different degrees of police enforcement.") But the media keep covering these events, and despite, or because of, the fuzz and the buzz, they manage to keep going.[1]

DIY (Do It Yourself) parties like Rubulad play an important part in the contemporary trend of urban renewal by pop culture. Places for cool cultural consumption develop an attractive image for an unlikely neighborhood, which then sparks a commercial revival, a residential influx of people with money, and, finally, the building of new luxury apartments with extravagant rents. It sounds like a typical process of gentrification. In this case, though, down and dirty hipster culture, rather than a sanitized version of entertainment, has produced a new kind of authenticity.

Like most of Williamsburg's cool scene, Rubulad began in the early 1990s for a small circle of musicians and hipsters but emerged into larger public awareness with media coverage, especially the new media of blogs and email listservs. Its success is connected to an influential turn in consumer culture that aestheticizes the city's gritty authenticity, in contrast to the bland homogeneity of corporate offices and suburban homes, and praises the found authenticity of do-it-yourself performances by artists and musicians. But Rubulad's success also highlights traditional urban factors of capital and the state. In this case, though, it's the *absence* of investment by either private sector developers or government that created an opportunity for new culture to thrive.

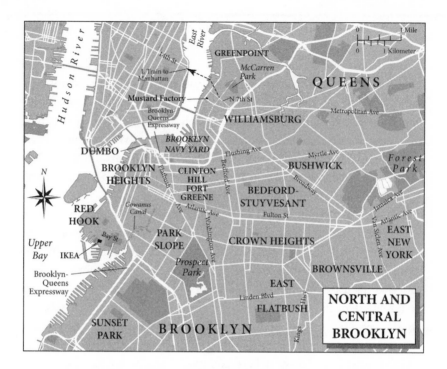

Williamsburg's growing prominence as a hipster locale during the 1990s confirms Jane Jacobs's idea that old buildings with low rents will act as incubators of new activities. In contrast, though, to her focus on a neighborhood's existing business owners and residents, the social, cultural, and economic capital of Williamsburg's new entrepreneurs reinvented the community as a new *terroir* for indie music, alternative art, and trendy restaurant cuisine. Together with gentrification in other neighborhoods, this remade Brooklyn's image as well. Cool cultural production created a new, ethnically white, cosmopolitan image of Brooklyn centered on the north side of the borough, in contrast to both more expensive neighborhoods in Manhattan and more traditional ethnic and working-class neighborhoods in Red Hook, Bensonhurst, and Bedford-Stuyvesant. This new image would not have worked, though, if new creative people had not moved into Brooklyn, reversing decades of flight.

I first became aware of the talent train to Brooklyn in the mid 80s, when, writing on architecture and design for the [*New York*] *Times,* I noticed

my Rolodex fattening with 718 [telephone area code] prefixes. Not long after, the borough started getting seriously cool, with all those Robert Wilson productions at BAM [the Brooklyn Academy of Music], plus the imports from the Royal National Theater at BAM's self-consciously 'distressed' annex, the Majestic....Restaurants followed, and soon reviewers rained stars on local chefs (who knew?).
—Joseph Giovannini, *New York* magazine, May 2, 2004

For most of the twentieth century Brooklyn had a sorry reputation as a place where artists and writers were born but were eager to escape from. Perhaps the best known writer to celebrate his flight was the literary critic Alfred Kazin, whose memoir tells how, by the 1940s, he had moved from Brownsville to Manhattan, leaving behind the hardships of his poor immigrant Jewish parents and newer black neighbors—and never looked back. Life in a working-class, immigrant neighborhood was ugly. Factories were Dickensian sweatshops of dirt and squalor, social life was lived on the street, and residents often turned on each other. As late as the 1930s most houses in Williamsburg and the adjacent neighborhood of Greenpoint lacked central heat and hot water; many of the walk-up tenements did not have private indoor toilets and bathtubs were in the kitchen, where water could be boiled in big pots on the stove and poured in the tub when needed. Daniel Fuchs, an Academy Award–winning screenwriter of the 1930s who set two novels in Williamsburg, paints a stark picture of the neighborhood when he was growing up, two decades earlier: "We saw almost everything that human beings did. It was a world marked by cruelty so pervasive as to be dazzling, of scavengers, pimps, gangsters shot down as they drank soda water at sidewalk counters." This was an authentic urban village, and there was nothing picturesque about it.[2]

By the 1940s however, a small number of literary men and women who were native-born Americans but not native to New York began to migrate over the Brooklyn Bridge, seeking a haven from the high rents and frenzied competition of Manhattan. From Walt Whitman to Truman Capote, writers who chose to move to Brooklyn delighted in it as an alternative space with a strong sense of place, with a "masculine" culture of piers and factories; it was proletarian, authentic, and not fully modern. Brooklyn especially attracted artists and writers who had lived in the Lower Manhattan neighborhood of Greenwich Village, which, during the 1920s, experienced both an early form of gentrification and an influx of tourists who wanted to see how bohemians lived. Pushed by rising rents and curious visitors, many writers were drawn to Brooklyn Heights, whose aristocratic brownstone townhouses and narrow streets looked very much like the Village, only quieter and less crowded and with a great view of the Manhattan skyline. Housing was cheaper there, especially to the south, where the Heights segued into a motley landscape of settlement houses, tenements, and modest apartments. There, in the 1930s, the poet and writer James Agee found a socially diverse population of "artists and journalists, communists, bohemians and barbers." This was a place a writer could call home.[3]

Writers found Brooklyn appealing because it was *not* Manhattan. Cheap rents were an important factor. But the borough's slower pace, neighborly interactions, and relative lack of sophistication made it seem more like the rest of the United States than Manhattan was; for this reason, Brooklyn seemed more "authentic" because it resonated with most writers' own origins. "Brooklyn is the small town—but on a gigantic scale—that the New Yorker [i.e., the Manhattanite] ran away from," wrote Betty Smith, a Williamsburg native and the author of the classic immigrant coming-of-age story *A Tree Grows in Brooklyn,* in 1943. This myth of return contrasts with the rejection of the borough by Brooklyn-born writers such as Kazin, Paule Marshall, and Pete Hamill, who grew up and left their parents' household and their strong, even repressive ethnic community, whether it was Jewish, Irish, Italian, or Caribbean. But it's a myth that, like Jane Jacobs's sanitized appreciation of the urban village of Hudson Street, lured more artists and writers to Brooklyn as those ethnic communities aged and grew smaller.[4]

Writers who migrated to brownstone Brooklyn after the 1970s found that the aesthetics of the streets and buildings confirmed their own sense of identity. "The scale and style of the architecture are more deliberately suited to small, personal lives, and we all lead small, personal lives," the poet June Jordan told an interviewer in 1984. Linking herself to an intimate sense of nature and culture, the novelist Paula Fox said she liked "to walk to the grocer on streets lined with old houses that don't hide the stars, to pass beneath sycamore trees, their changes from leaf to bare branch marking the seasons more intimately than the calendar." Such an aesthetic appreciation of the built environment was limited, though, to old bourgeois neighborhoods like Brooklyn Heights, Park Slope, Fort Greene, and Bedford-Stuyvesant, whose long blocks of stately, nineteenth-century houses still had an air of dignified distinction.[5]

During the 1980s and 1990s the migration of more journalists, artists, writers, actors, and filmmakers across the East River began to alter Brooklyn's image. Together with the Brooklyn Academy of Music's adventurous policy of sponsoring avant-garde performances to establish a niche among the city's major cultural institutions, these artists and writers created an unusual buzz about the borough. Like the novelist Paul Auster, their growing presence as both subjects and authors of Brooklyn novels, films, and articles in lifestyle media shifted the city's cultural geography. Noah Baumbach, the writer and director of the movie *The Squid and the Whale* (2005), recalls that in the 1980s Brooklyn was still "separated from Manhattan." Since then, the critic Philip Lopate adds, "Brooklyn has become an *extension* of Manhattan." Most of this change, though, was concentrated in only three of Brooklyn's forty-odd neighborhoods. Because by this time it was too expensive for cash-poor artists and writers to move into the brownstone houses of Brooklyn Heights, they rented apartments from gentrifying homeowners in Park Slope and lofts in Dumbo (the waterfront district of factories and warehouses Down Under the Manhattan Bridge Overpass) and Williamsburg. The critical density of new restaurants and

The epicenter of cool: Bedford Avenue, Williamsburg. Photograph by Sharon Zukin.

indie music bars in that neighborhood soon earned it a label in the media: Williamsburg was now "the epicenter of cool."[6]

Williamsburg was the most industrial of these areas, and for this reason the least likely in the 1980s to attract either gentrifiers or real estate developers. At least since the closing of New York's port in the early 1960s and the gradual decision by the city government to let Brooklyn's industries die, the neighborhood's warehouses and small factories had emptied, and many residents lost their jobs. Williamsburg and nearby Bushwick had been famous for breweries in the nineteenth century, but the last remaining brewery, F&M Schaefer, shut down in the 1970s, and the Domino sugar refinery, once the area's dominant employer, slowly phased out production. When factory owners complained about rising labor costs, congested truck routes, and competition from overseas, city officials didn't even try to help them. Business and political leaders saw Manhattan as the city's commercial center, and they saw Brooklyn as a dormitory for workers in Manhattan's corporate headquarters. After the fiscal crisis of 1975, when banks imposed control over the city government's budget, elected officials could not devise a rescue plan for anyone. Deep cuts in public spending left streets and highways in need of repair, with garbage often piled up on the sidewalks and firehouses and other basic services shut down. Though national attention focused on poverty and arson in the South Bronx, the industrial neighborhood of Williamsburg, then with mostly Italian and Puerto Rican working-class residents, suffered from what looked like terminal decline. During the 1980s, when the expansion of the financial sector encouraged city officials to think again about economic growth, they paid little attention to Williamsburg.[7]

Though elected officials did not support Brooklyn's manufacturers, they sometimes responded to political pressure to avoid creating "another SoHo," where, by 1980, art galleries and loft living had displaced metalworking shops and cardboard and rag factories. In the mid-1980s the city government evicted more than a hundred artists who were living illegally in lofts in the manufacturing zones of Williamsburg and Fulton Ferry (the area soon to be known as Dumbo), to keep space available for manufacturing. "What is at stake here is jobs," Deputy Mayor Alair A. Townsend said, in what was probably the last official statement to downplay the potential of artists to spearhead urban renewal.[8]

By this time, though, artists were already living in the lofts and small apartments of Williamsburg. In the early 1990s two thousand of them lived among 115,000 residents near the waterfront. Only 2 percent of a shrinking local population, they were nonetheless a visible presence in an area not previously known for the arts. During the 1990s the number of artists and writers, graphic designers, furniture builders, and new media producers quickly grew, especially in Williamsburg, Park Slope, and Dumbo. As many as 20 percent of residents of these neighborhoods worked in creative occupations, in contrast to 4 percent of all New Yorkers and only 2 percent of all Americans. Not only were new residents of these three neighborhoods creative, they were also "connected." Of more than two thousand blogs published in Brooklyn in the first years of the twenty-first century, most were based in Park Slope (318), Williamsburg (242), and Dumbo (31).[9]

After older generations of ethnic, working-class residents moved away or passed on and remaining small factories either shut down or were displaced by landlords aiming at higher rents, the new residents created a different image for these three neighborhoods. Moreover, by a kind of global brand extension, this image began to mark the entire borough. Brooklyn was no longer the butt of ethnic jokes made by Jewish comedians from Borough Park and Coney Island (familiar from the movie *Annie Hall*), the asphalt jungle where bouffant hairdos and black leather jackets were worn as tribal signs by Italian teens in Bensonhurst (seen in the movie *Saturday Night Fever*), or the nostalgic homeland of grown men who summoned tears when they talked about how they used to go to Ebbets Field in Crown Heights in the 1950s to see Jackie Robinson play for the Brooklyn Dodgers before the team abandoned Brooklyn for Los Angeles, and many of these men, now older and retired, moved to Florida or South Carolina. Instead the media presented a new Brooklyn with a different kind of authenticity that had little to do with its old working-class and ethnic origins. "Brooklyn-ness," as the *New York Times* art critic Holland Cotter wrote in 2004, is now "a *cultural* ethnicity."[10]

The contentious fate of the McCarren Park pool, a public recreational facility on the border between Williamsburg and Greenpoint, reflects this dramatic shift in Brooklyn's image. Built by Robert Moses in the 1930s with funds from the federal Works Progress Administration, the swimming pool served an overcrowded tenement district of the working poor. During hot summer months in the 1930s and 1940s more than six thousand swimmers a day would pass through the majestic arch of its entry pavilion. In the 1970s, though, when more black and Puerto Rican residents moved into nearby neighborhoods and began to use the pool, racial conflicts broke out over who belonged there, as well as over who was responsible for mounting incidents of crime and vandalism. Swimmers stopped going to the park because they felt unsafe. The city government, caught in the fiscal crisis, let the pool deteriorate along with the rest of the neighborhood, finally closing it for a planned restoration in 1983. At that point, however, already suffering from drastic cuts in city services and fearing more changes that they could not control, white residents organized protests to stop work on the pool.

For the next twenty years community groups and the New York City Parks Department sparred over alternative plans, with the Parks Department pushing for a larger pool to serve an expanded area of Brooklyn and local residents supporting a smaller pool that would be limited to nearby residents and would therefore be more ethnically exclusive. Continued conflict over the scale and type of new facilities, another dispute over designating some of the pool's buildings as historic landmarks, and repeated budget crises prevented any renovations from being done. Meanwhile Williamsburg was changing from an ethnic cauldron of working-class whites, blacks, and Puerto Ricans into a mainly white cultural mix of artists and musicians, some of whom took advantage of the unused public space in McCarren Park to begin organizing free concerts. In 2005, after a modern dance performance in the empty cement pool drew an audience of fifteen thousand, Clear Channel Communications decided that the pool would make a great venue for paying concerts organized by its Live Nation subsidiary. The company made a multimillion-dollar donation to the Parks Department to clean off graffiti and renovate the pool in return for a contract for its use.

Throughout the next three summers conflict over the pool focused again on who belonged there, but this time the dispute pitted Clear Channel, a major corporate promoter of mainstream, big-ticket concerts, against those who wanted to continue the Sunday-night "pool parties" that featured free concerts by post-punk bands, many of whom lived in the neighborhood. Because Williamsburg was now certifiably cool, corporate media would take a chance on it.[11]

As ... I trawled its cool-cat shops, soaked in the indie rock scene and walked the gallery- and café-lined streets, "Billyburg" still felt balanced on the cutting edge.
—Jennifer Barger, *Washington Post*, November 30, 2005

The story of hipster Williamsburg connects the neighborhood's reinvention as a cultural incubator with crucial stages in the product cycle of "authentic" cool. Like Chicago's Wicker Park in the 1990s, Manhattan's East Village in the 1980s, and SoHo in the 1970s, Williamsburg's new authenticity began with a low-rent and somewhat dangerous neighborhood, enabling moneyless twenty-somethings who wanted to be artists to form scenes, 'zines, and experimental art forms with little market value. Local media that were initially developed by and for insiders—alternative weekly newspapers, photocopied broadsheets, wiki, and blogs—were cannibalized by the mainstream media, which were hungry for content. First came glowing restaurant and gallery reviews in citywide newspapers and magazines, then stereotypical travel articles in national newspapers and guidebooks ("As...I trawled its cool-cat shops"), and finally corporate media websites that promoted the neighborhood for its shopping opportunities. Art and music critics who wrote for a specialized audience also promoted Williamsburg as the next new thing. Through the outreach of the media Williamsburg crystallized into an identifiable local product for global cultural consumption: authentic Brooklyn cool.

Tracing this process through the media shows how quickly the new authenticity was produced. LedisFlam, Williamsburg's first art gallery, opened in 1987. In 1991 the *New York Press,* an alternative weekly newspaper given away for free in take-out shops and grocery stores throughout the city, ran an article titled "Brooklyn Unbound," which praised the funky clubs and bars that were operating on "that huge stretch of eerie, magnificent, vacant waterfront with all those great rotting warehouses that are perfect to use as performance spaces." A few months later a cover story in *New York* magazine declared Williamsburg "the new Bohemia," a sure way to bring crowds of weekend shoppers and tourists. Typical of the magazine's air of underground discovery, this article described the scene in Teddy's, "a typical workingman's tavern in the Polish section," for middle-class Manhattanites and suburbanites who were not likely to find Brooklyn on their own. The bar's afternoon clientele included the unusual mix of a newly arrived couple from Eastern Europe, two young men in jeans, some middle-aged electricians, and "a cross-dressing performance artist." The next year the art world kicked in with an exhibition at the Krannert Art Museum at the University of Illinois; the exhibition catalogue proclaimed the discovery of "the Williamsburg paradigm." This drew the attention of both artists and patrons who were looking for a new arts community to replace the overly popular and increasingly expensive East Village.[12]

Jonathan Fineberg, an art professor who organized the exhibition, credited the paradigm to a synergy built up by different kinds of bohemian artists who like their earlier counterparts in nineteenth-century Paris and 1980s-era Lower Manhattan, organized unusual events that created a sense of community. Though Fineberg praised Williamsburg's artists for their lack of slickness, he could have praised them for their entrepreneurial energy, for the ephemeral clubs and gatherings that they initiated laid the groundwork for a dynamic cultural economy. In this sense Williamsburg operated very much like any other arts-based "industrial district," such as Wicker Park, Berkeley, Hoxton in London, or the East Village. In each place cultural producers build overlapping networks around the nodes of temporary events, which creates the social capital and media feedback for continued innovation. Participants in one event, club, art gallery, or blog likely join or organize others. It's like Silicon Valley without engineers and with much less venture capital.[13]

The East Village art scene that had burned so brightly in the early 1980s undoubtedly shaped both the hopes and the fears that artists held for Williamsburg in the 1990s. Like a 1984 show at the Institute of Contemporary Art of the University of Pennsylvania that quickly canonized the East Village art scene, the 1993 exhibition on "the Williamsburg paradigm" at the University of Illinois helped to establish the neighborhood's new reputation for creativity. Any ambitious young artist would want to be there. At first, the absence of other artists was an attractive feature. The cultural as well as the geographical distance between Brooklyn and Manhattan made it easy to see Williamsburg as an "alternative" space. As more artists moved in, however, their ability to find and entertain each other—through street parties, discussions, and DIY performances—created a hothouse of "authenticity."[14]

Like other arts districts, Williamsburg's viability depended not just on the presence of artists, writers, and musicians, but also on their ability to become cultural entrepreneurs. In truth, some of them brought their best creative efforts to this role. The clubs and galleries that they organized were small, but they became social centers for both fellow artists and young cultural consumers who wanted to be around them. These places also attracted art critics and music journalists because they were run by artists whose amateur status as business owners—an artist presenting other artists, a musician promoting other bands—emphasized their identity as insiders and made them appear even more authentic. For their part, the galleries and clubs presented themselves as being uninhibited, under the radar, and conspicuously poor. Because the owners made hardly any money, the places lacked heat and rarely if ever had a cabaret or liquor license, leading to occasional raids by the police and fire departments. Their names were as ironic as any indie rock band's, and it was often hard to find them in the maze of small streets and alleys near the derelict industrial waterfront. But these were all markers of their authenticity.[15]

In the early 1990s Williamsburg began to develop a wider reputation as the site of occasional, complex multimedia events that were somewhat like clubs and parties of the 1980s but also like mass be-ins and performances of the 1960s. Unused factories and warehouses in Williamsburg could hold crowds, and the potential audience for performances was even larger because of the growing popularity of alternative movements such as raves and culture jamming. All of these cultural events in and around the independent art and music worlds came together at the Old Dutch Mustard factory, a large, multistory loft building near the waterfront that had been vacant for several years. The factory's owners were already renting it out as a location for unadvertised parties, drawing hundreds of paying participants, when in June 1993 a group of more than a hundred artists and musicians rented it for an event they called "Organism." Described as the first web jam, Organism lasted from 6 o'clock one evening until 9 the next morning and drew two thousand participants. The organizers set up electronic systems, bionic sculptures, and computer projections, and instructed participants to engage this environment with their own bodies; *Newsweek* magazine called it "a sequel to the rave." It was no small achievement for such an event to get a write-up in the mainstream media, and the article in *Newsweek* celebrated Williamsburg as a cultural phenomenon.[16]

After a fire closed the Mustard Factory in 1994, one of Organism's organizers, Robert Elmes, opened Galapagos, a performance space and bar, in another old condiment plant, a mayonnaise factory, on a side street near the Bedford Avenue subway station. Elmes had moved to Williamsburg from Canada in 1989, and he wanted Galapagos to become a permanent place of artistic incubation and interactive performance as well as entertainment—a community institution for a creative community. Soon the shows at Galapagos were written up in the *New York Times* and *Village Voice,* and Elmes was bringing in all kinds of performers from Europe and

Former site of Galapagos Artspace: North Sixth Street, Williamsburg, looking toward the East River. Photograph by Sharon Zukin.

Asia as well as North America. In this way he became a prime promoter of Williamsburg's new cool.[17]

Warehouse parties and performance spaces were soon joined by small storefront art galleries, like those in the East Village, which attracted an older, more affluent group of media critics and cultural consumers. This constituency began to cross the East River in 1995, when a SoHo art dealer who specialized in exhibiting cutting-edge conceptual work invited four Williamsburg galleries—Sauce, Momenta, Four Walls, and Pierogi—to put together a show for his gallery. The SoHo exhibition put Williamsburg on the cultural map. Just as Manhattan collectors now prized Williamsburg artists as new talent, so the mainstream art media that was also based in Manhattan began to visit galleries there. Critics praised the neighborhood for its authentic feel, like SoHo before it was "discovered."[18]

During the 1990s, in addition to performance and art, Williamsburg began to develop production sites for two other sectors of the symbolic economy: food and fashion. New, inexpensive restaurants moved away from the "original" authenticity of the area's Polish bakeries and Latino bodegas to a new, bohemian combination of Asian exoticism and flea market chic. Oznot's Dish, a storefront restaurant offering Middle Eastern cuisine, opened in 1992 and received a good review two years later in the *New York Times*. At the same time, a young woman named Kitty Shapiro opened the L Café near the Bedford Avenue subway station. "She did it something like Greenwich Village," recalled a bartender at a Polish tavern down the block. Within a few years the café had become a neighborhood institution, selling bagels through the storefront window and offering high chairs and "Babyccinos" of steamed milk for residents' children. It was "an authentic environment, a neighborhood joint," said Dan Siegler, who bought the café from Shapiro when she moved on.[19]

Williamsburg's new authenticity took a giant leap when Brooklyn Brewery moved into another old factory just a few blocks from Galapagos. The first brewery to open in this area in about a hundred years, the operation was the brainchild of two Brooklyn-born men, a reporter and a banker, who decided to quit their jobs and go into the beer business when the trend for artisanal beer made by microbreweries swept through the country in the 1980s. They created a boutique beer called Brooklyn Lager that was brewed upstate and distributed from Bushwick, the neighborhood to the east of Williamsburg that had a working-class African American and Latino population but was racked by crime and dilapidated houses and factories. Because truck drivers were afraid to drive into Bushwick after dark, Brooklyn Brewery rented warehouse space in Williamsburg for deliveries. In the mid-1990s, around the same time that Galapagos opened, the owners decided to take direct control of their brewing operations and move them from upstate to Williamsburg. Though this attracted the unwanted attention of both labor union gangsters and armed robbers, archetypal figures who harked back to the neighborhood's origins, Williamsburg soon became safe enough for the brewery owners to offer guided tours for visitors. They also hosted a Friday night happy hour with local bands, games of pool, and three-dollar glasses of beer. In a way, artisanal beer production returned Williamsburg to its origins, but with higher-class commodities.[20]

Toward the end of the 1990s the "street fashion" company Brooklyn Industries added another cool cultural product to Williamsburg's growing entrepreneurial mix. In this case, the entrepreneurs, Lexy Funk and Vahap Avsar, were artists trying to make careers as designers in Manhattan while working at non-art jobs, Funk at an advertising agency and Avsar as the night manager of a restaurant. One day Avsar was inspired to recycle the discarded sheets of giant vinyl billboards that he found in a Dumpster near their studio-home in Manhattan. He cut the vinyl sheets into pieces, and then he and Funk sewed the pieces together into messenger bags that Avsar designed. Within a few years they had so many orders for their Crypto label that they needed a larger production space, leading them to rent an empty, one-story factory in Williamsburg. Avsar, Funk, and a few employees cut vinyl sheets into pieces on the roof, then took them indoors and sewed them together into messenger bags. Avsar drew the Brooklyn skyline of factory buildings and rooftop water tanks that they could see from their roof and used it as the company's logo; whether or not this was meant as a challenge to Manhattan Portage, a messenger bag company that was founded in Manhattan several years earlier and used the city's famous skyline as its logo, it turned Brooklyn into an aesthetic theme. Changing the name of their company to Brooklyn Industries, Avsar and Funk added T-shirts and pants to their line of bags and opened a retail store on Bedford Avenue in 2001. Within the next few years they opened seven more stores in Manhattan and Brooklyn and, like Brooklyn Brewery, began to distribute products outside the region. When Aesop Rock, a white indie hip-hop artist who wore Brooklyn Industries T-shirts played clubs in Europe, he was introduced as "straight outta Brooklyn"; this helped to turn the Williamsburg operation—and Brooklyn as a whole—into a global brand.[21]

Williamsburg's new entrepreneurs crystallized the neighborhood's "authenticity" into a product with cultural buzz and shaped their own new beginnings into a powerful story of origin. Art galleries, performance spaces, a microbrewery, and messenger bags shared an urban imaginary that was one part abandoned factories and two parts artistic innovation, all leading to a creative mix that was "made in Brooklyn." This story had no connection with Williamsburg's real origins, with either the "scavengers, pimps, [and] gangsters" of the early 1900s or the Domino sugar workers and Puerto Rican mechanics of the area's industrial prime time, or even with the Polish meat market and Mexican grocery store that are still doing business on Bedford Avenue, though less business now than before Williamsburg became so popular.

The origin story of Brooklyn cool is a romantic story of indie artists and culture jams, of participation and creativity; it's an anticorporate, anti-Manhattan rant. It also reflects the deliberate absence of economic involvement by private developers and public officials, who ignored manufacturers' pleas for protection from landlords when they refused to renew their leases or dramatically raised their rent when they saw artists coming. More than that, though, it represents a larger cultural transformation, with the creation of a nouveau grit aesthetic that telescopes Williamsburg's rebirth from a cheap, unremarkable, immigrant neighborhood near the docks to the "third hippest neighborhood" in urban America.[22]

A metamorphosis from gritty to cool was not unique to Williamsburg in the 1990s. Though it didn't affect cities with declining populations and little opportunity for economic growth, this same metamorphosis did extend the success of big cities with dynamic corporate financial and media sectors to rundown neighborhoods outside the center. Nouveau grit not only describes Williamsburg's revival; it also applies to the rebirth of San Francisco south of Market Street during the dot-com boom and the Seattle of Starbucks and grunge, as well as to the revival of a small number of industrial neighborhoods in Kansas City, Oklahoma City, Baltimore, and Philadelphia. Gritty's appeal was in the postindustrial spirit of the times and in the symbolic economy's ability to synthesize dirt and danger into new cultural commodities.

"I just love how gritty and industrial it is here," she said, indicating the trucks double-parked, motors running in the street, the guys in hooded sweatshirts pushing handcarts. "It's kind of like these are the raw ingredients, and then you go to the restaurant and have a meal."
—*New York Times*, February 9, 2007

Like Williamsburg, the word "gritty" hardly made an appearance in popular culture before the 1990s, and when it did, it carried the symbolic baggage of death and destruction. "Gritty" describes both the style and substance of old black-and-white films, especially the film noir movies made in New York and Los Angeles in the late 1940s and 1950s, films that suggested the alienation of the individual in modern cities and those cities' tragic loss of power to younger, more prosperous suburbs. The noir image suits a narrative of Brooklyn's economic decline, from the shutdown of the port and Navy Yard in the 1960s and the abandonment of the breweries to the changing social geography of upwardly mobile white ethnic groups who gradually left the borough's tenements and brownstones for high-rise apartments in Manhattan and split-level houses in the suburbs. "Gritty" is the word for what they left behind: crowded streets, rising crime rates, and blue-collar lives.[23]

By the 1970s the term was commonly used to describe factory towns and urban neighborhoods that were squeezed by plant shutdowns and out-sourcing of the basic manufactured goods, from textiles to steel, that had supported American families for so many years. *Gritty Cities,* a book of photographs published in 1978, emphasized the ruptured bond between people, place, and product that devastated cities such as Philadelphia, Baltimore, and Paterson, New Jersey. At their peak these cities were known by their achievements in manufacturing; they were the Iron City, the Silk City, the Steel City, and the Brass City, where "neighborhoods have the tough, proud look of the breadwinners who have come home to them from the mills for over a century." By the end of the 1970s, though, gritty cities were remarkable mainly for visual images of decay: long blocks of small red-brick homes, abandoned factory chimneys, and vacant storefronts. Like Brooklyn after the Dodgers left town, a gritty city's "drawing card [was] nostalgia."[24]

"Gritty" soon became the media's code word to depict the social ills and aesthetic blight of all older cities. In Youngstown, Ohio, the site of multiple steel mill shutdowns in the late 1970s, "grimy old factories whose hearths have been cold for years" filled "the gritty streets." Baltimore was "a seemingly endless strip of gritty row houses where on hot summer nights sweltering people hunch…on their stone steps for a breath of polluted air." In more prosperous cities "gritty neighborhoods" looked grim next to "prime areas."[25]

At the same time, journalists also began to apply the word to popular cultural forms they liked, especially those that had some connection with New York City. "Gritty" described both the punk rock club CBGB on the Bowery in Lower Manhattan and the highly rated TV detective series *Kojak* that took place on the streets of a fictional Midtown South. The changing use of "gritty," especially in the New York context, boded well for neighbor-hoods like Williamsburg, despite their physical decay and lack of public services.[26]

Journalists sniffed out that something in the gritty streets was chang-ing, but exactly what was changing varied according to which section of the newspaper was writing about it. The Careers section of the *New York Times* noted that new biotech firms were opening "in…gritty, loft-lined Hudson Street in the lower West Side." But the *Times'* Weekend section called attention to the trendy restaurants and clubs that were opening in this "area of gritty warehouses, ungentrified neighborhood bars, and century-old cast-iron buildings." Many articles identified artists as agents of change, beginning with "the gritty former industrial buildings" of SoHo and spreading to the "gritty city" of Newark, "saddled for two decades with an image of urban blight." Because of rising housing prices, though, the gap between gritty and prime areas began to narrow. "Manhattan's 'Fringes' Getting Voguish," a headline in a 1987 issue of the *New York Times* declared, for "rising housing costs in prime areas have pushed more and more people into gritty neighborhoods."[27]

By the mid-1990s, just when art galleries, performance spaces, and artisanal beer were starting to define Williamsburg's new authenticity, gritty neighborhoods became a destination for cultural connoisseurs. "Gritty West Chelsea Winning Over Art Set," the *Atlanta Journal and Constitution* said about Manhattan's newest gallery district. In London, said the *Financial Times,* "the gritty post-industrial wasteland climate" of the South Bank is now "a powerhouse for growth" fueled by theaters, trendy shopping, and a modern art museum.[28]

In the following years critics praised gritty novels, plays, and art for their honest aesthetic qualities, their ability to represent a specific space and time, and identified "gritty" with a direct experience of life in the way that we have come to expect of authenticity. "Photographs [the artist Ben] Shahn took of life on New York sidewalks in the '30s have an unmediated, gritty spontaneity," said the *New York Times.* The media also admired the "gritty urban aesthetic" of gentrifying neighborhoods from Philadelphia to San Francisco, where "gritty bars" and warehouses were now joined, paradoxically, by new restaurants, boutique hotels, and expensive condos. In all cities housing prices in gritty neighborhoods rose faster than elsewhere. Today the use of "gritty" in the media depicts a desirable synergy between underground cultures and the creative energy they bring to both cultural consumption and real estate development, not as an alternative to but as a driver of the city's growth. When the *New York Times* recommends "the gritty charm of Friday Night Fights" in the basement of a church, where the audience includes "thugs from the ghetto…blue-collar working class types…rich dudes and hipsters," readers know this is a positive recommendation. So is the comment of ninety-one-year-old Arthur Laurents, who wrote the book of the original musical *West Side Story* and directed its revival on Broadway in 2009; the new version of the play, said Laurents, should "achieve an authentic grittiness that the theater of the 1950s didn't allow." "Gritty," we now understand, means *authenticity,* and that is good.[29]

But a trace of the bad old gritty remains when it comes to race. While some industrial neighborhoods such as Williamsburg were becoming hip in the 1990s, other Brooklyn neighborhoods, inner-city areas where blacks and Latinos lived, were stuck with bad housing, failing schools, lack of jobs, and high crime rates. Most of these neighborhoods were also burdened with rapidly aging public housing projects that had been designed as towers surrounded by green park-like space but were experienced as vertical ghettos—the very design Jane Jacobs despised. Yet this racially other gritty, located in Bedford-Stuyvesant, Fort Greene, Clinton Hill, and East Flatbush, also developed a new image of Brooklyn as cool. Unlike in Williamsburg, however, these new beginnings entered popular culture through hip-hop music and black films.

Jay-Z, Big' Smalls, n— s— ya drawers
Brooklyn represent y'all, hit you fold
You crazy, think your little bit of rhymes can play me?
I'm from Marcy, I'm varsity, chump, you're JV.
—Jay-Z, "Brooklyn's Finest," 1996

In the mid-1990s, when Spike Lee adapted the novel *Clockers* to the screen and changed its location from the fictional town of Dempsy, New Jersey, to the real streets of Brooklyn, he brought the borough's gritty black neighborhoods into the virtual core of popular culture. Lee had set his movies in Brooklyn and filmed on location there since beginning his career a decade earlier. His first film, *Joe's Bed-Stuy Barbershop: We Cut Heads* (1983), is very much a neighborhood movie. His second film, *She's Gotta Have It* (1986), begins with a shot of the Brooklyn Bridge. Unlike other directors, who tend to shoot the bridge in front of Manhattan's skyline, Lee focuses on the Brooklyn side of the river. He uses such local landmarks as the downtown Fulton Mall, Brooklyn Heights Promenade, and Fort Greene Park, site of a six-minute-long color fantasy sequence. To introduce the character Mars, played by Lee himself, Lee shows him bicycling down a hill in Dumbo. If the audience needs a more literal sign to identify blacks with Brooklyn, Lee dresses Radio Raheem, a character in his later film *Do the Right Thing* (1989), in a T-shirt labeled "Bedford-Stuyvesant." And the song that opens

Clockers (1995) declares, "Brooklyn is the borough." Using all these devices, Lee's films replaced the long-standing icon of African American urban identity, Harlem, with the black neighborhoods of Brooklyn.[30]

Lee's images of these neighborhoods follow a model set by the African American film directors Oscar Michaux and Charles Burnett, who portray everyday life in working-class areas of the inner city. But they also follow classical New York "street" movies like *Dead End* (1937) and *A Tree Grows in Brooklyn* (1945) that claim to show authentic urban life through the lens of a single block. Unlike these earlier films, though, that were shot on Hollywood sets designed to look like New York streets, both *Do the Right Thing* and *Crooklyn* (1994) take place on a real street of brownstone houses in Bedford-Stuyvesant. Lee uses the street theatrically, as if it were a set. In this place, which is not so different from the gentrified street of Park Slope in *The Squid and the Whale,* anger and frustration boil over into violence. Yet at the center of each film loving families and familiar characters watch over the comings and goings of neighbors and friends and comment on them like a Greek chorus. As Mos Def, the hip-hop artist and actor who grew up in Bed-Stuy, says, echoing the current view of Brooklyn, "It still has that spirit about it. Like small town neighborhoods. People know each other. People are very loyal to their neighborhood." But *Do the Right Thing* does not gloss over the hateful ethnic and social tensions that were so much a part of New York and other American cities in the 1980s. The tragedy of the black community in Brooklyn at this time is the conflict between insiders and outsiders, pitting African American residents against each other as well as against the Italians who own the corner pizzeria and the recently arrived Korean greengrocer.[31]

Though Lee was also filming music videos for hip-hop performers, Brooklyn was not yet known for this kind of music. The D.J.'s who developed the beats and techniques of sampling in the 1970s came from the Bronx. Not until the 1980s and 1990s, when M.C.'s were rapping lyrics rather than laying down beats, did a new generation of rappers make a vocal claim for the "authenticity" of the other Outer Boroughs with sizable black populations: Brooklyn and Queens. If Jay-Z and Busta Rhymes "represented" an African American neighborhood like Bed-Stuy or East Flatbush or a public housing project like Marcy Houses, this said their product was authentic—to both the black audience who expected the music to be "real" in terms of evoking racial experience and the whites who liked it because it spoke of danger. Like movies by black directors, hip-hop moved during the 1990s from depicting an abstract space called "the ghetto" to naming specific streets and landmarks of "the hood." And some of these neighborhoods were in Brooklyn.[32]

Naming neighborhoods gave hip-hop artists a means of branding their products in terms of origins, and branding was important to them because the economic and cultural stakes of success in the music business were so high. Just as Nike and Adidas bought endorsements by black athletes, so other corporations that sold clothes, cars, and cell phones hired hip-hop artists to promote them. This created a multibillion-dollar sports-fashion-and-entertainment complex that included Def Jam, Roc-a-Fella, and Bad Boy Records in New York and Death Row Records in Los Angeles, all record labels that were started by hip-hop entrepreneurs. When gangsta rap made the fortunes of these labels in the mid-1990s, its lyrics represented, and reinforced, the "authenticity" of black neighborhoods. Prominent among them was Bedford-Stuyvesant, home of Jay-Z as well as Biggie Smalls, the "notorious B.I.G.," a heavy-set rapper and, briefly, the most important hip-hop artist at Bad Boy Records.

Taking his stage name from a character in a 1970s gangster comedy directed by Sidney Poitier, Biggie Smalls was larger than life in more than body size. He rapped about being a drug dealer and spending time in jail, using explicit language to depict a neighborhood of gun battles and cocaine deals. By his persona no less than his lyrics he represented his home borough as a cradle of "authentic" hip-hop culture—the good, the bad, and the ugly, from illegal drug sales to gold chains. When Biggie and Jay-Z rapped "Where you from?" on the chorus of "Brooklyn's Finest" (1996), they offered a shout-out to the neighborhoods spanning central Brooklyn that had gone through a racial transformation from white to black in the 1960s and 1970s and developed a more complex ethnic identity in the 1980s and 1990s with growing Caribbean and African immigration. The rising popularity of gangsta rap cast these neighborhoods as an epicenter of cool, though in a different way from Williamsburg and for a different part of the public.[33]

Even if black Brooklyn was cool, it was not always easy to survive there. Biggie Smalls was shot to death in 1997 in what was presumed to be a battle in the lethal rivalry between hip-hop record labels and the moguls who run them. Other Brooklyn rap artists were regularly arrested for illegal weapons possession or involved in fights in music clubs—a mirror image of the violence in many of their songs. Like Williamsburg's artistic entrepreneurs, hip-hop artists created a story of origin that became the basis for Brooklyn's new authenticity. But unlike hipster Williamsburg, black Brooklyn was dangerous.

Spike Lee's movie *Clockers* dramatizes black Brooklyn's power to entrap and immobilize people in the central character's thwarted love of trains. The film scholar Paula Massood connects the image of trains in the film with the history of black migration, beginning with the African slave trade, passing through the Great Migration from the rural south to the industrial north, and ending with the move into formerly white neighborhoods. Brooklyn is more than a temporary stopping point in this history, she says: "Brooklyn is the literal end of the line after multiple journeys." But Strike, the successful neighborhood crack dealer who likes to play with a model electric train in his rundown apartment, has never been on a train. Only when Rocco, the homicide detective who has been trying to solve a murder in the neighborhood, realizes that Strike is innocent and helps him to get away is Strike able to take his first railroad journey and leave the city. The golden light that filters through the train window in the last scene, Massood observes, is "a marked difference from the gritty cinematography" of the rest of the film. Like Lee, she interprets this contrast between golden light and gritty atmosphere as both an aesthetic and a moral choice.[34]

Unlike Williamsburg, black Brooklyn neighborhoods do not benefit from the growth machine of cultural production. Though they are the birthplace of rappers, they don't have the critical cluster of "clubs, radio stations, cable access TV stations, record labels, and mix-tape producers" that supports Manhattan's hip-hop music industry. The perspective established so forcefully, then, by the opening shot in *She's Gotta Have It* didn't create the same value for black Brooklyn that practically the same shot of another bridge created for Williamsburg six years later, when *New York* magazine's cover story established Williamsburg as "the new Bohemia." If Williamsburg's artists and musicians "feel a dialogue with Manhattan," as that article said, Bed-Stuy's rappers still live very far from this border.[35]

A story of cosmopolitanism runs alongside the story of origin in Brooklyn's rebirth as cool. While cultural entrepreneurs have come to Williamsburg from other regions of the world, so have many rap artists' families come to central Brooklyn from Africa and the Caribbean. And just as Williamsburg exports Brooklyn art, bands, lager, and T-shirts around the world, so Brooklyn hip-hop is a global brand. But black cosmopolitanism confronts the demographics of a gradually "whitening" Brooklyn. Before

1980 white twenty-somethings tended to be working-class youths who lived in traditional white ethnic neighborhoods like Bensonhurst and Bay Ridge: the urban village. After 1980 these nodes of youthful whiteness disappeared with the aging of the white population and the suburban migration of the upwardly mobile among them, along with growing Caribbean, Latino, Asian, and African immigration; Brooklyn became blacker and browner. By 2000, though, the map of Brooklyn showed young white adults living in different places: the three creative neighborhoods—Williamsburg, Park Slope, and Dumbo—that represent a new, more affluent, and more aesthetically attuned "urban village."[36]

Most people call this gentrification. But that is too narrow a term to describe the demographic and economic changes that have reshaped both Brooklyn's physical fabric and its reputation. In-movement by whites, coupled with African Americans' out-migration, suggests a process of ethnic succession in reverse, with whites now replacing blacks and Latinos and the corner bodega selling organic whole wheat pasta. Brooklyn's new "authenticity" reflects a different, upscale social character, where *upscale* means richer people on the one hand and taller buildings on the other.[37]

"It was generally felt that Brooklyn was a good place for parents ambitious for their children and a kind of up-and-coming super-gentrified area," said Mr. Hampton, who is British.
—*New York Times*, March 29, 2009

Though the collapse of financial markets in 2008 stalled funding for new construction and left many condos unsold, the rezoning that New York mayor Michael Bloomberg's administration started three years earlier is bringing taller, denser buildings, "Manhattanization," to Brooklyn at last. This was Robert Moses's dream in the 1950s, but the dream was long deferred because private real estate developers did not believe people with money would move to Brooklyn. They have moved in, though, and rising housing prices coupled with new luxury apartments have already fueled further change in Williamsburg. Brooklyn Brewery's rent has tripled, Galapagos Artspace has decamped to Dumbo, and artists and musicians are moving eastward into Bushwick, farther afield to Flatbush, and even out to Queens, seeding new areas with cool bars and restaurants as they migrate from the hipster core.

When the New York City Planning Commission rezoned 170 blocks in Williamsburg in 2005, they explicitly aimed to upscale the waterfront, ridding it of its remaining industrial uses and reclaiming the prime space for high-rise residential construction. Now twenty- to forty-story apartment houses stretch along the East River from the old Domino sugar refinery to the former Schaefer brewery site, and the area upland, away from the waterfront, is dotted with shorter steel-and-glass condos such as the Steelworks Loft, its name reflecting only an aesthetic interest in the neighborhood's past. This kind of redevelopment represents the future the city government desires.

In the rezoning process the Bloomberg administration respected the letter of the laws Jane Jacobs inspired but paid no attention to her broader social goals. The City Planning Commission held public hearings on a 197a community development plan created by neighborhood residents, a coalition of working-class families and artists, who strongly supported keeping facilities for light manufacturing and building low-rise, affordable housing. But the commissioners rejected the residents' proposals. At the next level of public hearings, Mayor Bloomberg and the City Council ignored an eloquent letter supporting the community plan that Jacobs herself sent them shortly before she died. "What the intelligently worked out plan devised by the community itself does not do is worth noticing," Jacobs wrote. "It does not destroy hundreds of manufacturing jobs.... [It] does not promote new housing at the expense of both existing housing and imaginative and economical new shelter that residents can afford.... [It] does not violate the existing scale of the community, nor does it insult the visual and economic advantages of neighborhoods that are precisely of the kind that demonstrably attract artists and other live-work craftsmen." But the council members proceeded to rezone the waterfront from manufacturing to residential use, permitting tall—and presumably luxury—apartment towers to replace empty factories and rundown warehouses.[38]

City Council members compromised with community demands for reasonably priced housing by offering tax subsidies, and the right to build bigger buildings, to developers if they agreed to include about 20 percent "affordable" rental apartments in their projects. These agreements, though, are strictly voluntary, and developers and building owners upland most often ignore the incentives, preferring to charge rents as high as the market will bear. For these reasons, a developer tore down the Old Dutch Mustard

Factory—arguably a monument to Williamsburg's new authenticity—and replaced it with loft-condos and townhouses, a "private zen garden," and rooftop cabanas.[39]

The story of how Brooklyn became cool, and of the upscale real estate development that followed, shows the effects of capital investment and government policies, to be sure, but also demonstrates the cultural power of the media and new middle-class consumer tastes. These have produced a sense of Brooklyn's authenticity different from anything that came before.

If you ask Paul M., a middle-aged man who was born and raised in the borough, why Brooklyn is now cool, he doesn't think of the Old Dutch Mustard Factory or parties like Rubulad. He smiles shyly and says, "Hasn't Brooklyn *always* been cool?" Paul sees Brooklyn's authenticity in the movies about World War II that he grew up with, whose ethnically balanced casts of actors, except for the absence of blacks, who fought in segregated units until 1949, symbolized America's cultural diversity. The soldier who came from Brooklyn, Paul says, was always "the salt of the earth." But this is an image of Brooklyn's old authenticity, and it speaks of a time when the borough not only was an urban village, but the motherland of all America. In those years one of every seven Americans, regardless of where they lived, had a family member who came from Brooklyn.

The new Brooklyn is different. It's a place people come *to*, not a place they come *from*, and where residents don't have a traditional, urban village way of life but are very proud of the "authenticity" of the neighborhood where they choose to live. Brooklyn's urban imaginary today combines hipsters and new immigrants, lifestyle media and blogs, and both desire to become the next cultural destination and yearning for an urban village that disappeared after World War II. For each generation, though, the idea of Brooklyn's authenticity shows an aspiration to connect the place where people live to a timeless urban experience.

Brooklyn's older generation, who grew up with Jackie Robinson and watched him break the "color barrier" in 1947, is defined by nostalgia for *yesterday*. They look back to the years before the Dodgers left town, the Navy Yard shut down, and many of their neighbors left for the suburbs as Brooklyn's prime time. Now they live in retirement in the South or in lower-middle-class neighborhoods with new immigrant neighbors.

The middle-aged generation of new immigrants arrived in Brooklyn after 1985, when U.S. immigration laws were changed and the flow of people from the Caribbean, Mexico, China, and Africa increased, and the

Soviet Union broke apart, bringing other new residents from Russia and Central Asia. This generation is defined by hope for *tomorrow*. Working hard in small factories, driving taxis, or caring for children in other people's homes, they look forward to the success of the next generation.

The third generation is the twenty- and thirty-somethings who define themselves by *today*. Gentrifiers as well as hipsters, they find the aesthetic tools to fashion a looser, hipper identity in their Brooklyn neighborhood, from fading shop signs and loft buildings to new art galleries and cafés. Though they claim to admire the old authenticity of Brooklyn's origins, they have created another authenticity that reflects their own story of origin.

Not everything in Brooklyn is relentlessly upscale. While Williamsburg suffers from a glut of unsold luxury condos, the popular free concerts have moved from the McCarren Park pool to a new waterfront park. A few neighborhoods away, in gentrified Park Slope, the food co-op inspires at least as much dedication—and idealization of community—as the old corner candy store. The new development project planned for Atlantic Yards has been halted by the economic crisis, and in Coney Island, the city government is fighting a developer who wants to turn the historic but seedy amusement park into a theme park with shopping mall. Yet development, says Brooklyn Borough president Marty Markowitz, makes all of Brooklyn cool.[40]

Development has brought many changes to Brooklyn in recent years. Together with dramatic decreases in the crime rate, it has encouraged middle-class people to venture into neighborhoods where they had never gone before. Race used to be considered a barrier to these changes. The recent whitening of Brooklyn, though, has expanded gentrification into working-class black neighborhoods while new immigrants as well as white gentrifiers have made other areas into an ethnic mosaic. If racial barriers still hold back gentrification anywhere, however, we would surely see their effects in Harlem, "the capital of black America." The historical connection between race and place should be even more "authentic" there than in any neighborhood of Brooklyn.

Why Harlem Is Not a Ghetto

Every person in this room can remember thirty years ago,
when Harlem was a community with a rich past, but an
ominous future—when it was a neighborhood with block
after block of vacant lots and derelict apartment buildings,
when it was a community that seemed to be locked into a
downward spiral of abandonment and decay. Take a look at
Harlem today. It has become one of the hottest residential
neighborhoods in the five boroughs. Families are snapping
up its magnificent 19th century townhouses. Harlem's
population, which was shrinking just fifteen years ago, is
growing again.
—Mayor Michael R. Bloomberg, New York/National Housing
Conference, December 2002

It's noon on a warm Saturday in the middle of June, and a bright sun is
shining on Settepani Bakery's sidewalk café at 120th Street and Lenox Avenue. You didn't think to bring sunscreen to eat brunch in Harlem, so you
choose a table under the red awning, put on your dark glasses, and settle
down to read the menu. The small, square, white tables and lightweight
aluminum chairs remind you of cafés in Italy or Greenwich Village, and

the dishes on the menu also inspire dreams of other places. Smoked turkey panini with brie on pumpernickel bread. Mozzarella, tomatoes, and basil on rosemary focaccia. Bucatini pasta with an almond, basil, and tomato pesto. Cappuccino and latte, of course, but also decaf Masala chai.

You understand why Settepani is popular among Harlem's new movers and shakers. You've heard that Maya Angelou, the distinguished poet, playwright, and actor, who lives in a restored brownstone townhouse nearby, often has lunch here. The famous basketball champion and author Kareem Abdul-Jabbar has been seen walking by. The restaurant's website lists former president Bill Clinton, whose office is on 125th Street, as a corporate customer. And when your graduate students stop in for coffee while doing a research project for your class, they meet Daniel Tisdale, the founder and publisher of *Harlem World* magazine, who is having a business meeting a few tables away, and Eric Woods, the chief financial officer of *Uptown* magazine and cofounder of Harlem Vintage, the neighborhood's first wine store.

Harlem has other well-known restaurants: the venerable Sylvia's, the soul food restaurant that is on every tourist itinerary and sells its

"New Harlem Renaissance": Settepani café, Lenox Avenue. Photograph by Sharon Zukin.

own bottled sauces; M&G Diner, known for its smothered pork chops, collard greens, and candied yams; and Amy Ruth's, offering dishes named for local celebrities, like the waffles and bacon that honor retired police chief Joseph Leake and the chicken and waffles that pay tribute to the Rev. Al Sharpton, a friend of the former owner. Since it opened in 2002, though, Settepani, with its red awnings, outdoor café, and rosemary focaccia, has taken a special place in what the media calls "the new Harlem Renaissance."

The first Harlem Renaissance was the period of extraordinary creativity in the 1920s and 1930s when African American and Caribbean writers, painters, and intellectuals joined with white literary critics to create a "capital of Black culture" in Uptown Manhattan. Poets such as Langston Hughes, novelists such as Zora Neale Hurston, and social critics such as W. E. B. Du Bois, who are now admired figures in the modern American canon, lived and worked in a gritty area of the city that had been developed for middle-class whites but, in a frantic sequence of overbuilding, targeted marketing, and overcrowding, quickly filled with working-class blacks.

Racism forced Harlem to grow into a ghetto. College-educated black professionals, successful entrepreneurs, and celebrity entertainers lived in exclusive pockets of the neighborhood in expensive homes surrounded by tenements and apartment houses rented to domestic workers, unskilled porters, and factory laborers, often recent migrants from the South. The concentration of talent and social frustration in this one place spawned literary salons and political journals as well as influential churches, Black Nationalist leaders, and white-owned nightclubs with black performers that drew a downtown, whites-only clientele. Out of these conditions, in the first half of the twentieth century, Harlem shaped an authentic space of racial identity, a "black cultural sublime." It was a space that both oppressed and freed the soul.[1]

These days, though, "Harlem Renaissance" refers to a neighborhood that has become gentrified. Aristocratic brownstone townhouses are being newly restored to Victorian splendor from use as crack houses and single-room-occupancy hotels. Luxury rental apartments and condos are springing up in place of rundown tenements and vacant lots. Modern chain stores and interesting cafés and boutiques, notable for their long absence, dot the streets. "Harlem Renaissance" is both a slogan for marketing the neighborhood's new commercial growth and a sign of its historic cultural distinction.

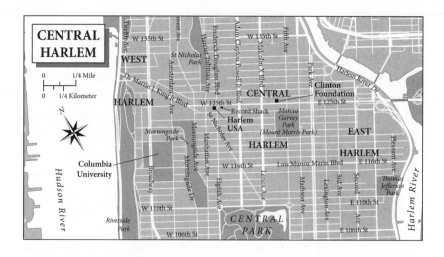

Like the upscaling of the waterfront in Williamsburg, Harlem's gradual redevelopment relies on outside capital and the state, aided and abetted by new lifestyle media. In the first years of the twenty-first century Settepani got a small loan from the Upper Manhattan Empowerment Zone, established by the U.S. Congress during the 1990s to jump-start the area's commercial revival. Then, when the café had trouble finding clientele, the Clinton Foundation, founded by the former president after he left office in 2001, supplied a grant to pay student consultants from New York University's graduate business school. Based on their advice, Settepani added salads, sandwiches, and pasta to the pastries already on the menu. At that point a *New York Times* profile described it as a setting for "a new Harlem gentry in search of its latte," meeting and greeting each other in the "pale mist curling from pastel-hued scoops of gelato in porcelain bowls."[2]

Settepani's cultural distance from the soul food heritage that Harlem still tangibly represents makes it a source of both pride and anxiety in the community. The owners, Nino Settepani and his wife, Leah Abraham, bring to Harlem two different cultural traditions. Nino Settepani belongs to an Italian American family with a thirty-year history in New York's baking industry. After he left the original family business in Greenwich Village still run by his brother, he opened a commercial bakery in East Williamsburg, Brooklyn, and for a time operated restaurants in Chelsea and Westchester County. While still managing the Brooklyn plant, he devotes most of his energy to the Harlem café. Leah Abraham, who comes from Ethiopia, is Settepani's public face. Often interviewed in the media, she is a visible member of the far-flung African diaspora that has moved into Harlem in recent years.

Neither "native" enough to be considered African American, nor "down home" enough to dispel fears of gentrification, Abraham admits that Settepani sets a new tone for the neighborhood. "We are catalysts for some of the changes," she says, and regrets that not everyone welcomes these changes or can adapt to them: "A lot of the people who were here when we first opened are no longer here, or not here as much." Despite her efforts to offer neighbors and customers a personal touch, "be it advice, be it guidance, be it mentorship—just introducing something new to people," she acknowledges the resentment, even anger, many longtime residents feel. No need to mention the Harlem man who complains that the genial atmosphere Abraham strives for is "faggoty" and unattractive. He neither welcomes this style nor feels welcomed by it. The waist-high grids of metal fence, covered by squares of red canvas that match Settepani's awnings, are a symbolic barrier between him and Harlem's new upper middle class.[3]

Some members of this middle class are sitting at tables around you today: young brown-skinned couples, some with braids, a family with small children, all well dressed and chatting politely. Your server, a young man with golden honey-toned skin and close-cropped dark hair, looks North African or Middle Eastern, but he tells you he is a free-lance photographer from Latin America who is working on a photo essay on the renovation of a Harlem brownstone for an architecture magazine. It's easy to imagine you have seen this cosmopolitan brunch crowd featured in the video profiles of housing renovations that float around the Internet and cable TV, such as "Harlem Homecoming" on *House and Garden* magazine's television channel: "Young professional couple returns to Harlem to live in a century-old home."[4]

Framed by the late actor Ossie Davis's dignified voice-over narration, this "return to Harlem" features the family of a thirty-something, African American investment banker who was born and raised on Strivers' Row, a street of nineteenth-century townhouses, now part of a historic landmark district, and educated at the Wharton School of the University of Pennsylvania and Harvard Business School. Commuting to a job on Wall Street, married to a corporate businesswoman of Jamaican descent, and the father of an attractive toddler, Howard Sanders praises both the cultural and the economic value that owning a home in Harlem represents. "I'm a pretty cheap guy," he says. "I don't like to pay more than things are worth. So I think the best housing value in the city is in Harlem." Ossie Davis reinforces this point. The hundred-year-old house, "brought back from the brink of destruction," features its original mahogany woodwork, a fireplace in almost every bedroom, and a small, charming backyard garden. It offers a setting for "elegant living."

The video's crucial message, though, is that Harlem is a spiritual home for a widespread diaspora of people of African descent who have grown up in different countries and ethnic cultures. "It's got the culture that we're from, both West Indian and African American," Sanders says. "Those are firmly rooted here."

At Settepani you see this new cosmopolitanism all around you, and in an even broader sense. After the middle-aged black couple seated next to you finishes brunch and leaves, two young white women in their twenties take their table, and one of them tells you she lives in an apartment house nearby. You wonder if this is a Harlem building that the *New York Times* has described as an "urban dorm," where young, single, and often white college graduates share large apartments because they can't afford the rent downtown. Their migration reminds you of the black families who came to Harlem in the early 1900s.[5]

This is now, though, in part, a *white* migration. You look at the white couple in their thirties sitting near the doorway under the red awning. Perhaps they are the new homeowners you have seen in the video *Building Green in Harlem,* a ten-part series of short films on the website of *Dwell* magazine. You know from the video that they, like the Sanders family, were attracted to Harlem because they could not afford to buy a home this big in any other Manhattan neighborhood. But the white couple was not born here and has no connection with the African diaspora. They found their way to Harlem by reading an article about an earlier townhouse renovation, published under the very title "Harlem Renaissance."[6]

After paying the bill you take a last look at the other café patrons still sitting at tables in the sun. When you arrived at noon, practically everyone already eating brunch was black or brown or tan. Now, though only an hour has passed, just about all of Settepani's patrons are white.

You know you can't jump to conclusions. The vast majority of Harlem's residents, 75 percent, still identify themselves as black. More than 50 percent of the households are in the two lowest-earning quintiles of the city's population and another 20 percent hover around the middle. Asthma rates in the area are high and birthrates low. For most of the area's longtime residents who live in subsidized housing, owning a home on Strivers' Row, where the price of a smartly renovated brownstone now exceeds four million dollars, or paying a thousand dollars a month in rent to share an apartment in an "urban dorm" is a distant prospect.[7]

But so many new affluent men and women are moving into Harlem that the neighborhood is rapidly changing its character. Cheap mom-and-pop stores are losing their leases, some of them evicted by churches that use the windfall profits from selling their property to improve facilities and programs; luxury housing is bringing in a new, black bourgeoisie. "You can still find a semblance of Harlem, but it is vanishing quickly," says Sikhulu Shange, owner of the celebrated Record Shack on 125th Street, who lost his lease in 2007. "What we have built, they want it now. They want the culture."[8]

If for many years Harlem embodied the dual racial consciousness of African Americans that W. E. B. Du Bois described at the turn of the twentieth century, today it represents what Henry Louis Gates Jr. calls blacks' *social class* hyphenation. On one side, you have new high-rise office and

"The capital of black America": Sikhulu Shange outside Record Shack on 125th Street in 2006. Photograph by Sharon Zukin.

residential towers, million-dollar brownstone townhouses, and rosemary focaccia: the cultural signs of the "new Harlem Renaissance." On the other side, you have old high-rise public housing projects, social service agencies, and "chicken shacks": the dark ghetto's *terroir*. There's such a deep split between these spaces it has pushed Harlem into a crisis of authenticity.[9]

This is a broader problem than the historical "crisis of definition" that black neighborhoods have felt ever since the great northward migration of rural blacks began in the early 1900s, when urbane, highly educated, middle-class residents who saw themselves as guardians of morality stood on one side on the cultural divide, and their poor, country cousins, who engaged in a raucous public culture of alcohol, cheap cabarets, and low-life amusements, stood on the other. Today claims to represent Harlem's best interests have been put in play by a wider spectrum of groups: old and new black residents in both the middle and the working class; new and future white residents, all middle class; real estate developers, new retail entrepreneurs, the media, and a host of government agencies, all of whom are pushing Harlem to be less like the ghetto of its recent past and more like other Manhattan neighborhoods. Despite the halt to many new construction projects brought by the financial crisis, small stores catering to black customers have been forced to close and longtime residents have been forced out. This presses Harlem to confront a previously unimaginable challenge: Does any neighborhood in the city today have the right to be both poor and black? Has Harlem lost its authenticity as a dark ghetto?[10]

He was from the Harlem of Charlie Parker and LeRoi Jones, of
Dizzy Gillespie and W. E. B. Du Bois.
—Michael Hunt on Kareem Abdul-Jabbar, *Milwaukee
Journal-Sentinel* online, November 20, 2007

When the psychologist Kenneth Clark called Harlem a "dark ghetto" in 1965, at the height of the civil rights movement, he evoked a space of almost hopeless desolation, where men and women born with darker skin are condemned to live isolated behind "invisible walls" built by whites with privilege and power. Within these walls houses crumble from lack of repair. Streets are seldom cleaned, parks not cared for, and consumers badly served. No one in power pays attention to the "cumulative ugliness" of "social, political, educational, and—above all—economic colonies," reinforcing the lesson residents learn every day: that they are worth less than whites by every measure. "The only constant," Clark said, "is a sense of inadequacy."[11]

This has been the dominant image of American ghettos since at least World War II. It is so firmly rooted in whites' perceptions and popular culture that most urban neighborhoods where African Americans live cannot escape the conceptual overlay of blackness and poverty, what sociologists call the "intersectionality" of race and class. Even John Shaft, the successful private detective at the heart of one of the first, and best, Hollywood Blaxploitation films, *Shaft* (1971), matter-of-factly underlined this point. When he phones his girlfriend to tell her he won't be able to see her that evening as planned, she asks, "You got problems, baby?"

"Yeah, I got a couple of 'em," Shaft says. "I was born black. And I was born poor."

For a mass audience that did not know Clark's book, the movie offered a quick way to read the dark ghetto. Shaft's authenticity enables him to move—not without friction—between two worlds. He lives in a cool bachelor apartment in Greenwich Village and keeps an office in Times Square, both areas of the city that are ethnically diverse but mainly white. He mixes easily with all the social groups who were becoming visible in New York movies during the 1970s: white taxi drivers and gay bartenders, Black Power activists, Latino street characters, Italian American cops and gangsters. But when the white police officers need information about what's happening "up in Harlem," they send for him. And when the kingpin gangster of Harlem, a character named Bumpy Jonas, a reference to the real gangster Bumpy Johnson, who died in 1968, also sends for Shaft to investigate the Mafia's kidnapping of his daughter, he says, "My people aren't worth a damn outside of Harlem." Shaft's value to both sides reveals the dark ghetto's complex authenticity. It is both impenetrable by outsiders and powerless against them, very much like a traditional urban village.

To portray the ghetto's sense of place in visual terms, the director, Gordon Parks, an important African American photographer as well as a filmmaker, made specific aesthetic choices, looking back to noir films of the 1940s and 1950s and pointing forward to Martin Scorsese's *Mean Streets* (1973) and *Taxi Driver* (1976). When Shaft strides through Times Square or goes downtown to the Village, it's daytime. But when the movie travels uptown with him to Harlem, it's nearly always night. Street scenes are dark, as dark and threatening as the brick and brownstone tenements that Shaft visits. Paint is peeling on both the buildings' façades and inside walls. Building numbers are crudely painted on the doors. Glass and garbage litter the sidewalks, and little groups of men stand idly by. This was indeed the "dark ghetto" in those years before whites rediscovered the Harlem Renaissance: authentically black and poor.[12]

People were scared by the illegal drug violence that reached notorious proportions in Harlem in the 1970s, between the careers of the movie detective Shaft and of the real-life black gangsters Frank Lucas and Nicky Barnes, who became famous when he was profiled as "Mr. Untouchable" in the *New York Times Magazine*.[13] Whites were also put off by blacks' new willingness to speak out in public against white paternalism, especially on issues concerning the "authentic" representation of Harlem's cultural heritage. Everyone knew this was a struggle for control.

When the Metropolitan Museum of Art organized an exhibition called "Harlem on My Mind" in 1968, at the height of the Black Power movement, African American and white artists vented their outrage at "the white man's distorted, irrelevant and insulting" picture of the neighborhood's history, as well as the failure to include work—in an exhibition at an art museum—by contemporary black artists. Many blacks also took offense because the show was held outside of Harlem, in a museum on Fifth Avenue, the stronghold of white cultural power. "Originally greeted by the Harlem cultural establishment with enthusiasm," according to the *New York Times,* the exhibition drew fierce protests at its opening. During the first few days pickets marched up and down in front of the museum, three African American professionals who had served as consultants to the planning committee resigned, and unknown "vandals" defaced several European paintings in the Metropolitan's collection, including a Rembrandt, by scratching small *H*s on them.[14]

The most contentious issue, though, was the exhibition catalogue, which protests on all sides forced the museum to withdraw. The catalogue featured essays by the exhibition's curator, Allon Schoener, a white administrator in the New York State Council on the Arts, Thomas P. Hoving, the white director of the museum, and Candy Van Ellison, a black teenager in NYSCA's Ghetto Arts Corps. Each of these pieces infuriated a substantial constituency: Schoener's because it drew attention to the fact that a white man had organized the first comprehensive view of Harlem's history; Hoving's because it dramatized the lack of understanding between affluent whites and the African Americans who worked with, and for, them; and Van Ellison's because it referred to tensions in New York between blacks and Jews.[15]

This last essay was bound to create a storm of protest. Like an earlier article by James Baldwin in the *New York Times Magazine* and the movement for community control of public schools that provoked a lengthy teachers' strike around the same time as the exhibition, Van Ellison's essay stirred enormous hostility within the Jewish community. She was referring to a situation that had already been described in Nathan Glazer and Daniel Patrick Moynihan's 1963 book, *Beyond the Melting Pot:* conflicts of interest between Jewish landlords and black tenants, and between Jews who had won and blacks who were still seeking jobs in public sector bureaucracies. But the footnotes that would have labeled her sources were removed in the editing process, and as a result both blacks and Jews found the essay incendiary. Both groups picketed the exhibition, each reaching out to powerful allies for support. To his amazement, Allon Schoener later wrote, the City Council threatened to stop sponsoring "Harlem on My Mind" if the museum did not withdraw the catalogue, and the Met soon buried twenty-six thousand copies in its basement.[16]

By the end of the 1970s most casual visitors had stopped going to Harlem. The Apollo, the famous theater for live performances on 125th Street, closed in 1976, and few jazz clubs or good restaurants remained. During these years of fiscal crisis, when the entire city seemed to reach rock bottom, the shabby neighborhood, from the tenements on the East Side to the brownstone townhouses of Sugar Hill, lost its hope for the future. Walking around Central Harlem a *New York Times* reporter saw "empty, boarded-up stores along the once-bustling 125th Street shopping corridor; burned-out abandoned buildings demeaning almost every block…; hundreds of idle men clustered at corners, drowning empty days in wine and whisky; youths barely into their teens selling drugs as openly as other boys hawk newspapers."[17] The scope of decay defied massive anti-poverty programs.

The dark ghetto's inescapable overlay of race and poverty was ground in by the illegal drug trade—this was when Frank Lucas says he earned a million dollars a day selling dope on 116th Street—and by the government's increasing unwillingness to rebuild. "It's a bitter harvest after ten years," said the archdeacon of New York's Episcopal diocese. "But looking back on them, we have no reason to expect anything else. The will for change, real change, never was there."[18]

Life grew ever more violent in the 1980s because of the crack epidemic, when more buildings were abandoned and boarded up. During these years the New York City government became Harlem's biggest property owner by seizing buildings *in rem* when landlords didn't pay their taxes. Small landlords decided it was more rational to walk away than to make needed improvements, for no one wanted to buy these buildings and tenants couldn't pay higher rents. Drug addicts squatted in vacant houses, and safe passage through the streets became a risky matter for visitors and residents alike.[19]

For all these reasons experts believed that Harlem would prove immune to gentrification. White homeowners, who made up the largest portion of "urban pioneers" in all American cities, were reluctant to settle in poor black neighborhoods. Most of them wanted to live far away from drug dealers, corrupt or incompetent policing, inadequate public services, and inferior stores. They feared being robbed, or even killed. These fears were kept alive by periodic television images of brown-skinned crowds attacking stores in their own neighborhoods, from the 1960s, when African Americans in many cities protested the assassinations of Martin Luther King Jr. and Malcolm X, to the 1990s, when they protested the arrest of Rodney King in Los Angeles. Whites felt intimidated too by blacks' own fears, which were fanned by whites' hateful assaults on black men who ventured into white neighborhoods, such as Yusuf Hawkins, who was killed by four young white men in Bensonhurst, Brooklyn, in 1989. Few whites wanted to gentrify Harlem under these conditions.[20]

Money was also a problem. The sale prices of houses in Harlem were low, especially when Mayor Edward I. Koch's administration tried to auction them off for a few dollars each. But because of persistent redlining, banks and other big lenders did not make private investment capital available in black neighborhoods. Like landlords, potential homebuyers, white or black, could not get loans to finance the extensive renovations old houses in Harlem required. When they did get loans, often by putting up their homes as collateral, they faced high interest rates and the risk of foreclosure, very much like in the later subprime mortgage crisis.

Neither was it possible, even if developers had wanted, to build the same kinds of apartment houses above retail stores that filled the Upper East and Upper West Sides, for much of Harlem was zoned for the "towers in the park" design of high-rise public housing projects. Most important, there was not yet an affluent black middle class, a potentially significant agent of change that would be attracted to Harlem's stately townhouses and cultural authenticity and could anchor gentrification.

Little by little, though, a new black middle class holding professional, financial, and media jobs began to buy the cheap, dilapidated, but still stately houses and to spark a small cultural renewal. Eric Sawyer, an investment consultant and AIDS activist, bought a Harlem brownstone for twenty-six thousand dollars in 1981, when it was one of only three occupied buildings on the block, and decided to "tough it out." The Studio Museum, founded in 1968 to sponsor African American art, renovated a late nineteenth-century building on 125th Street and moved into it in 1982. Eight years later the National Black Theatre, which was founded, like the Studio Museum, in 1968, renovated and moved into another old building nearby. Both cultural institutions got significant outside support: the Theatre, from New York State's Urban Development Corporation, Manufacturers Hanover Bank (now part of JP Morgan Chase), the National Endowment for the Arts, city agencies, and big media corporations whose headquarters were in New York City. Although many commercial projects "came close to foundering because of investors' poor perception of the area, a lack of financing or government paperwork," said the New York Times, redevelopment plans began to gain support "almost by their sheer persistence."[21]

It wasn't only persistence. It took at least a generation for would-be Harlem entrepreneurs to develop the social capital that assured them, to some degree, of access to financing. When Dark Ghetto was published in the 1960s, black politicians did not hold major leadership roles in either the city government or the city's dominant Democratic Party. Neither did they have any influence over the state's Urban Development Corporation or the banks. By the same token, though black cultural entrepreneurs in the arts had little reason to believe that white politicians or business leaders, or white cultural producers and audiences, really wanted to join them uptown, they had already established credibility with nonprofit organizations, private foundations, and government agencies.

By the end of the 1980s redevelopment plans began to reflect the emergence of a new black middle class, college graduates and cultural entrepreneurs, men and women with civil service jobs and positions in business corporations, who were able to network as officers of banks and local economic development organizations. They found their story of origin not in the low life of the dark ghetto—the alienated youth, radical activists, and gangsters of the 1960s—but, reaching farther back in time, in the high life of the Harlem Renaissance. Daryl Bloodsaw, an advertising executive who grew up in the South and bought a four-family house in Harlem in 1998, recalls a "state of emergency" with drug dealers when he moved in. "[Yet] when I walk these streets," he says, "and think that Langston Hughes lived here and Duke Ellington and all the others, it's wonderful. I can feel all of that history alive again."[22]

This powerful image of the Harlem Renaissance reflects a new understanding of American culture that gives credit to its varied ethnic roots. Since the 1970s many colleges and universities had begun to pay greater attention to black cultural history, and high schools were assigning and performing classical African American works. But it also parallels what was happening in Williamsburg during the 1980s and 1990s. Off-the-radar performance spaces, the L Café, and Pierogi art gallery were making Williamsburg feel cool. Harlem, though, was becoming a different sort of place, where a selective vision of the distant past created a new sense of authenticity.

The narrative of the first Harlem Renaissance highlights those parts of Harlem's culture that most people aspire to: the affluence of Strivers' Row rather than poverty and vice, good times at the Cotton Club rather than at tenement rent parties, the aesthetics of Langston Hughes and Duke Ellington instead of the more critical racial politics of W. E. B. Du Bois or Marcus Garvey. There's no place in this narrative for the fact that the Harlem Renaissance "occurred precisely as Harlem was turning into the great American slum," with New York's highest rates of death, disease, and joblessness.[23]

But as Kareem Abdul-Jabbar points out in his history of the Harlem Renaissance, Harlem in the 1920s and 1930s was a complicated place. Five different neighborhoods, "each with a distinctive personality," formed a city within the city, or what the writer Claude McKay called, in 1940, a "Negro metropolis." There were churches and theaters on Seventh Avenue; pool halls, dance clubs, nightclubs, and Prohibition speakeasies on Lenox Avenue; the aristocratic townhouses of black elites on Strivers' Row and Sugar Hill; a YMCA and public library branch, where writers gathered, on 135th Street; and the commercial hub of 125th Street, home to the Harlem Opera House and the Apollo and Victoria theaters, as well as to small department stores such as Blumstein's, owned by Jews and boycotted time and again by blacks who wanted jobs.[24]

Like Williamsburg, Harlem's gritty authenticity, with a distinctive aesthetics, politics, and sense of place, reflects a history of exclusion. The second Harlem Renaissance prefers to take a different view. But unlike the working-class Brooklyn neighborhood, the reshaping of Harlem in the first years of the twenty-first century would depend not only on new residents, cultural entrepreneurs, and media coverage, but on aggressive actions taken by the state.

Around the world, people know Harlem as the spiritual and cultural capital of Black America. It's increasingly becoming the economic capital as well.

—Kenneth J. Knuckles, president and CEO, Upper Manhattan Empowerment Zone, August 2005

If you stood on the corner of 125th Street and Lenox Avenue in the mid-1990s, almost a decade before Settepani opened, you would not see a neighborhood getting ready for change. The buildings were mainly low and old, and the stores were modest, small, and cheap. Only a few chain store logos would stand out amid hand-lettered shop signs and often shuttered iron gates. Though the Apollo had been renovated with new broadcasting facilities, it had not yet reopened. The Victoria was also closed. Black ownership of stores, as low as 2 percent in the 1960s, had risen above 35 percent by the end of the 1970s, mainly because white merchants were chased away by residents' aggressive behavior as well as by impossibly high insurance rates that reflected the threat of violence. Even in the 1990s many commercial properties were held by the city government or local, not-for-profit corporations.[25]

You would see new faces. Changes in U.S. immigration laws in 1985 brought new entrepreneurs to Harlem, especially in storefronts where they didn't have to pay high rent and in businesses where ethnic ties connected them to wholesale distributors and customers. By the mid-1980s around three dozen Korean merchants had opened stores on 125th Street, where they sold clothing, wigs and beauty supplies, and groceries. By the early 1990s a larger number of vendors from West Africa and the Caribbean had set up tables on the sidewalks, where they sold clothing, CDs, and food. There was a bustling trade around the peddlers in this informal African market, and buses ferried in European and Japanese tourists to eat soul food at Sylvia's a couple of blocks away and hear gospel services at several of the neighborhood's churches.[26]

Though two new office towers housed state agencies and nonprofit corporations, most of the development projects that had been announced from time to time since the late 1960s were never built. The ground floor of Blumstein's Department Store had been divided into three small clothing boutiques and a jewelry store, but none of the big projects that were publicized in the press—the Commonwealth Shopping Center, Harlem International Trade Center, Inner City Broadcasting Company studios and headquarters, and Harlem on the Hudson, a mixed-use development along the Hudson River to be financed by Japanese investors—broke ground.

Private investors still lacked confidence that there was money to be made in legitimate ways in Harlem. A stock market collapse in 1987, followed by a real estate recession and federally financed mortgage scandals in 1991, made investment capital scarce, and the city and state governments lacked the means and the will to either leverage private investment or reward investors enough to reduce the risk.

Opening a business in Harlem was a risky investment. In the 1980s African American residents boycotted Koko's, a Korean-owned grocery store on 125th Street, where a Korean employee had mistakenly accused a black shopper of theft and assaulted him with a knife. Despite generally civil relations, community residents could still show anger against white merchants. One of these hostile situations concerned Sikhulu Shange, who lost his space for the Record Shack in 1995, when Freddy Harari, the Jewish owner of Freddy's Fashion Mart, told him he was ending his sublease in order to expand his own store. When neither Harari nor the primary landlord, a church called the United House of Prayer for All, would change their plans, community residents firebombed and then boycotted Freddy's. Then a local black resident attacked and shot seven of its nonblack employees before killing himself. These violent events echoed in the media, and in many New Yorkers' minds, for months. The dark ghetto was very much alive.[27]

At the same time, though, despite appearances, 125th Street hovered on the brink of revival. Chain stores were beginning to lower their resistance to opening branches in the inner city, persuaded by the Harvard Business School professor Michael Porter that these low-income neighborhoods offered the advantages of a central location and captive consumers, as well as by the reports published by the Clinton administration of residents' pent-up spending power. A more entrepreneurial approach to the inner city also followed from a decade of Reaganomics, the conservative Republican view that the poor should be weaned from dependency on government aid by business development. This idea found support in New York City's black community. Leaders had grown tired of trying to tear down the wall of public disapproval and investors' apathy that circled the dark ghetto, and a new generation of African American lawyers and MBAs were eager to become entrepreneurs. These professionals had little in common with the separatist movements of the past that had spoken up for black capitalism and black power. Some even joined the Republicans, who were eager to recruit them to their political base.[28]

Most important, when the Clinton administration spearheaded efforts to reduce the welfare rolls during the 1990s, the redevelopment strategy in New York's public sector also changed direction. The city's neoliberal think tank, the Manhattan Institute, urged political officials to shift their priorities from social welfare policies to "making markets." When New York City voters elected Republican Rudolph Giuliani mayor in 1993 and New York State voters chose Republican George Pataki to be governor two years later, both leaders led the way to using public money for entrepreneurial investments. In Harlem a few local development corporations—notably, that of the influential Abyssinian Baptist Church—stepped up to the plate, ready to invest their social capital as not-for-profit partners of commercial developers. The dark ghetto was being coaxed to bear fruit.[29]

At this point, prodded by Representative Charles B. Rangel, who had served Harlem in Congress since 1970, the federal government established the Upper Manhattan Empowerment Zone (UMEZ). Though a few small branches of chains—the Body Shop, Ben & Jerry's, and McDonald's—had already begun to locate on 125th Street, now larger companies started negotiating with UMEZ for major funding to open stores in Harlem. Despite Congressman Rangel's involvement, mainstream developers who earlier had hesitated to do business there believed the empowerment zone might offer a way to avoid the old patronage relationships of the black political community. A Business Improvement District—a beefed-up, market-oriented form of commercial property owners' association that had proved successful in promoting richer shopping streets downtown—was organized on West 125th Street. And Mayor Giuliani sent in the police to move the West African vendors by force from 125th Street to a vacant lot on 116th Street owned by the Malcolm Shabazz Mosque.

While city, state, and federal officials would now back investment in Harlem, conditions in the area truly changed. By 2000 crack use had hit its peak and declined; crime rates were down to 1960s levels. Many young men had died or gone to jail; others had grown older, wiser, and decidedly less scary to men and women who might want to open a business. "So to me," a middle-aged man in West Harlem told an interviewer, "I look at things now in terms more of individual[s] than when I was younger, and I was one of those guys that I'd be throwing bricks and stuff to get these Jews out of Harlem."[30]

Under these new conditions the empowerment zone took on the task of "making markets" with zeal. They courted chain stores, of which Harlem had never had enough to meet residents' needs, as well as upscale retailers such as Starbucks that would both satisfy middle-class residents who already lived in the neighborhood and attract newcomers. Everyone understood that, without good restaurants, stores, and bars, demand for new housing and offices would die.

Between January 1995 and May 2006 UMEZ approved more than $335 million in grants, loans, and bonds. Their first big project was Harlem USA, a 275,000-square-foot shopping and entertainment complex, which opened on West 125th Street in 2000. Harlem USA was striking in many ways. It was a large, new, glass-fronted, commercial development in one of Central Harlem's most prominent locations. It brought a nine-screen multiplex showing first-run films to an area that had had no movie theaters for years. Surrounding the multiplex were a modern bookstore and café, Hue-Man Books, and branches of Old Navy, HMV Record Stores, Modell's Sporting Goods, and a Disney Store (though HMV and Disney soon closed). The key to this commercial development was the use of public sector funding to leverage loans from the private sector; UMEZ loaned the developers—Magic Johnson, the basketball star turned entrepreneur, and his partners, Drew Greenwald of Grid Properties and the Gotham Organization, a construction and development firm—$11 million, which led to additional loans of $48 million from Chase Development Corporation and $3 million from the state's Empire State Development Corporation. Chase also opened a bank branch in Harlem USA, subsidized by the state's program to encourage more bank facilities in underserved areas. Soon, on East 125th Street, UMEZ funded another big project, issuing $17 million in tax-exempt bonds to build the city's largest auto mall, developed by General Motors and the Potamkin Auto Group, a New York–based, family-owned, national network of car dealerships.

But luring developers and chains was a slippery process. Though a 50,000-square-foot Pathmark supermarket opened on East 125th Street in

1999, supported by the not-for-profit Abyssinian Development Corporation, local merchants complained about the competition, and neither public nor private entrepreneurs found it easy to line up commitments by big commercial tenants. "In Harlem it was nearly impossible [to get them to sign on]," Greenwald of Harlem USA recalls, "until we could show retailers the value in having 500,000 people in Upper Manhattan." Greenwald claims that Harlem has "the largest income density in the United States—something like $800 million per square mile." Yet retail stores waited to see if other chains would succeed before making a commitment.[31]

Neither did firms rush to rent offices in Harlem, despite finding lower rents there than in Midtown or Downtown. Only after President Clinton moved into an office on 125th Street, according to a former CEO of the Abyssinian Development Corporation, did they begin to show even the slightest interest. By that time, though, in addition to Harlem USA, Harlem Center, a small office building with three chain store tenants—Marshall's, CVS, and H&M—had opened on the site where the Harlem International Trade Center was never built. Unlike plans for the Trade Center, which had always interested local politicians more than developers, Harlem Center emerged from negotiations between powerful outsiders in the public and private sectors: the state government, city officials, and the big commercial developer Forest City Ratner, who needed government support to build a much bigger mixed-use project, Atlantic Yards, in Brooklyn. Harlem Center was cosponsored by a powerful insider as well: the Abyssinian Development Corporation.[32]

Though most residents welcomed new shopping opportunities, some expressed discontent that commercial gentrification was destroying Harlem's authenticity as a place for low-income black residents. "At a June [2002] town hall meeting at the Schomberg Center for Research in Black Culture," a reporter writes in the *Village Voice*, "audience members heckled forum speakers, including representatives from banks, UMEZ, the city's Housing Preservation Department (HPD), and the public housing authority. One elderly woman, whose voice was stronger than the fragile fist she threw in the air, screamed: 'Where the hell are the politicians?'" The changing face of 125th Street, in these residents' view, was unmistakably connected with higher rents and *residential* gentrification. They sensed that upscale stores would bring about their own displacement.[33]

But UMEZ continued trying to reshape the retail landscape. In 1995 only 3 percent of more than six hundred stores in Central Harlem were branches or franchises of chains. Five years later there were 568 stores, but 7 percent of these, twice as many as in 1995, were chains. A sign of the desired upscale trend of retail development, the first Starbucks in Harlem opened at 125th and Lenox, near the former site of the African market. By 2006, with many old buildings torn down or boarded up for redevelopment and new stores occupying larger spaces, only three hundred stores remained, but 16 percent of them, almost three times as many as in 1995, were branches of chains. Even more remarkable was the appearance in Central Harlem of upscale, individually owned boutiques, restaurants, and cafés such as Settepani. The share of this new entrepreneurial retail capital rose from zero in 1995 to 10 percent of all establishments in 2006, while that of old-style, cheap, locally owned stores fell from 84 to 74 percent.[34]

The New York City Planning Commission also pressed forward with zoning changes. As they did in other neighborhoods, in Harlem they rezoned the wide avenues for taller, denser development—apartment houses with stores on the ground floor—while preserving the low-rise scale of the brownstone side streets. These height and density limitations would bring a double bounty: keeping the neighborhood character that attracted gentrifiers while enabling developers to create a bustling retail landscape like those of the Upper East and Upper West Sides. The City Planning Commission also approved a long-simmering seven-billion-dollar plan by Columbia University to expand its campus many blocks to 134th Street, through a commercial area of West Harlem that held storage facilities, garages, and a few apartment houses. Then in 2008 the City Planning Commission approved a controversial rezoning of 125th Street, popularly known as "the Main Street of Black America," for high-rise, mixed-use towers. This plan offered developers the right to build taller buildings in return for renting storefront space to arts and cultural facilities, though these could include commercial movie theaters owned by chains. All three plans were approved by the New York City Council, despite residents' fiery protests and efforts by Harlem's city council representatives to get more affordable apartments.[35]

Rezoning 125th Street in this way crystallized the community's fears about losing Harlem's cultural authenticity. Residents were bitter that the city government ceded a large chunk of West Harlem to the university. They knew that rents would rise in the new buildings on 125th Street, as they already had elsewhere. They believed that small-scale, locally based cultural producers, from visual and graphic artists and theater groups to individually owned music stores, would be displaced in favor of more chain stores. Though the City Planning Commission argued that rezoning 125th Street would create more growth for the community, including a regional cultural hub and jobs, longtime residents and merchants did not agree. As in Williamsburg, the local community board pressed for its own plan, which in this case would limit new residential towers to 124th and 126th Streets and restrict retail trade on 125th Street to fairly small stores. A planning group affiliated with Columbia University devised another alternative that would give priority in the "cultural zone" to small, local cultural groups.

Neither alternative had a chance. "You're destroying Harlem. You're getting rid of all the black people," the architectural historian Michael Henry Adams "screamed" as he was "ejected" from the public hearing room after the City Planning Commission voted in favor of its own plan. "Soon it will all be millionaires and the native people won't be able to live in their homes," warned Sikhulu Shange, the owner of the Record Shack. "Soon there won't be any black-owned businesses."[36]

The harshest fact for residents to absorb, though, was that black folks were actively involved in pushing out other blacks. Harlem's role as an incubator of black culture had always been supported by small, black-owned businesses, many of which now found it impossible to survive. Record Shack, where "the VINYL is precious, the staff is wise & Brother Sikhulu Shange is a wealth of BLACK HISTORY & MUSICAL KNOWLEDGE!," had staved off eviction by Freddy's and the United House of Prayer for All in 1995, but lost its lease for good in 2007, with its owner ending up selling CDs on the street next to incense merchants and bootleg cigarette vendors. Bobby's Happy House, a music store whose black owner had been doing business in Harlem since the 1940s, also lost its lease, along with Manna's Soul Food and Salad Bar, both properties sold as part of a 100,000-square-foot commercial redevelopment project on 125th Street.[37]

To be sure, all music stores were threatened by changes in the music industry led by consumers who downloaded songs from the Internet onto iPods. But Record Shack's storefront was owned by a black church, and the deal that threatened Bobby's and Manna's was arranged by the influential Harlem real estate broker Eugene Giscombe, who has managed commercial properties in Central Harlem for years and chairs the 125th Street Business Improvement District. "Change is inevitable," Giscombe said, "but as long as people don't get hurt, it will be fine." Yet the audience at the hearing on 125th Street hurled "shouts of 'Uncle Tom' and 'sellout'" at minority group members of the City Planning Commission who voted in favor of rezoning.[38]

Taking pictures of a double storefront on East 125th Street near Park Avenue almost every year since 1977, the photographer Camilo José Vergara has documented the gradual transformation that the public sector engineered. His first image shows the brightly painted, deep red doors of Purple Mist, a bar; a few sparse potted plants hang in the window, and paintings of wine glasses decorate the panes of the large front doors. After the space is subdivided into two smaller storefronts, it goes through a rapid succession of tenants, steadily becoming shabbier as it hosts a series of clothing stores, a take-out shop for fish and chips, a sketchy smoke shop, and a hair braiding salon. In 2001, after UMEZ is formed and before the attack on the World Trade Center, both sides of the storefront are emptied, reunited, and treated to a renovation. Three years later—a pause partly due to economic uncertainty after the attack—Sleepy's, a branch of the national mattress chain, opens. It manages to get "one of the last cheap leases signed in the booming neighborhood," *Crain's New York Business* says. The Upper Manhattan Empowerment Zone has succeeded in its strategy of "making markets," for now "hungry retailers gobble up the available commercial space, trying to capitalize on Harlem's burgeoning upscale retail market."[39]

Research on the empowerment zone's effect shows that five of a sample of fifteen new entrepreneurial retail businesses that opened in Central Harlem between 2000 and 2006 received UMEZ loans, and three of those five also received help from the Clinton Foundation. A sixth new retail merchant got a loan from the U.S. Small Business Administration; the other nine relied on their own capital and that of outside investors. Funding was not easy to get from UMEZ. Not surprisingly for a state agency that aims to leverage public "resources to facilitate private investments," UMEZ holds successful applicants to rigorous financial standards. Cynthia Harris, the owner of a flower shop, said it took her three years to work up the forms she needed to file with her application. During that time she financed her start-up with savings and credit from a local bank, and her husband helped out with deliveries. That she had savings reflects the fact that Harris had worked for fifteen years before setting out on her own, in university administration, a nonprofit corporation, and the private sector.[40]

As Harris's career suggests, many of Harlem's new retail entrepreneurs are members of the new black middle class. These entrepreneurs have bachelor's, master's, and law degrees; they have established themselves in financial, administrative, or professional careers; and some are fairly affluent. Unlike previous generations of small shopkeepers, these store owners have access to funding, often from black investors. Carol's Daughter, a black-oriented cosmetics firm on 125th Street, was founded in Brooklyn during the 1990s by Lisa Price, who had worked in TV and film production. Before expanding to Harlem, Price gained a successful branding consultant, Steve Stoute, as her outside partner. He brought in ten million dollars of investment capital from the rap star Jay-Z, the actors Jada Pinkett Smith and Will Smith, and the record producer Tommy Mottola. Another black-owned business, Hue-Man Books in Harlem USA, was founded by Rita Ewing, a novelist, attorney, and former nurse, as well as the former spouse of the professional basketball player Patrick Ewing, and Celeste Johnson, the wife of another pro basketball player, Larry Johnson; a third partner, Hue-Man's president Marva Allen, worked as an executive in the high-tech sector in Michigan and was named one of the Top 100 Most Influential Women there. Both Carol's Daughter and Hue-Man Books received UMEZ loans.

Though many new businesses have an Afrocentric theme and a Harlem name and market products mainly to black consumers, not all of their owners are black or come from the surrounding community. Slightly fewer than half of all the owners and co-owners of the fifteen firms in the research sample are Harlem natives or residents. Among the others are a restaurateur from India, a café owner from France, and an art gallery owner who moved to Harlem from Chicago. It is more crucial here, though, than in other areas of the city for new entrepreneurs to have a personal narrative that connects them with the origins of Harlem's black community, even if the story blurs some facts. This is how the new retail entrepreneurs confirm Harlem's authenticity while using it to establish their own.

Nubian Heritage, a cosmetics company with a flagship spa on 125th Street, is a good example. Though the media like to depict the Liberian cofounders, Nyema Tubman and Richelieu Dennis, as former street vendors who sold "incense and soap on the sidewalks of 125th Street," both majored in business at Babson College in Boston, where Dennis, like Lisa Price, the founder of Carol's Daughter, tested family recipes for skin-care products on the kitchen stove. After Dennis was fired from his day job, he and Tubman sold these homemade products on the street, but they also organized street vendors into a distribution network. They opened their first store in Brooklyn, on a major shopping street for African and Caribbean Americans. But with both an UMEZ loan and help from the Clinton Foundation, they moved the company's offices to Harlem in 2004 and created the flagship spa. By 2005, when UMEZ gave them another loan, for one million dollars, they were manufacturing products in their own plant, operating a third store in Queens, and distributing to consumers through a website.[41]

As Brooklyn Industries and Brooklyn Brewery did for Williamsburg, so these retail entrepreneurs created a new authenticity for Harlem by making products based on a local identity and networking with local institutions. In Harlem, though, the new authenticity resonates with both cultural images of the past and marketing opportunities of the present. Speaking with an interviewer, a manager at Carol's Daughter thoughtfully constructs a narrative that bridges a story of origins in community and the new beginnings of an entrepreneurial venture. "We can definitely feel the strength of ALL of Harlem's community empowerment groups," she says.

Rev. [Calvin O.] Butts and Abyssinian [Baptist] Church were extremely helpful in putting us in touch with the right people to find our space. Project Enterprise [a microbusiness lender associated with the Grameen Foundation] and their micro loans in the community with small business are wonderful, and company founder Lisa Price has been awarded by them and speaks to their students. Last holiday season, managing partner Steve Stoute and his marketing and brand imaging firm…participated in the Harlem Hospital toy drive. Lisa has also spoken and or participated in seminars at Harlem Hospital, Sisters in the Black, and the Harlem Empowerment Zone. We stand firmly behind empowering our communities.[42]

Like Carol's Daughter, Eric Woods and Jai Jai Greenfield, the MBAs who founded Harlem Vintage, also sell identity-based products—in their case, wines from small, minority-owned wineries—and network with community organizations. They explicitly connect the design of their store with Harlem's cultural history to claim a role as insiders in the community—to become, in short, an *authentic* part of Harlem. "Designed to evoke 'the style of the Harlem Renaissance,' Greenfield says, Harlem Vintage resembles a comfy living room with warm wooden floors and candlelit shelves. Many talents of the 1920s first performed in this type of setting." But this description, like the street vendor cred of Nubian Heritage's founders, obscures some crucial facts. It's not likely that a modern, well-stocked wine store would resemble a 1920s apartment, and still less recall a rent party in a tenement apartment. Yet the wine store's narrative connects with the powerful image of the Harlem Renaissance. This rhetorical act legitimizes as rightfully belonging in Harlem an entrepreneurial venture by two black MBAs that intrinsically, *authentically,* contradicts the old ghetto culture.[43]

Harlem's new authenticity does refer to cultural heritage. Unlike in the charged political climate of the 1960s, though, gatekeepers no longer make a point of excluding others who can't claim that heritage by birth or direct experience. Authenticity is now available to a socially and ethnically diverse community of consumers and entrepreneurs. They have the cultural capital to appreciate the aesthetics of heritage and the financial capital to buy into it. Most important, membership in the new Harlem Renaissance is open to the white, as well as the new black, middle class.

You can be from a place spiritually and not necessarily from a place physically.
—Aaron Levinson, music producer, *The Harlem Experiment,* WNYC-FM, December 20, 2007

Though public and private capital has created the new Harlem, media coverage has opened it to a larger public, making the neighborhood desirable to a wide variety of new residents and visitors. Beginning in the 1980s mainstream media such as the *New York Times* and *New York* magazine published occasional stories of gentrifiers, more black than white, who bought brownstone houses cheap because of the neighborhood's decline and then confronted drug addicts, gangs, and rubble-strewn lots. Through the 1990s, when the empowerment zone set up shop, the stories about new residents grew more optimistic, and after 2001 they focused on more whites than blacks. The media highlighted new boutiques and cafés and the way they made a gracious lifestyle possible, conforming to the tastes of all the urban middle class. Not just the local media, but *Vogue, O* magazine, and *Black Enterprise* published profiles of new businesses and their owners, who were that much more newsworthy for being *black* entrepreneurs.

During the next few years the Internet greatly increased the means of promoting Harlem to a worldwide audience. New stores created their own websites; travel and lifestyle websites featured reviews of restaurants, bed-and-breakfast establishments in private homes, and stores; design websites offered step-by-step video documentaries of adventures in buying and restoring an old house. After the 2005 rezoning, when new apartment houses began to come on the market, developers created websites for each building that connected such lifestyle comforts as marble bathrooms and an in-house gym to both the neighborhood's cultural heritage and its new restaurants and boutiques. Altogether the media created a buzz about Harlem as an interesting place with a unique sense of authenticity, complementing new investment by private developers and the state.[44]

But a closer look at the media representations reveals two problems. First, despite pro-development coverage in the *New York Times* and online real estate promotion, articles in the black-oriented *Amsterdam News* expose dramatically rising property taxes, difficulties in selling dilapidated homes, and rapid residential and commercial gentrification, with black tenants and shopkeepers being displaced by speculators, both black and white. The *Amsterdam News* expresses both the community's pride in members of the new black middle class who come, or come back, to live in Harlem and its anxiety about whether these new residents will destroy the low-rent housing and stores on which poorer blacks rely.[45] The second problem reflects the gap between virtual representations of Harlem on the World Wide Web and the bricks-and-mortar reality on the ground. Reading the many articles, blogs, and reviews of new restaurants and stores gives the impression of a much grander set of amenities than Harlem really offers. There are in fact many magnificently restored old brownstone houses, and new cafés and bars offer pleasant places to socialize. But these places are still few and far apart. To their owners especially there is too great a distance between them to make a viable cluster that would attract a critical mass of customers throughout the day and night. Supermarkets and gourmet food stores are still in short supply, and the economic crisis has increased the number of business failures. Media images, then, may overstate the success of the new Harlem Renaissance.

At the same time, though, another kind of media, real estate wikis and blogs, provides a powerful means of opening Harlem to potential new residents. In a city where chronic housing shortages and continually rising prices lead to a general obsession with real estate, these websites attract avid readers and detailed posts. Though it is impossible to know for sure who the authors of these posts are and whether they are reliable or objective observers, the real estate blogs are filled with rumors, information, and lots of opinions about changing buildings, businesses, sale prices, and rents. For those readers who are not looking for a home, these blogs offer a voyeuristic voyage through unfamiliar neighborhoods. More seriously, they provide a way to investigate the balance between the agony and the ecstasy of neighborhood change.

The arrival of luxury apartments, high rents, and affluent residents in Harlem has sparked a lot of debate on real estate blogs. Few posts explicitly raise race as an issue; this is a great sign of change, in both Harlem and general public discussion. Because crime rates in Harlem are much lower than in the past, neither is there much mention of danger. Posts focus instead on the same issues that are talked about in any neighborhood: the quality and price of housing, access to stores and transportation, and how quickly apartments are being rented and houses sold. But it is impossible to avoid subtle references to the dark ghetto. Lurking just beneath the online musings about apartment size, amenities, and rent is concern about the emotional issues that drive the middle class away from Harlem: the presence of public housing projects and social service agencies and longtime residents' resentment of gentrifiers, both black and white.[46]

A recent thread on Curbed.com gives a good sense of the tone of these discussions.[47] It begins with a request for information about The Ellington, a new condo development in Central Harlem named for the jazz composer Duke Ellington, and also about "a nicely renovated brownstone" at 117th Street and Lenox Avenue, near the Mt. Morris historic district. "Joey" likes the brownstone house's location and balconies, but finds fault with the bedrooms' size and bathroom sinks. "Kablowie" claims that a penthouse apartment in Loft 124, a converted warehouse on 124th Street, recently sold for more than one thousand dollars per square foot, which may be "a record for a project north of 110th Street." But Kablowie adds, in a not-so-subtle reference to the dark ghetto, "I guess buyers aren't that turned off by the block and neighborhood afterall!"

"Bing" admires the landscape from the roof deck of another house, but cautions, "As always, it's Harlem and having the city views means you're kind of an outsider looking in." "Central Harlem anonymous" dislikes Harlem's aesthetics but realizes that the housing market is hot. Speaking of Loft 124, he says, "The block looks ugly to me, but the building does seem to be impressing people." Yet he is also lured by the possibility of making money here from real estate speculation, for he knows someone who is "financing the purchase [of an apartment in Loft 124] by selling a shell he owns elsewhere in Harlem."

Other bloggers indicate that they are not convinced that moving to Harlem is worth the high prices. "First of all," a blogger who signs herself "Anon" says, "you should get a major discount for living across the street from the public services & clinics directly across the street. They are a magnet of a 'type,' and those types line up there all the times in huge numbers. You're buying into a NIMBY [Not In My Backyard] factor right out your front door." Though this post expresses social status anxieties more than anxieties about race, it evokes images of the dark ghetto. Whether the blogger is white or black, though, she doesn't think that someone who pays one million dollars for an apartment should tolerate living next to welfare offices and methadone clinics.

Anon also dislikes the heavy truck and taxi traffic on 124th Street. But "Central Harlemite" puts this criticism in historical perspective by reminding her that not so long ago, taxi drivers were reluctant to drive into Harlem and even to pick up black passengers for fear of being robbed. Central Harlemite likes Loft 124, she says, because "you can actually GET a cab in that area. For those of us who like to take cabs, it's a godsend that they're relatively readily available on and around 124th St."

This positive view is picked up by another "Anon," who recently bought an apartment in Loft 124. "We were at first a little turned off by the block," she says. "But as we've spent more and more time there are more comfortable with it. There are a few 'characters' that you see on the block but we have never ever felt the least bit unsafe (including late at night). I think this block has great potential." Significantly, she focuses not on the block's present residents and users, but on "a large very high-end residential tower (with new Harlem retail)" that is planned across the street. Though the new development will almost certainly overwhelm the public clinics and social service agencies, if not completely drive them away, "that will have a very positive impact on the block." Clearly, the demise of the dark ghetto is far from certain.

Disagreement on this point also shapes a recent discussion about middle-class black communities on City-data.com, where people from around the United States post comments and questions about the quality of life in different regions. This thread begins with a posting by "moeshak," who says he is moving to New York "and is looking for upper middle class african-american communities," especially in the northern suburbs and in the city itself.[48] Most replies talk about the three northern suburban counties that Moeshak has mentioned—communities with nice houses, tree-lined streets, good schools, and a Baptist church. Some posts suggest that Moe-shak look at suburban communities on Long Island and in Queens. When a post by "Sweetz" recommends Harlem, though, others jump in, strongly denying that Harlem is "middle class."

According to Sweetz, Harlem "is getting pricey and a lot of gentrifica-tion [is] taking place!" But "Hustla718" (718 is the telephone area code for Brooklyn and Queens) immediately contradicts him: "Hahaha! Please tell me your kidding. [Stuyvesant Heights in Bedford-Stuyvesant and Harlem] are FAR from middle class Black neighborhoods."

"No I'm not," Sweetz fires back. "I love the progressiveness of Harlem and like I said—cost are going up—so it is not as scary as it used to be—and with the hospital and all—there is a growing population of the 'pro-gressive' and upper middle class black folk."

Hustla718 then attacks with data on residents' incomes:

Have you ever took a look at the census on congressional district 15 (Uptown Manhattan). Third poorest district in the USA. Factor in living cost and it is the second poorest.

Rent cost may be going up when it comes to market rate property, but so is the number of strictly low income housing. And by far the majority of that neighborhood is low income.

Harlem is not a middle class Black neighborhood in any way whatsoever.

He ends this posting by suggesting that Harlem is just "a ghetto with a few yuppies." Expensive homes surrounded by poor people are a "bubble," he says, not "a middle class neighborhood."

At this point "scatman" enters the discussion, mentioning Maya Angelou's restored brownstone house, which has been written about in the *New York Times* and is now worth $3.4 million. "Seems like famous and upper income people are trying to hop to Harlem," he says. Then he challenges Hustla to come "and see Harlem for yourself! I did, and, even with the hangouts at 125 and Lex, it's better than it was in the late 70s! Oh, yeah, how do you explain British guys giving my mom directions on 125th Street?"

But Hustla brushes Scatman off with what he claims to be his own first-hand observations: "As for E 125th Street and Lex. I know that location well. It's a robbery hot spot. That Pathmark is home to a lot of illegal activity, which is why so many people hang out there."

Scatman argues for a different view. If *whites* are moving to Harlem, and *European* whites at that, the neighborhood must be middle class. "Oh, by the way," he says, "my friend's condo in Harlem went from 90 percent black 20 years ago to 30 percent black today! And how do you explain a British guy giving my mother directions?"

Toward the end of the thread a new writer raises a question about the initial post. If Harlem is becoming less poor and less black, he asks, how can it be an "upper middle class *African-American*" community? "I guess Harlem would be a good answer for now," he says, "but it is being stripped of all its African American culture and I think the O[riginal] P[oster] will be back at square one in 5 to 10 years."

Most posts in the Curbed.com and City-data.com discussions do not stress out about the dark ghetto's loss of authenticity. They prefer the individual houses and tree-lined streets of the suburbs, or at least the brownstone townhouses around Mt. Morris Park—if only the African drummers in the park would stop playing loud music. Their desire to live in a place that corresponds to their social status is typical of middle-class tastes. "Middle-class people tend to value status over convenience," Herbert Gans wrote in the early 1960s, "and thus they reject neighborhoods in which residence and business are mixed—or in which there is any real diversity in population." Members of the black middle class are no less likely than their white counterparts to prefer traditional, middle-class neighborhoods that are quiet, orderly, and comfortable. At best they are ambivalent about sharing space with lower-class blacks and, despite expressing appreciation for African-American heritage, they usually prefer Settepani to a chicken shack. These consumption preferences point to a significant black constituency for more gentrification.[49]

Blacks' ambivalence about Harlem resonates with larger social questions about black cultural diversity. In a recent survey by the Pew Research Center, more than half of black respondents said there is so much "diversity" among blacks today that they cannot "still be thought of as a single race." Though this survey was taken one year before the election of President Barack Obama and the many discussions about a "postracial" society, it raises the issue of whether Harlem can ever return to being poor and black. Not just rising rents, but the ambiguity of who is really black—and the opportunity of some individuals to escape the historical overlay of blackness and poverty—continue to drive a crisis of authenticity.[50]

Pack your bags and come uptown! The second Harlem Renaissance
is underway, and now is the time to join in the excitement. But being
a pioneer doesn't mean roughing it. From the Italian kitchens to the
soaring ceilings to the views of the city, every aspect of Loft 124 has been
painstakingly conceived to bring you the best in modern living while
preserving a historic loft building.
—www.loft124.com, 2007

We can't ignore the real desires to remake Harlem into a more comfortable
place, to change it from a dark ghetto into a middle-class, racially integrated, cosmopolitan community. For every business owner like Sikhulu
Shange who is evicted from his rented store and every longtime resident
who is displaced from a single-room-occupancy hotel, there are younger,
more affluent residents who are putting down roots. They don't buy music
from an elder in a dashiki, they download it to their computer. They post
on Curbed.com that "the neighborhood is really coming together" and
that a new D.J. lounge is going to open soon. Their tastes and desires create
a market for Harlem's new entrepreneurial authenticity.

Political officials share the eagerness to rewrite the story of the area's
origins. Representative Rangel, in his foreword to a new edition of the catalogue of that contentious 1968 exhibition Harlem On My Mind, sets out
an official view. He does not refer to the controversy about the exhibition;
he downplays the unique history and culture of African Americans, their
segregation from the rest of the city, their struggles for jobs and services
and decent housing. Rangel downplays, in short, Harlem's history as a dark
ghetto. Instead he praises the cosmopolitan culture created by successive
waves of residents, black and white, African, African American, Latin American, and European. He talks about a wide variety of ethnic restaurants
with offerings ranging from gumbo and fried chicken to mufongo, pas-
tilles, and Basque chicken yassa, then on to tamales, bagels, and "European
nouvelle cuisine" before he even mentions Harlem's churches; he speaks of
real estate markets before affordable housing. Rangel offers readers a good
sense of Harlem's desired authenticity now.[51]

Despite the absence of yearning for the dark ghetto in Harlem's past, its
shadows hang heavily on Harlem's future. Persistent high unemployment
rates, bad schools, and public health problems are evidence that racial
inequality is still real. The financial crash has halted many new construction projects, leaving empty lots next to unsold condos. But the gradual

reshaping of the dark ghetto's physical environment—and the winnowing of its population as well—continues to erase Harlem's contentious history. Yet this is not the only old neighborhood where the urban imaginary is being revised. This happens in the East Village in Lower Manhattan, too, where artists, actors, low-income residents, and students consciously evoke the ghosts of a radical past to battle gentrification. In the East Village the slogan of the day for many years has been "Die, yuppie scum."

Living Local in the East Village

I think there are unbelievable things that are going on in
Lower Manhattan. The deli is gone, and the BMW is in.
—*New York Times*, May 30, 2007

You're waiting to meet the Japanese college students at 10 A.M. on the corner
of Broadway and Astor Place. It's a cool and drizzly day in June, passersby are
buttoned up against the chill, and at this early hour downtown doesn't have
its usual buzz. When the students show up, you're surprised to see they're all
young women, led by a middle-aged male professor who has some contacts
in the city. They're excited to be in New York, especially in Greenwich Village,
and they whip out their digital cameras when you show them the colored
tiles that Jim Power, the otherwise unemployed "Mosaic Man," has spent the
past twenty years gluing onto lampposts in a single-handed effort to beau-
tify the neighborhood. They giggle in soft, high voices when you point out
the Japanese pastry shop around the corner. "Beard Papa's," you hear them
say to each other. They know the name of this chain from home.

But they don't know about local institutions such as Astor Place Hair
Stylists, which occupies a basement in the building behind you, with its
multiethnic team of eighty barbers who use their old-school expertise
with the clippers to style the most eye-catching, gravity-defying Mohawks

of the Lower Manhattan punk scene. In the 1980s young men used to make the pilgrimage to Astor's barbers in the East Village from the suburbs and overseas, walking in with a shaggy mane and walking out with a towering crest, sprayed and lacquered and often dyed an unnatural black or red or green that went much better with their black leather jacket and metal studs. Opened in 1945 by an Italian American barber, the salon is still family owned and run. Now it shares the block with a branch of Cold Stone Creamery, the ice cream chain, Arche, the French shoe store chain, and a big Barnes & Noble bookstore.

Neither do the Japanese students know that the Walgreen's drugstore on the corner was until recently Astor Wines. Opened in the 1960s as a neighborhood liquor store, it rode the wave of Americans' growing enthusiasm for ever finer alcoholic beverages to become one of the largest wine merchants in the city. Like Astor Hair, Astor Wines is still owned by the family that opened it, but last year it moved two blocks farther down Lafayette Street after the landlord raised their rent to a level only a chain store could afford.

Astor Place, Starbucked: the Astor Cube, surrounded by history and commerce. Photograph by Richard Rosen.

On a traffic island at the center of the next intersection you point out the Astor Cube, a large black steel sculpture that has mysteriously balanced itself on point since 1968. The cube is a gathering place for teens and college students, punks and skateboarders, panhandlers and sidewalk vendors. Across the street the orange Mud Truck is selling freshly brewed, anti-Establishment coffee. Customers like to say they are protesting the way Starbucks has colonized the area in the past few years, with an outdoor café on one side of the street, a big indoor café on the other, a third café inside Barnes & Noble, and yet another Starbucks a block away.

Who remembers the Digger Free Store on East Tenth Street, where during the 1960s volunteers gave away used shoes, clothing, and odds and ends to "Negro and Puerto Rican children, old women speaking Middle European dialects, barefoot runaways with glazed eyes, stumbling winos, and gaily ornamented hippie couples?" Now the neighborhood has been Starbucked. Though in Harlem it may be a welcome attraction, in the East Village Starbucks is a dire sign of a free fall toward gentrification. No wonder Jeremiah Moss, the pseudonymous blogger of Jeremiah's Vanishing New York, calls Astor Place the "epicenter of evil."[1]

The East Village has always been an area where protest is a way of life and history is important. These are the sources of the neighborhood's reputation for authenticity, and they have been preserved in the low rents and social spaces of a sometimes shabby, often funky locale of tenements and small stores. Now, though, after decades of anchoring the loose lifestyle of the 1960s, the East Village's quirky shops and poets' cafés are being overwhelmed by trendy restaurants, chain stores, and expensive, renovated apartments. New residents and visitors are literally consuming the local.

Across the street from the schmaltz herring store, they sell raspberry apple cider. Next door to the herb teas and unsulfured dried fruits, sfogliatelle and cannoli are dispensed just as they have been since 1904.
—"East Village Food: Tradition and Change," *New York Times*, November 16, 1985

You cannot know the East Village without knowing its local history, and there's almost too much history for any one neighborhood to have. Unlike Harlem or Williamsburg, the East Village's story of origin has been shaped less by race and crime than by generations of social protest—against landlords, the rich, the government, and every other form of authority. It started long before *Rent,* the Broadway musical and film, dramatized the romance of bohemian rebellion on Avenue A to a generation for whom most social protest is, well, history.

The East Village was built as cheap housing for immigrants on swampland near the East River docks between Houston and Fourteenth Streets, and between the Bowery and the East River. It was part of Kleine Deutschland, Little Germany, as the much larger Lower East Side was called in the mid-nineteenth century, but as a later addition to the street grid it had to make do with lettered rather than numbered avenues, bringing it the nickname Alphabet City. The area always simmered with economic grievances and political conflicts; it was also a hotbed of ethnic and social class tensions. In 1849, when Astor Place was the center of the commercial theater district, young Irish immigrants clashed with native-born Americans of English descent in a culture war over rival Shakespearean actors: a Brit who was seen as an arrogant Anglo aristocrat and an American who represented the underdog the Irish felt themselves to be. In 1863, during the Civil War, working-class draft resisters who resented rich New Yorkers' ability to buy their way out of military service put up barriers against the police just north of Tompkins Square Park. In the decades that followed, German and Czech cigar makers, Jewish and Italian garment workers, and Eastern European carpenters rallied in the park, held mass meetings in the Great Hall of Cooper Union and nearby Webster Hall, and argued about socialism, anarchism, and labor rights. The labor union patriarch Samuel Gompers is said to have escaped arrest at a rally near the park in 1874, and the fiery leader Emma Goldman lived on East Thirteenth Street around 1900.

For years the gradual deterioration of the buildings and the successive arrivals of new immigrants from Poland, Ukraine, and Puerto Rico kept this northernmost part of the Lower East Side off most New Yorkers' radar, especially if they had gone to college and made enough money to move to the suburbs or uptown. During the 1950s, though, after World War II, the area drew penniless artists and writers who couldn't afford to live in nearby Greenwich Village. They hadn't yet made it to mainstream markets—or refused to try. Abstract Expressionists showed their work in galleries on Tenth Street near Third Avenue, and Beat poets wrote verses in coffeehouses and jazz musicians played in clubs a few blocks to the east. Later, in the 1960s, a new wave of college students, teenage runaways, and community activists moved into the East Village, carving out a neighborhood with a new name on the gritty streets. Their thrift shops and sketchy little stores selling psychedelic posters and drug paraphernalia re-created the neighborhood as a haven for hippies. Poets and dancers performed in the historic St. Marks Church-in-the-Bowery, and actors worked in off-off-Broadway theaters in the area's basements and storefronts.

During the 1970s and 1980s, as in Williamsburg and Harlem, when landlords left their rent-controlled buildings to rot and drug addicts settled in, punk artists, poets, and rockers found a home in the East Village. Patti Smith, Blondie, and the Ramones all performed at CBGB, a music club on the Bowery, which was still "a drab, ugly and unsavory place," as its owner Hilly Kristal recalls. "But it was good enough for rock and rollers. The people who frequented CBGB didn't seem to mind staggering drunks and stepping over a few bodies." Low rents and the gritty local character of the streets generated an art scene that keyed Lower Manhattan's new creative energy. Young graduates of art schools moved to the city, found out they couldn't afford to live in SoHo, and formed communes in the East Village's dilapidated tenement storefronts where immigrant butchers and bakers had once plied their trades. They needed cheap space to live and work, but they were also chasing the dream of earlier generations; they were refugees from one place or another.[2]

Though there were always conflicts, the neighborhood tolerated many different lifestyles. Each group of new arrivals settled in alongside aging Jewish and Eastern European immigrants, recent migrants from Puerto Rico, and a smaller number of African Americans. The legendary jazz saxophonist Charlie Parker, a black man, lived here with his white companion; Avenue B on the east side of Tompkins Square Park is now named for him. Allen Ginsberg, the Beat poet and gay rights activist (among many other causes), lived here too and often ate pierogi at Odessa, a Ukrainian diner on Avenue A. Miguel Algarin, the fierce cofounder, with Miguel Piñero, of the Nuyorican Poets' Café, still lives near Avenue C. In the 1980s the painters Jean-Michel Basquiat, Keith Haring, and Kenny Scharf, the performance artists Ann Magnuson and Karen Finley, and other would-be masters of the art of life hung out at Club 57 on St. Marks Place and the neighborhood's many performance clubs, seat-of-the-pants art galleries, and cafés. "Unlike today," recalls a former East Village artist who still works in New York's art world, "the galleries were *social* spaces. People hung out in them *all day*."[3]

From the 1950s through the 1980s most cultural migrants came to the East Village because they felt "different," and they believed the neighborhood was "authentic" because of its concentration of difference. "I probably came Downtown for the same reason everyone else did," says Carlo McCormick, an art writer and editor, "because we were too different to be anywhere else." In contrast to the high crime rates and drug dealers that made the neighborhood dangerous, the East Village offered safe space to be as different as possible. "If you lived in SoHo, you couldn't go outside of the neighborhood," a gay artist recalls. "If you walked in Little Italy, you'd get beaten up." Until the 1980s, even in New York City, some neighborhoods were so hostile to artists, gays, and gentrifiers that their homes and cars were vandalized and covered with graffiti, and they themselves were beaten and mugged. During the 1980s, around the time the artists moved in, the police began to use large-scale crime-fighting strategies. Targeted drug sweeps and zero tolerance of "quality of life" crimes resulted in a large number of arrests and gradually made the East Village safer.[4]

Meanwhile the cultural infrastructure of Beat poets, cheap cafés, avant-garde theaters, and eccentric performance spaces created another kind of authenticity. The area was an incubator for new and experimental culture and was promoted as a creative *terroir,* like the later scene in Williamsburg, by independent local media and artist-entrepreneurs. Carlo McCormick moved to the East Village in 1979, but says, "I was hanging around in the '70s, more as an observer than a participant. I was a kid who picked up the *SoHo Weekly News* and checked out stuff. I'd end up at the Mudd Club, Tin Pan Alley, ABC No Rio, the *Times Square Show* [performance spaces, alternative art gallery, temporary art exhibit], just because it all seemed so much more interesting than official culture."[5]

The cultural dissidents of the 1980s joined the politics of protest they found embedded in the East Village. In the blocks around Tompkins Square artists and activists squatted in abandoned tenements and warehouses. Together with their Puerto Rican neighbors they cleared debris from empty lots where derelict tenements had fallen or been torn down and in their place they built community gardens, which the administration of Mayor Rudolph Giuliani tried to auction off to real estate developers in the late 1990s, leading to protest demonstrations and arrests of protesters. Even today struggles over turf still shape the East Village's local character. But many longtime residents feel a real despair about the threat of both abandonment and renewal. They are equally afraid of landlords who refuse to repair a broken boiler and of the higher rents that come with gentrification.

At times this fear boils over, the culture of protest acting as a cauldron that heats and stirs a deep anger against authorities and market forces. During a hot August in 1988 homeless men and women built and occupied a tent city in Tompkins Square Park, defended by punks, rockers, self-declared anarchists, and others who wanted to assert a free right to the city's public spaces. For more than a day and a night the police clubbed these protesters when they tried to stop them from tearing down the encampment. The homeless, though, had aroused the anger and dismay of the local community board, of many residents, and of Mayor Ed Koch himself.

Today the East Village looks like a great place to live: its old buildings gentrified; its interesting little noodle bars, Japanese hair salons, and Moroccan, Afghan, and vegan restaurants; and not least, its ethnically varied but mostly young population out walking the streets 24/7. Even Tompkins Square Park, renovated after the police violence of 1988, is calm and homey. Old men pushing shopping carts loaded with their belongings sit on benches to rest and chat, children too young for preschool sway back and forth in black rubber toddler swings, and young men play basketball on a fenced-in court.

On these streets, though, you can feel the hum of another kind of time. The Greeks called it *kairos:* a sense of the past that intrudes into and challenges the present. It's different from *chronos,* our usual sense of time as a simple, unending arrow of progress from yesterday to today and on to tomorrow. The streets and buildings of the East Village are reminders of an alternative time that doesn't make the present look like the culmination of the past; these are "kairological images" that create "a sense of authentic origin and justification for present hopes." They make you feel you're re-creating a unique story of origin, and the storefronts and tenements give material form to the comfort you take on living in an old neighborhood with a history of artistic energy and resisting authority. You sense that in this space you could be living in any time and you could take on any of these roles: artist, poet, rebel, *flâneur.* Or maybe you could take on all these roles at once.[6]

With *kairos* comes a particular kind of authenticity that connects your sense of the old East Village with your desire to *consume* it. And suddenly you see that this projection of your own self-image on the shabby chic streets is exactly what the marketing theorists expect authenticity to be: a sympathetic vibe between consumers and the objects of their desire.[7]

So it's not surprising that selling *kairos* in the East Village today brings big bucks. Three adjoining houses on St. Marks Place that were once a Polish social club called Dom ("Home"), and then, beginning around 1960, in rapid succession, a performance space for the antiwar band the Fugs, a club run by Andy Warhol, and a discotheque called the Electric Circus, have all been renovated into apartments renting now for more than two thousand dollars a month. Sotheby's recently auctioned a canvas painted by Basquiat in the 1980s for fourteen million dollars. These prices contradict the neighborhood's carefully nurtured sense of authenticity. They say the East Village of beatniks and hippies is dead, and that the neighborhood's deep local character, its ability to incubate art and protest and dissident culture, cannot be maintained. Gentrification deprives these social groups of the low rents and social spaces they need to reproduce local culture.

The most unusual thing about the East Village, though, and about bohemian neighborhoods in other cities, is that it attracts both rich and poor in close proximity. This is historically true of Astor Place, where, in the mid-nineteenth century, two broad avenues and the social classes they represented met and collided. "On the west," Edwin Burrows and Mike Wallace write in *Gotham*, their history of New York City, runs "Broadway, with its retail shops, department stores, monster hotels, and porpoise-parade of the fashionable. On the east: the Bowery, the thoroughfare of sportsmen, dandies, gangsters, and fire laddies." These two "class worlds" existed in a tense immediacy just a few blocks apart, with the rich folks tasting danger by slumming with the poor folks in working-class saloons and the poor living in fear that the other group, or at least their agents—landlords and the police—could kick them out of their turf.[8]

Today these class worlds overlap. Gentrification, the overlay of renewal on top of abandonment, has moved steadily eastward from Broadway to the Bowery and on toward the letter-named avenues of Alphabet City, creating a new sense of place where the culture of resistance is consumed. A luxury high-rise apartment house towers over Astor Place, a branch of Chase Bank occupying its entire ground floor. To the south, on the Bowery, a high-class French chef has opened a bistro that jokingly copies the old CBGB logo: DBGB, Daniel Boulud Good Burger. To the north, near Fourteenth Street, a twenty-six-story New York University dormitory looms over the skyline. Like the three Starbucks on Astor Place, these upscale places bring to a visible high point the changes that have gradually crept through the East Village in the past thirty years.

Downtown—crime-ridden, sparsely inhabited, practically restaurant-free—was just beginning to boom when the SoHo *News* folded, in 1982.
—"Downtown Girl," *The New Yorker,* September 24, 2007

I have lived near the East Village since the 1970s, and my home reflects the neighborhood's new beginnings. All around us old industrial buildings have gradually been renovated into offices for architects, psychotherapists, and literary agents and living quarters for artists, writers, designers, and lawyers, all of them part of the new urban middle class. I moved into a loft in one of these buildings when my husband, then just starting his career, designed and built furniture. Though our small building already had a few live-work tenants like us, it was still used mainly for light manufacturing.

An elderly couple who had worked together all their married life made men's hats on one floor; two business partners who looked as old as the comedy routines in vaudeville manufactured cases for traveling sales-people on another; a woodworking company owned by two young archi-tects rented a floor in the middle; and in the loft beneath ours a silkscreen printer and his two employees made signs. An artist used one of the lofts as her studio, but lived uptown. A woman photographer lived in another loft, and a guy our age who built loft beds, a new kind of furniture in those days, lived several floors below.

Within five years the old people who made traditional things in tradi-tional ways moved out of the building when they retired or the landlord raised the rent too high. They were replaced by younger residents engaged in more creative occupations: a couple of graphic artists, a young woman from Paris who designed fur coats, and a commercial photographer from Milan who lived in our building but rented a studio for work in SoHo. After a few years the landlord turned the building into a co-op by sell-ing the individual floors to some of the residents and newcomers. Prices weren't too high, but we had to invest our own money to make the raw space livable. So we installed hot water heaters, ran the building's boiler seven days a week instead of five, and replaced old, leaky windows. We also exposed brick walls and refinished wooden floors to make them shine. You know what I mean: loft living.

A few decades later most of the lofts have changed hands several times, and the sale prices have climbed to levels we would not have believed back in the 1980s. My new neighbors sell financial investments and real estate, work in the music industry, and practice law. One owns an antiques store, another makes promotional films, and three are interior designers.

Changes in who my neighbors are give you a capsule version of how Lower Manhattan has been transformed in recent years, but in my building you can also see how the East Village retains kairological images of past and present. In the fading sign painted on the redbrick wall of a nearby building I can still read the East Village's origins in the words "Cloak World," a ghostly reminder of the factories that used these lofts before we came. On the sidewalk, though, I see the area's new beginnings in the college students, gentrifiers, and hipperati sitting at sidewalk cafés. The movement from origins to new beginnings occurred in stages, beginning in the 1960s and 1970s with the gradual disappearance of the factories, and the hardware stores and diners that catered to their workers, and the growth of banks, law firms, art schools, and universities. This shift was amplified by new tastes for loft living and media buzz. Like Harlem and Williamsburg, our neighborhood was reimagined. Its reputation for authenticity still reflected local character, but the meaning of "local" had changed.

The East Village still enjoys the image of an oasis of authenticity in a Wal-Mart wasteland, which tends to make living here even more expensive. Almost everywhere, lofts and walk-up flats have been transformed into luxury housing. "Blight," which urban planning officials in the 1950s sneeringly said was the problem with old neighborhoods like ours, has yielded to chic.[9]

Redevelopment began in the 1950s, to the south of Washington Square Park, when Robert Moses used federal government funds for urban renewal to demolish manufacturing lofts and replace them with faculty housing for NYU. Since then NYU has expanded northward and eastward block by block. Tompkins Square Park has been cleaned up and pacified by the Parks Department and the police. Bars have overtaken ethnic grocery stores; rising rents have pushed old tenants out. Real estate markets have been supported by the actions of government agencies: policing by the NYPD, rezoning by the City Planning Commission, liquor licensing by the State Liquor Authority. As a result, life in the East Village is safer and more interesting than ever. Most important, though, the local character that draws so many people to the neighborhood is experienced through consumption: eating, drinking, and most often shopping.

It is late afternoon, and Momofuku Ssam Bar in the food-fixated East Village is idling in self-service mode waiting for the cocktail crowd—pretty much indistinguishable from the pierced and tattooed waiters—to saunter in.
—*New York Times*, May 18, 2007

Stores on East Ninth Street, between First and Second Avenues, recycle the loose lifestyle of the 1960s into low-key, downtown chic. It's an unusual block even in this heavily commercial part of the neighborhood. In contrast to St. Marks Place, one block to the south—the headquarters for teens who want goth, schlock, piercing, and tattoos—the shops on Ninth Street offer fine quality at fairly modest prices. There are several vintage clothing and furniture shops, stores with custom-made bridal gowns, a shop that sells handmade wooden toys, and boutiques of emerging designers. The boutiques on the block draw shoppers in their twenties and thirties, college students, and tourists who want items with a unique look, such as old eyeglass frames, jelly jars, and wind-up alarm clocks; these flea market finds are specialized goods for a niche market. In their own way, the shop owners on East Ninth Street are selling kairological images of consumer culture. They know the value of authenticity,

The "authentic" East Village: stores on East Ninth Street. Photograph by Sharon Zukin.

the kind of authenticity that connects the self-awareness of the 1960s counterculture to the "mobile awareness of personal and individual life-style" typical of consumers today. Their shops reflect the "class worlds" that dominate the East Village now: both elegant and derelict, hippie and yuppie, distinctive and diverse.[10]

This block of East Ninth Street is distinctive in several ways. Leafy trees shade the sidewalk, which is unusual in Lower Manhattan. And the block contains an astonishing number of stores, more stores than buildings, forty-six separate stores in thirty-five four- to six-story tenements and small apartment houses. Most of them are ground-floor storefronts, but some are below street level in the basements, and others stand in matching pairs on both sides of the doorways. These buildings are not the aristocratic brownstone townhouses with high stoops that you find in the center of Greenwich Village near Fifth Avenue, in some parts of Harlem, or in Park Slope. These are typical Lower East Side tenements. Most were built in only two years, 1899 and 1900, when the small developers and contractors who built tenement housing heard about the impending passage of a new law that would require them to make a new kind of low-rent apartment in which every room had access to daylight and fresh air. At that time tenants in the neighborhood were recent immigrants from Eastern or Southern Europe who worked in the garment industry, in small metal workshops or food stores, or as street peddlers, and their apartments were crowded with family members and boarders. The toilet was in the hall, shared by all the tenants on a floor, and each apartment had a claw-footed bathtub in the kitchen, just inside the front door. In some apartments these bathtubs remained in the kitchen until the 1970s or 1980s because the landlord refused to make improvements on rent-controlled apartments. Even today some buildings still lack elevators.

During the past few decades all of the buildings on East Ninth Street have been renovated; several façades have been modernized, and doors and window frames freshly painted. But the block still has an old-fashioned feel. Black iron fire escapes run up the fronts of buildings; low, crumbling stoops lead to the doorways. Most apartment rents are regulated, either "controlled" or "stabilized," by New York State laws. There is no commercial rent control, but the size of the stores on East Ninth Street is too small to interest chains. The same little shops seem to remain in place for years. You can imagine this block in Paris or on some of the less modern parts of Lexington Avenue. It's low-key, charming, and more than a little funky: it's *local*.[11]

At the eastern end of the block, where rents are lower, a few storefronts offer everyday services on which residents rely: a bakery, laundry, shoe repair shop, watch repair service, and photocopy shop, a dry cleaner, and a veterinary clinic. Some store owners say the bakery and shoe repair shop have been there since the 1920s. The rest of the block, on both sides of the street, is filled with stores that can only be called, for their small size and selective stock, boutiques. As on many shopping streets, the largest number of them, seventeen, sell women's clothing; these include the first store opened in the 1980s by Eileen Fisher, a designer of basic, casual clothing in natural fibers, before she expanded her company into a national chain. There are also five shops selling design objects and home accessories, four furniture stores selling "semi-antique" tables and chairs, two furniture repair shops, two shops offering personal services and products for body care, an eyewear store that provides unusual eyeglasses for films and Broadway shows, an art gallery, and stores selling handmade purses, jewelry, children's toys, messenger bags, candles, and supplies for Wiccans who practice modern witchcraft ("Come in for a spell," says the sign in their window). Unlike the broad avenues that border the block, which bristle with little restaurants and bars, this street has no bars, and its three restaurants serve only beer and wine: the tiny, dark Ninth Street Market, Mud Truck's indoor café, and Veselka, a diner for "Ukrainian soul food" that opened around 1960. In place of the aspirational shopping of designer labels that you find in so many downtown neighborhoods these days, East Ninth Street offers motivational shopping: it's not about social status, but about expressing yourself.[12]

This rich variety of shopping doesn't reflect the decades of decline and disinvestment in the mid-twentieth century, when the immigrant population aged, landlords refused to renovate apartments, and drug dealers ruled the streets. Joe, whose family owns and runs Veselka, points to the late 1960s and 1970s as the worst time: "There were a lot of drugs in the neighborhood, a lot of crime. It got more dangerous." He came to the East Village as a college student in the 1970s, got a job in the restaurant, married the boss's daughter, and moved to the area permanently in 1988. But when he moved into an apartment on Tompkins Square Park, he says, "the park was a gathering place for the homeless, where they continuously camped. It was a mess, it was dangerous—a very dangerous place. Twenty-four hours a day, homeless people were in there sleeping with tents and making fires at night. It was a mess, a real mess. And nobody in the city had the political courage to clean it out." These were the conditions that led Mayor Koch to call on the police to clear the park, a signal that the urban middle class, backed by business leaders, were cracking down on the 1960s' tolerance of difference that was felt to threaten public order. Even in the East Village the confrontation came down to "community residents" on one side and "anarchists, punks, and homeless" on the other. "Nobody else in the neighborhood could use the park," Joe continues. "Too dangerous. Too dirty."[13]

Eleanor, who opened an accessories store on East Ninth Street in 2001, also remembers the East Village as unbearable. When she first moved to New York City in the early 1980s, she and her friends often went to bars in the neighborhood. After a few years, however, she didn't want to be around "all these dirty kids."

Lana, a Ukrainian-American woman who has lived her whole life in the East Village and owns one of the vintage clothing stores on the block, recalls that throughout the 1970s most storefronts were used as apartments by groups of young people. Next to her store, "about fifty anarchists" lived in a commune. She remembers that they often smashed windows of parked cars to steal radios or anything they could sell for money to buy drugs. She suspected a store at the other end of the block of being a center for producing illegal drugs. Another store owner thinks that a former owner of the candle shop sold drugs.

But longtime store owners also say that conditions were different here, "west of First Avenue." "This block has always been good," Joe says. "Even in the middle seventies, when the neighborhood was bad, when there were some very bad blocks, and some very bad areas, this block was always one of the better blocks in the neighborhood—if not the best." Like other old ethnic neighborhoods, the East Village had old-style gangsters who looked out for the residents. Joe remembers "a little Mafia clubhouse down the street, with all these gangster guys hanging out there in the evening." They "didn't disturb" the neighbors; "they were joking around...like 'wise guys.' They weren't a problem because we knew them and we knew where they were." Lana remembers that they offered to help her "whenever somebody gave [her] a problem." Maybe they were Italian, or maybe they were "the Ukrainian Brotherhood," as another store owner recalls," but what is important is that they watched over the block.

East Ninth Street was different in another way: it "was popular," says Susana, a saleswoman who has lived on the block since 1962 in a rent-controlled apartment. "This block has all the time been popular. People would come out of the subway at Astor Place and they would walk towards this street." In fact, the path from the subway leads directly to St. Marks Place, but people could have been coming to Ninth Street too. "This block has always been trendy," says Glenna, who owns a store for home accessories. "Back to the fifties, maybe even the forties. It has always been an eclectic street, very eclectic."

Joe suggests that this local sense of authenticity comes from the history of stores on East Ninth Street. "There was a long tradition of shops," he says. "Little shops, owned by artists and craftsmen. In the sixties and seventies, in this street, there were a lot of handicraft people. There was one guy who used to make chess sets, and every one of them was different. Another guy had a leather shop, and several women designed and made clothes. A lot of these people lived in there, too. They had their little shop in front and they lived in back....It was not much different than it is now."

Though the atmosphere on the block may have been like it is today, residents socialized differently in the past. Partly this reflects the postwar decline of the urban village. "There were not as many people living in this neighborhood," Joe recalls. Like other urban villages, the East Village lost residents when tenants moved to better neighborhoods and landlords refused to maintain their buildings, even abandoned them. The number of residents has increased by about 12 percent since 1980, but more important, today there are fewer of the very old and the very young. "It was a working class neighborhood," Joe says, "so everybody got up in the morning and went to work. And the neighborhood was really quiet. Not much traffic, not many people....And then, at 5 or 6 o'clock, everybody came home. And there was a lot of activity, especially in the summertime, when the weather was nice. People would bring chairs and sit outside, talk to their neighbors. Kids would play in the street. There was a repair garage down the street, and there would be cars in the street that he was fixing....It was more of a social scene on the street"—very much an urban village.

Today the block's rhythm is set by the stores instead of families. Most open after 11 A.M. and stay open until seven or eight in the evening, when neighborhood residents come home from work or school and visitors who come to the East Village for dinner are window-shopping. The restaurants keep the block lively around the clock.

In the early 1980s, Joe suggests, you could feel these changes coming. "The neighborhood got younger," he says. "And it got more popular. . . . In an apartment where maybe a husband and wife [had lived], now there might be three or four students living . . . so [there was] more of a concentration of people, and a younger population. Then slowly . . . a big thing [happened]. A lot more people [were] in the neighborhood during the day."

Joe focuses on two big changes in the East Village at that time: the aging of the working-class residents and the arrival of artists and yuppies. Lana talks about how NYU started to expand into the area from its campus on Washington Square. Joe mentions the East Village art galleries. Like the artist who recalls hanging out in the galleries all day, they also remember young people, students, and artists practically taking up residence in the area's growing number of cafés. Because rents remained low, many cafés could survive with patrons who nursed a single mug of coffee for hours.

Veselka managed to adapt to these changes and even thrive. The restaurant's original owner, Joe's father-in-law, was an immigrant who fled Ukraine with his family during World War II. In the 1950s he opened a candy shop and newsstand on Second Avenue in the heart of "Little Ukraine." Within ten years he had expanded into the luncheonette next door. In 1970, when the Fillmore East, a famous rock and roll concert hall, was still in business nearby, he bought the store around the corner on Ninth Street and enlarged the dining area. In 1992, with the Ukrainian immigrant population getting smaller and the number of college students and recent graduates growing, Veselka changed its menu, adding pierogi made with arugula and goat cheese to the traditional beef- or pork-stuffed dumplings and introducing vegetarian plates next to traditional Ukrainian meat stews. A few years later the restaurant opened a sidewalk café, a visible sign of gentrification.

The block's turning point came in the mid-1980s, just after the East Village art scene began to fade but downtown still drew a lot of media attention. While more creative young residents moved in, equally creative retail entrepreneurs opened vintage furniture stores. There were, at the peak of this wave, as many as eight furniture stores, which helped to create the block's reputation for distinctive shopping. Then clothing stores began to cluster there. An African American jazz musician opened one in 1980, and Lana started her consignment store for vintage clothes in 1986. Eileen Fisher opened her store around 1984. At first she shared a single storefront with another merchant; then, as sales increased, she moved into her own store across the street. Other store owners believe the company keeps the original store for nostalgic reasons, but business isn't bad. As Glenna says, "When they have a sale, there is a line in front of the store."

Despite their different specialties, the new store owners who came to the block in the mid-1980s shared a modern aesthetic. They liked big plate-glass windows, brightly lighted interiors, walls painted white. Like The Gap, which promoted the same kind of store design at that time, these small shops looked distinctly modern. "Before, [the stores were] very hippie looking," Lana recalls of their dark, makeshift interiors. "But then, very pretty stores started to open. The *New York Times* started to write about [the block], and it became known."

National and local media had already covered the meteoric rise of the East Village artists. Maureen Dowd wrote a cover story for the *New York Times Magazine* in 1985 on how the neighborhood was being hyped as a new Bohemia.[14] By then, however, the meteor had crashed. Many artists died from drug overdoses or AIDS, and successful survivors moved away. Most of the art galleries and performance spaces closed. Though the illegal drug traffic was seriously threatening and prostitution was rampant on many blocks, journalists wrote about the new shops and restaurants that were popping up in the midst of squalor. These became a part of the new phenomenon of "lifestyle shopping," a way of selling the authenticity desired by the counterculture to the next generation of consumers.

Lana remembers when The Paris Apartment moved into the storefront next to hers. The owner sold flea market finds that she carefully repaired and painted and presented as one-of-a-kind Baroque and Art Deco treasures. In a book that the owner wrote about the store, she described it as a place "where visitors can step back in time and immerse themselves in the beauty and romance of antique furnishings. Reflecting an unusual mix of design influences...and personal taste, its style is luxurious, playful, and wholly original." The Paris Apartment, as its name implies, was both in the East Village and apart from it, balancing between the self-conscious authenticity of urban squalor and chic consumer culture. "In stark contrast to the dark neighborhood," the owner's current website recalls, "[the store] flowed with French boudoir furniture and accessories." In its time The Paris Apartment attracted sophisticated shoppers, interior designers, and lifestyle reporters to East Ninth Street. When that store disappeared (to be resurrected years later on the Web), it was replaced by another shop that also sold unusual home accessories.

"All the rich ladies used to come to them," Lana says. After that store too was written up in the *New York Times,* "they made it really big" and moved uptown to Lexington Avenue.[15]

Store owners pinpoint the mid-1990s as the next turning point. "It changed in 1996," Glenna says. "That's when women's dresses started. It happened just as I opened my store here.... Very different shops were here before that. This shop was a camera store. Another used to sell pianos. Another was a candle shop...Paris Apartment...Hex.... But now...more and more clothes."

A third wave of store owners arrived in the first years of the twenty-first century. Like shoppers, they were drawn by the block's reputation for aesthetic distinction. By this point, East Ninth Street was not only an incubator of new boutiques and designers, it also represented a step up from cheaper neighborhoods. "It made sense [for me to move here]," Eleanor says about her move from a studio on the Lower East Side. "I had not even thought about the East Village before. It was not upscale enough in the past."

While changing types of stores have shifted the block's focus over the years, their products have become even more distinctive. "They are all designers here, and they all have their own styles," store owners say. "It's all different styles." Like Eileen Fisher when she began, many of the store owners design and even make their wares. "I have my own look, it's not the same as the others,'" Alexandra says. "My background is in design." As the MySpace profile of another store asserts, there is a continuing connection between local design, local production, and local character: "Our clothes are edgy. They speak for themselves.... We design and make our own line here, in NYC. Our collection is exclusive, and cannot be found anywhere else."

Alexandra believes, as do other store owners, that each shop's exclusive merchandise reinforces the attractiveness of the block as a whole and reduces competition. "Everybody has unique products, so that's not a problem. Nobody has my stuff 'cause I design it, of course." Carole, who sells handmade cloth purses across the street, says about her store, "It's definitely a 'different' shop." Ken, the owner of the vintage eyewear store, says he gets a lot of publicity "because [his store is] so unusual": "Nobody has this stuff....We have eyeglasses from the 1600s! And...who [else] has a leather cowboy shirt from the fifties?"

It takes the media, though, to confirm the *interesting* quality of the block, to suggest a sense of discovery about it. "That's why they come," Ken says. "They think they have discovered something, and they want to write about it." This in turn attracts more shoppers. "This block has got written up in the *New York Times* and in guidebooks as a good shopping block," Joe says. "So now a lot of people come in from Westchester [County]. It's become a destination."

According to Maria, who designs and sells evening gowns, the block attracts two different types of shopper, both of whom are looking for the "utterly Ninth Street" outfit. One type is "the little rich girl from Park Avenue" who comes with her father's credit card: "Some people who come here, they're label-conscious, but here it's not about the label. Some things I do in only one piece, and they like that. They like the fact that, unlike something with a brand name, if they get something here, it will be special…and her friends will not know where it is from." In contrast, the other type of shopper, seeing a young designer working in her storefront shop, expects to buy a custom-made wedding gown on the cheap. "The other day," Maria continues, "a girl came in and told me she wants a wedding dress, and I said okay. She described what she wanted—the best material.…But she said she could only pay me six hundred dollars max! I said I can't do it, and she was surprised I didn't want the business. Well, with six hundred dollars, I can maybe cover [the cost of] the material, but custom-made is a lot of work. I would have to close my shop for so many days [to work on it]. So I said, 'Look, girl, custom dresses are not for everybody. That's why it's *custom*.'"

With these two types of shopper, the "little rich girl" and the bargain hunter, the block carries on the neighborhood's history of representing two contrasting class worlds. Today, however, the East Village is not so deeply torn between "fashionable" people on one side and "dandies" and "gangsters" on the other, but between consumers who want to experience authenticity and those who are just looking for a bargain. Often the two types overlap, for prices on East Ninth Street are lower than they are uptown. Bargains are still a part of the local character.

Housing is a different story. The current asking price for a six-story, walk-up tenement building on East Ninth Street, with sixteen apartments and two stores, is six and a half million dollars. Because of rent control there hasn't been much interest in buying buildings like this until recently. By now, however, so many longtime tenants have died or moved away and landlords have been so aggressive at pushing other tenants out, that a lot of rents have been "decontrolled" or "destabilized." Tenement buildings like this are a checkerboard of speculative opportunities.

Only three of the sixteen apartments in this building are still rent-controlled, and six others are rent-stabilized; the remaining seven apartments' rents have been deregulated. The difference is dramatic. Although the rent-controlled apartments all bring in less than two hundred dollars a month, rents on the destabilized units are ten times higher. No wonder the class world of the East Village has tilted toward gentrification.[16]

Shop owners insist, though, that the block still has an "authentic" East Village feel. "The past is here," Eleanor says, contrasting East Ninth Street with shopping streets on the Lower East Side and with SoHo. "I like it very much that it is not totally upscale. Not like in SoHo. There are stores that have been here for twenty years." But since Eleanor found the East Village upscale enough to move her shop here in 2001, the block must have found a balancing point between class worlds on which it, like the Astor Cube, is tenuously perched. Ironically it is the longtime tenants, who live in the rent-controlled and rent-stabilized apartments, who create the sociability on which Eleanor thrives. "Another nice thing," she says, "is the people who live here in this block. When I was renovating the store, they would come in and introduce themselves. Ever since, if I happen to be looking up as they pass, we say hello to each other. We are very friendly." She especially enjoys how another owner, the musician who opened his store in 1980, plays his keyboard on the street in the evening.

Eleanor is indebted to the bohemian class world of rebels, artists, and immigrants who sought a refuge from persecution here and now fear gentrification. "I think it's probably due to the past of the East Village," she says: "all this hippie culture, the friendliness, the openness. I think this is a very solid neighborhood and I like that quite a lot. Not only the shops, but the neighborhood."

Yet the easy sociability that Eleanor admires, and the neighborhood that nurtures it, are threatened by rising rents. On the Bowery CBGB's rent rose from six hundred dollars a month in 1973 to nineteen thousand dollars a month in 2004; the next year, the landlord, a nonprofit organization that helps the homeless, evicted the club and raised the rent again, to sixty-five thousand dollars a month. On St. Marks Place a ground floor with a storefront rented for twenty-eight dollars a month in 1959; by 2005 rents had reached ten thousand dollars a month. Rents are lower on East

Ninth Street, where there is less foot traffic, but recent increases of up to 25 percent have caused some stores to close or move out.[17]

If rents continue to rise, the neighborhood's authenticity will rest more on the historic look of the old tenements than on the historic compromise between opposing social worlds. The lower-class world has already been pushed as far east as Avenue D, where the public housing projects are. Almost everything that's new in the East Village—the condos, the boutique hotels and restaurants, and certainly the two Whole Foods Markets on the neighborhood's northern and southern borders—is geared to upscale consumption.

SOLEX Frederick Twomey, who owns the Bar Veloce Group, and Christophe Chatron-Michaud have opened this French wine bar with food to match from Eric Hubert, who was the pastry chef at the Ritz Carlton: *103 First Avenue (Sixth Street).*
—*New York Times*, November 14, 2007

The rise of the East Village as a destination coincided with the emergence of America, especially in big cities like New York, as a "gourmet nation." Before the 1980s few New Yorkers, even those who regularly dined at expensive restaurants, knew the names of the chefs; cooking was still a working-class profession. But during the 1970s a generation of young college graduates who had traveled through Europe, where they learned to enjoy fresh food and good wine, decided to spread their tastes through the rest of the country. Some became restaurant chefs, others decided to write about food, and still others turned to careers as organic growers or opened gourmet food stores. These were the people who did the cultural work of re-creating the authentic foods of other times and places from local food supplies and shaping them to meet contemporary tastes; they were both retail and cultural entrepreneurs. Giorgio DeLuca, a founder of the gourmet food emporium Dean and DeLuca, which opened in SoHo in the early 1970s as a small imported cheese store, gladly claims this role. "I was trying to show people things," he says. "An artist shows people things that they can't see themselves."[18]

New stores and restaurants lured food lovers from more affluent neighborhoods and the suburbs to areas of the city that, like the industrial lofts of SoHo and the drug-dealing streets of the East Village, seemed closed to outsiders and even dangerous. They were not the only outposts of change in these areas. But together with art galleries, performance spaces, and residential lofts, new gourmet food stores and restaurants presented Lower Manhattan as a cradle of cultural innovation for the new middle class. Stores like Dean and Deluca and the Greenmarket at Union Square attracted middle-class visitors and tourists who wanted to consume both "authentic" food, meaning European cheese and freshly picked produce, and the "authentic" city: old brick buildings, cobblestone streets, and lively crowds. This aesthetic attraction to authentic foods and places found an echo with architects and planners who were thinking about how to redevelop the wastelands of the inner city.[19]

Pike Place Market, on the Seattle waterfront, offered a strong case for food as an anchor of redevelopment. Like many open-air public food markets in city centers, Pike Place had been established in the early 1900s but fell into disuse by the 1950s and 1960s, when many shoppers deserted the downtown for suburban shopping malls, or at least for more modern and more sanitary supermarkets. The area became derelict and dangerous, very much like St. Marks Place in the 1950s, SoHo in the 1960s, and Union Square in the 1970s. But Pike Place had its local defenders. They insisted that saving the market would be "about saving a way of life, especially the presence of local farmers," and in 1971 they persuaded Seattle's voters to approve a referendum to revive the market. Partly an opportunity to buy locally grown produce and freshly caught fish, and partly a colorful tourist attraction, Pike Place Market marked Seattle as a city that appreciated authenticity. Later, of course, this point was taken up by Starbucks, Seattle's most successful chain.[20]

As in Seattle, the decay and destruction of old neighborhoods in New York in the 1970s also inspired men and women to organize around preserving the "authentic" city. Historic preservationists, many of them mobilized by Jane Jacobs's work, had recently succeeded in persuading the city government to set up a Landmarks Preservation Commission, and new laws made it harder to destroy old buildings that gave a sense of the city's past. Unlike in Seattle, though, there wasn't much feeling for reviving New York's old public food markets. The wholesale fruit and vegetable market at the World Trade Center site was relocated in the 1960s to the Bronx, and the indoor retail markets that were built in working-class neighborhoods from the Lower East Side to East Harlem during the Great Depression by Mayor Fiorello LaGuardia had mostly been abandoned. Like city-built public baths, gradually made obsolete by bathtubs in every apartment, the public markets steadily lost customers to supermarkets and suburban malls. Then in the 1970s local activists who wanted to support regional agriculture lobbied the New York City government for help in setting up a new kind of market, an outdoor farmers' market, that would bring "real food" to consumers in the city. It would also, they believed, bring to New York "the social amenity of the European 'village square' markets."[21]

Union Square Park was both a good and a bad location for this kind of amenity. On the northern edge of the East Village and served by many bus and subway lines, the park was city-owned property that needed little new investment to host an outdoor market. Local businesses like Consolidated Edison and the Guardian Insurance Company, and the private New School University, which would soon form a Business Improvement District at Union Square, were concerned about the area's declining reputation and welcomed any project that promised to improve it. But it wasn't clear that farmers or shoppers would be willing to come to such a dicey location, even on a Saturday morning. The first Greenmarket, already open for business uptown, was doing so well, the farmer Ron Binaghi recalls, "that [his] father told [him] that [he] could keep any money [he] made at Union Square." He laughs heartily because he knows he got the better part of that bargain.

Today the farmers' market at Union Square is the flagship of the city's extensive Greenmarket organization, the largest of more than fifty farmers' markets spread around the city. Seventy farmers, bakers, cheese makers, beekeepers, and vineyard owners sell their products at Union Square four days a week. The Greenmarket is a hotspot of locavore food culture; everything sold there must be grown, raised, or processed in the greater New York region, extending from northern Vermont to southern New Jersey and including northern and central New York State. Some farmers drive for as long as six hours to bring apples or poultry to the Greenmarket, loading their large trucks at 1 A.M. and arriving at Union Square by dawn. They set up their stands and remain on their feet all day, dealing with shoppers' questions and comments, before returning to the farm late at night.

I shop often at the Greenmarket, as often as three days a week if I can manage it. First drawn there by a friend who praised the tomatoes, I soon began to depend on it for most of my food supplies during the summer and for a kind of public life as well. The people who shop there and the farmers who sell there are neither neighbors nor strangers. But the market provides me with a sense of local authenticity, of living local both in my neighborhood and on the land. I have seen some farmers every week, most often on Saturday morning, for years, and we always exchange greetings and casually chat. It's not the most serious conversation, but it's an important part of my local social world, and it gives the East Village another layer of local character.

Like many local worlds, though, this one has been globalized in recent years. The Greenmarket prides itself on helping to maintain small, regional, family-owned farms by providing them with direct access to consumers. This being the twenty-first century, few of the farmers are from the Dutch, English, or German families who migrated to the Hudson Valley or central New Jersey centuries ago and have remained on the farm since then. Stokes Farm, "since 1873," as their white truck says, is one of the exceptions, for Ron Binaghi is a fifth-generation farmer. In addition to the Binaghis, the farmers include a Taiwanese family who sell organically grown long beans and bok choy and a New Jersey farmer who grows uchiki kuri, a Japanese squash, along with heirloom varieties of American tomatoes. Elizabeth Ryan, who grew up on a farm in Iowa and owns Breezy Hill Orchards, hires Central Americans who have migrated to the Hudson Valley both to work on the farm and to sell apples and cider at the market. Other farmers employ Tibetans to work at the stands.[22]

Besides these changes in who performs the role of local farmer at the market, there have been changes in farming practices as well. Small, family-owned farms have shifted from wholesale production, where they depended on a middleman to distribute their produce and set prices, to the retail trade, and some have moved into small-batch production for niche markets, selling exotic herbs and free-range chicken to restaurant chefs. They learn from each other, from their customers' preferences, and from food and fashion writers in the media who introduce them to the latest trends. With all this cross-fertilization, many products now on sale at the Greenmarket are not historically local products, but cultural hybrids. Sure, there are tons of apples and yellow onions. But there are also long red Tropea onions, wild arugula, and Tuscan kale, all grown locally from Italian seeds. The Taiwanese farmers bring homemade kim chee to the Greenmarket, and the American owner of a New Jersey dairy farm learned to make sheep's milk cheese in France.

Unlike most other farmers' markets, the New York City Greenmarket system demands that all goods sold there be locally produced. Though the reason for this is to protect sustainable agriculture in the region, the market's local "brand" also reinforces its reputation for authenticity. Yet applying the rule creates problems, for it is often difficult to determine what is truly, authentically *local*. Imagine the debates that broke out when the owners of Coach Farms, a small, family-owned dairy that makes goat cheese in the Hudson Valley, sold the cheese-making part of their business but kept the thousand-goat herd whose milk went into the cheese. Because *local*, according to the Greenmarket's restrictive rules, means that vendors must make all their products from start to finish, the new owner of the cheese-making part of the business was not allowed to sell at the market. Experts say that Coach Farms' cheese is *fresh* because it's locally made from the milk of goats who live on a farm just two hours away; you know where it comes from, "it was produced just down the road, just over the river." But according to the Greenmarket's rules, because the goats are no longer owned by the dairy that makes the cheese, the cheese is not a *local* product and can't be sold at Union Square. This Talmudic wrangling over the definition doesn't just romanticize, it makes a fetish of "local" production—like the man waiting beside me to buy trout raised in the Catskills, which he planned to carry to New Jersey in his briefcase on the PATH train and then drive two hours in his car to his home.[23]

In contrast to the Greenmarket's official emphasis on preserving regional farmland, shoppers value the market for the quality of the food and the experience of shopping there. One Friday at lunchtime in early fall, I ask eighteen shoppers at Union Square what they like about the farmers' market. Half of them say, "The quality of the food" or "The stuff is so good." Four speak about fresh vegetables. A man in his fifties, shopping alone, says, "Wednesdays, there's a fish vendor that sells the freshest fish." A Latina woman in her thirties says, "I come from the Bronx, and the markets up there can't compare. The farmers don't bring nearly as much variety as they do here." Other shoppers talk about the "authenticity" of the social experience. "I like the whole feeling of community," says a woman in her fifties, walking her dog, "and Union Square too. Just look around—there are ten thousand protesters—and people get together." The man who likes fresh fish says, "It's such a scene. You can stand back and enjoy the pageant of city life!"

What is so *local* about the Greenmarket? It's not as if we're harvesting okra on the streets of the East Village. Many of the people we buy from, and some of the farmers, are immigrants from other regions of the world. And it's not as though you see the friendly interdependence among shopkeepers, housewives, and passersby that Jane Jacobs described as the ballet of the street. Instead you feel a real sociability at the Greenmarket, which is born of personal interaction, identified by product and provenance, and honed by habit. In a way it creates a story of origin for this part of the neighborhood. It also recalls the sense of local authenticity that visitors and tourists believe is "natural" at weekly food markets in Provence and Tuscany. Like the Greenmarket, though, that authenticity is a carefully produced social construction.

During the course of a year the French anthropologist Michèle de la Pradelle made detailed observations of the weekly market in Carpentras, a town in Provence that has been famous since ancient times. She notes the air of festivity, the joking back and forth among shoppers and vendors, and the freshness of the produce, whose regional provenance is chalked on a sign along with its price. The vendors contribute to the experience of authenticity by acting the role of local farmers. They dress in blue peasant smocks, speak a mixture of standard French and local dialect, and personally vouch for the quality of the strawberries, green beans, or melons at their stand. But this is a performance, for the vendors do not grow what they sell. The shoppers, for their part, play along with the vendors' performance. They anxiously ask the vendor for reassurance that *his* peaches are the best in years; they request the charcutier's *own* pâté; they search for the carrots that still bear traces of soil. In fact, as de la Pradelle finds out, the "local" produce sold in Carpentras wends its way through a centralized, nationwide system of food distribution and comes to the stands from a nearby wholesale market. But both shoppers and vendors pretend that the produce is local and is being sold by the farmers who grew it in order to give the social occasion as a whole and, by extension, the whole town the *sense* of authenticity. They collude in constructing the appearance and feeling of local character so they can *experience* authenticity.[24]

Maybe that's not so different from what we experience as authenticity at the Greenmarket. We feel attached to our neighborhood by shopping at the farmers' market, and this attachment is strengthened by the aesthetic quality of the local produce we consume. We know that "local" at the Greenmarket really means as far away as upstate New York or New Jersey, and that our interdependence with the farmers is limited to an economic transaction and a fairly brief social exchange. We are also aware, in the East Village, that local character can be manipulated to expand gentrification. If market day brands Carpentras as an authentic experience of Provence, then the Greenmarket brands New York City as a "green" city, brands Union Square as a good place to live, and brands the East Village as a great area for consuming and living local. An authentic *experience* of local character becomes a local *brand*.

Unlike many New Yorkers who inhabited the East Village of the 1980s, Mr. Nersesian seemed to remember every aspect of that gritty and often dangerous time with fondness. Even as he described the endless parade of prostitutes down East 12th Street or the bonfires set by the homeless in Tompkins Square Park, there was a palpable tenderness to his voice.
—*New York Times,* September 14, 2008

Like Harlem and Williamsburg, the East Village has been reshaped by new tastes and lifestyles that rely on continual exchanges of people, products, and capital. The more "local" the neighborhood's character seems to be, though, the more it attracts media attention; and the more media attention it gets, the greater the risk that it will become a cultural "destination": local character will become more expensive, give way to standardization, and disappear. Already the East Village's history of protests and struggles, its unfashionable edge and shaggy intellectual charm have been submerged by too much publicity on the Web, too many branches of chain stores, and too dramatic an upscaling of an ethnically diverse, socially underprivileged population. I don't mourn the old days of drug dealers and crime, but I do resent everything that Starbucks represents, including the new high-rise hotels and restaurants that make the Bowery shiny and expensive and the real estate speculation that drives rents so high. I mourn the end of the local struggles against wealth and power that have produced the East Village's reputation for authenticity.

Of course I benefit from many of these changes. Like the London novelist Hari Kunzru, whom we met in the introduction, "I am partial to a nice piece of raclette." The wheels of the market forces that upscale both our neighborhoods are greased by our own tastes—for imported cheese, cool boutiques, and locally grown tomatoes. In the East Village as in the East End of London, we are literally consuming the local.[25]

Since the 1970s changes in consumer culture have made neighborhoods like ours more desirable. People come here because they want to experience a historic "authenticity," and these neighborhoods offer a toolkit of places and products to do so. Visitors and residents come to the East

Village to shop at stores for unique vintage clothes and to inhale the aura of a radical, intellectual, and artistic past. This style of life usually appeals to men and women who have more cultural than financial capital and can't afford to pay high rents. But they can pay more than longtime residents. By connecting in some way to the growing sectors of the mainstream economy—working as a free-lancer, getting a teaching job at NYU, or consulting for an investment bank—they are willing and able to pay more for the consumption of history that the East Village represents. For a long time the neighborhood offered a visible image of the jagged edges of the city's uneven development, with its tenements and storefronts and dangerous, derelict streets. Today it's another gentrified locale.

Neighborhoods like Harlem, Williamsburg, and the East Village play with space, time, and scale in ways that challenge the homogenizing forces of modernism and redevelopment. To the degree that they preserve a variety of streetscapes, with old and new buildings at high and low rents, they will, as Jane Jacobs said, attract different uses and different types of people. But these uncommon spaces offer something more, something that Jacobs did not write about. They offer kairological images of living simultaneously in the past and the present and in contrasting class worlds of poverty and privilege. Like the Astor Cube, though, the East Village has been teetering on point between its origins and its new beginnings. Cool boutiques and farmers' markets convince us that we are helping to keep the balance by living local, but with land values rising and our strong desire to consume, we are pushing the neighborhood over the edge.

Williamsburg, Harlem, and the East Village are not typical neighborhoods. Each has a distinctive history and population that has enabled it to maintain an outsize reputation for "authenticity" despite recent upscale changes. When we move to the common spaces of streets, community gardens, and parks, we find a different situation: recent changes have enhanced rather than reduced the experience of authenticity. This is a surprise, considering that many of these changes have "privatized" the city's public spaces, giving control over public resources to private, not-for-profit groups and commercial activities. For me, this is a suspicious change of view that conflicts with my feelings about privatization, especially when I look at Union Square Park, located just to the north of the East Village on Fourteenth Street.

Common Spaces

Union Square and the Paradox
of Public Space

We're constantly trying to attract a specific demographic:
young, moneyed consumers who know New York City from
New York magazine...and who watch *Friends*. We can train
these young consumers to think of urban living on Union
Square.
—Spokesperson, Union Square Partnership, 2006

At 6 o'clock on a weekday evening in early July, Union Square is most alive. The small, oval park at its center, three acres of green nestled between four broad streets, throbs with music and conversation, with voices rising and swelling to join the steady drone of traffic on all sides. You see children swinging under their parents' eye in small playgrounds on the park's northern edge; at the southern end you pick your way carefully through a swarm of a couple hundred young men and women who are milling around the wide, shallow stone steps leading up to the park's main entrance. Tourists browse the T-shirt and art vendors' tables while other shoppers stop at the Greenmarket on their way home, and every fifth person in the crowd is making a call or reading a text message on their cell phone. The crowd skews young, mostly under thirty-five, their faces are mainly white but also black and brown and several shades of tan, and you hear a girl ask, "Where are you? Are you in front?" in Japanese on her phone. Next to the subway entrance a lone political demonstrator uses a portable loudspeaker to make a speech against the U.S. president; nearby, under a statue of George Washington on horseback, two New York City police officers, also on horseback, interrupt their early evening patrol to chat with a park cleaner in a bright red uniform and a private security guard in navy pants and a matching cap.

So many people are sitting on green wooden benches under the trees that you can hardly find two seats together. Most of the occupants are watching the parade of passersby; some are listening through earbuds to portable music players, others read a book, and one or two doze. In the fenced-in dog run, pets frisk about while their owners laugh and talk. A trio of young musicians sits on benches in the middle of the park, setting up a cello and two violins for an informal outdoor rehearsal. Though you see them vigorously scraping their bows, you can't hear the music from only twenty feet away.

It's a normal evening at Union Square, but in this normality you find all the fascination of city life. Unlike in Jane Jacobs's sidewalk ballet,

Union Square Park on a summer evening: main entrance, statue of George Washington in background at right. Photograph by Sharon Zukin.

COMMON SPACES

the participants don't know each other by name or face, and there is only limited interaction between them. In contrast, though, to Georg Simmel's classic description of the modern metropolis, they're not rushing past each other so quickly and so intent on their business that there's no feeling of connection. You like to think of Union Square as an endless arcade of possibilities, reflecting and refining city dwellers' creative ability to shape their own, spontaneous social space. It's an authentic public square, not a place for contemplating nature, but a marketplace for meeting, trading, and gaining intelligence about social life. Yet this high degree of face-to-face sociability hides a paradox, for the public space of Union Square is controlled by a private group of the biggest property owners in the neighborhood.

Union Square is typical of the public spaces in city centers that since the 1980s have been taken in charge by private associations of local businesses and rich patrons with a vested interest in renovating them and restoring their civility. In New York City, where some of the biggest, most prominent associations of this type thrive, they take several different forms, from Business Improvement Districts to Local Development Corporations and park conservancies, depending on the type of space they oversee. The Union Square Partnership, which was the first Business Improvement District to be set up in New York State, in the early 1980s, is both a BID and an LDC; by either name, it is a private organization of commercial property owners that carries out public functions of financing, maintaining, and governing public space.[1]

The purpose of all these organizations is to keep shopping streets, commercial districts, and public parks clean and safe at a time when city government budgets are grasping for funds and city dwellers are repelled and frightened by the litter, odor, panhandling, and other nuisances they find when they step outside their front door. To pay for the program, BID members agree to assess themselves a small percentage of their local property taxes over and above what they owe the city government; the city government collects the self-imposed assessment with the other local taxes and returns it to the BID. Most important, if rarely stated, these associations work to raise property values in and around public spaces, which cannot be done if homeless men and women sleep on park benches, muggers threaten shoppers, walls and lampposts are covered with graffiti, and cities fail to provide the basic services of street cleaning, trash collecting, and policing on which the urban public, including the businesses that rent commercial real estate, relies. The vitality of Union Square is really a sign of the city government's defeat by the public's expectations. In this defeat the public both gains the use of a clean, safe space and loses control over it.[2]

Most people who use Union Square don't see the situation this way. They like the feeling of security and order that such a public space offers, a result of the privately hired guards and cleaners that the Union Square Partnership pays for. Not only do the Partnership's members tax themselves to do so, but they also raise revenue by renting space in the park to private promoters for outdoor product demonstrations, photo shoots, and festivals. These entrepreneurial sources of income, added to the budget allocation of the city's Parks Department, which still owns the place, also pay for spring flower planting, reseeding the grass, food tastings prepared by local restaurant chefs, concerts performed by local bands, and public art installations, all of which make the experience of using the park more pleasant and broaden its user base. Many people come to Union Square to shop at the four-day-a-week Greenmarket. Though the Union Square Partnership did not invent this attraction, the BID and farmers' market have enjoyed a productive synergy since they began independently in the mid-1970s. The other elite public parks that are managed by BIDs, such as Bryant Park and Madison Square, offer somewhat different amenities, but they all aim to make the place they manage a destination. And all of them operate by the same rules of private management, public ownership, and public access.

What exactly are these rules? Critics argue that the very idea of private management betrays the public's trust; that private organizations control public spaces more severely than government dares to do; and that these control strategies exclude social groups—usually homeless people, pushcart vendors, street artists, and the young—who have no other place to go. Exclusion from public space literally means expulsion or eviction, giving tangible, violent expression to the property rights more often identified with *private* property. Privatized public space, in other words, tends to reinforce social inequality. Exclusion of some social groups from public space weakens the diversity of experiences and contacts that define urban life. It makes the centers of cities more like the premier privately owned public space of our time, the suburban shopping mall: clean, safe, and predictable.[3]

Privatized control would seem, then, to reduce the traditional authenticity of public spaces whose origins are not in a modern shopping mall but in the agora of ancient Athens and the forum of ancient Rome, places where many different kinds of men and women gathered for politics and commerce. Those ancient cities excluded women and slaves from citizenship and also from meaningful political participation. But they still gave us an ideal of public space, in contrast to the ancients' bathhouse or banquet hall, that is open to all and, for this reason, democratic. In modern times the idea of political democracy has been worked out, in large part, by gradually opening public spaces to everyone. In the eighteenth century, before the French Revolution swept away social class distinctions, the marketplace of the Palais Royal in the center of Paris allowed men and women, aristocrats and commoners, the respectable and the criminal to mingle in ways they could not do in private spaces. In nineteenth-century London and New York public libraries, museums, and parks made the city's cultural wealth freely available to all before all groups got the right to vote. Though the rich often thought of these urban public spaces as instruments for improving the minds and behavior of the lower classes, and didn't design them for everyone's needs, the ideal of open access confirmed the spaces as "authentically" public and helped to define the modern public as well. Public parks, museums, and libraries broke down traditional barriers that excluded women, the poor, and children from taking their place in the same public space as everyone else.[4]

"Authenticity" in this case means democracy, which in politics as well as physical space can often be loud, unruly, and unpredictable. And also dangerous: allowing the bodies of strangers or members of unlike groups to mingle arouses fears of danger. Though recent decreases in crime have reduced fear of physical harm in public spaces, many people still have such deep fears of being bothered by forces beyond their control that spitting, begging, drinking alcohol, and sleeping in a public place are felt to be as nasty as an outbreak of moral pollution, the first steps down a slippery slope toward chaos. Like the broken windows or subway turnstile-jumpers who experts believe will lead to violent crimes if left unchecked, these "distasteful, worrisome encounters" are signs of a fragile social order. They offer a much darker vision of urban life than Jane Jacobs's when she praised storekeepers and housewives for enforcing sidewalk safety with their "eyes on the street."[5]

Keeping order at Union Square Park: main entrance, looking toward Fourteenth Street. Photograph by Sharon Zukin.

Distasteful behavior in public spaces has been the moral scourge of urban revival in many times and places, and certainly in New York since the 1970s. Panhandling and prostitution in Times Square, drug dealers in Union Square Park, and vandalism in neighborhood parks too numerous to mention: these have provided the visible signs of both a more permissive, narcotized society and a widespread alienation from the dual disciplines of the work ethic and state power. They also signal a city, or a neighborhood, on the skids, where men and women can't find good jobs in the mainstream economy, property owners can't or won't maintain their buildings, and businesses pack up and leave. What begins as an "image crisis" of a derelict city leads, on the one hand, to middle-class outrage about the quality of urban life and, on the other, to business people's anxiety about the investment climate. This outrage and anxiety are the cultural sources of the current era of privatization.[6]

You cannot understand the struggle for authenticity in Union Square without relating the park, and the streets around it, to economic arguments for privatization when the government's resources are stretched thin. But you must also look at the cultural sources of this struggle in a general anxiety that the city is out of control. You must see Union Square in relation to its own contradictory history of political expression and real estate development, to the changing neighborhoods around it, to other elite parks that are managed by BIDs, and to commercial spaces of civility such as Starbucks.

Most important, though, you must understand Union Square as a living contrast to Lower Manhattan's most prominent yet entirely different public space: the World Trade Center site. If, despite privatization, Union Square is the most "authentic" public space in New York City today, it is because of the attack on the Twin Towers on September 11, 2001. Jane Jacobs rested her argument about authentic public space on microsocial rules of interactive behavior: the ballet of the street. But looking at Union Square in a broader framework shows that its authenticity also reflects other levels of governance, from social norms of political control and capital investment to metasocial norms of citizenship and national identity. A public park is much more than green space and wooden benches. Its experience of "authenticity" is produced by local culture and national power.

Sweet 14: We're making it the livingest street in town!
—Promotional slogan, Fourteenth Street–Union Square Local
Development Corporation, late 1970s

Union Square has such a deep historical connection with political protest that many people think its name refers to labor unions or some other form of organized solidarity. Though the formerly powerful garment workers' unions, the Socialist and Communist parties of the United States, and Tammany Hall, the city's Democratic Party Machine, all kept their headquarters near the square in the twentieth century, the name in fact reflects the park's location since the early 1800s at the junction of two major roads, which later became Broadway and Fourth Avenue. In 1831 the New York State Legislature designated Union Square a public place, suggesting a grander vision for the vacant lots on the site of a former potters' field, a burial ground for people whose families could not afford to buy a plot in a private cemetery. Around the same time, a wealthy lawyer and real estate developer named Samuel Bulkley Ruggles bought a lease on land in the area and persuaded the city government to build out the streets around the square, enclose it, and acquire it from the state as a public park. An early forerunner of today's public-private partnerships, Ruggles's contract with the city government required him to pay for building curbs and sidewalks along the new streets around the park—and allowed him to reap the eventual profits from higher property values.[7]

When the park opened at the end of the 1830s the neighborhood around it was an exclusive place to live, and the park's design, with beautiful landscaping, a decorative fountain, and an iron picket fence, mimicked the elegant private squares of London. The steady northward movement of the city's commercial center pushed the upper class to migrate too, though; within a generation the fine houses on Fourteenth Street, at the park's southern edge, were replaced with theaters, restaurants, concert halls, and hotels, and Union Square became a popular entertainment district. Just as Times Square served as the city's central public space in the twentieth century, during the age of the Motogram news display and giant neon sign, so Union Square was a major gathering place for crowds and information in an earlier era, when the newspaper tabloid and telegram were new media.

During the 1850s protesters rallied at Union Square to support a variety of causes: European political radicals, the distribution of free food to the poor, and, significantly, the preservation of the Union against the threat of secession by southern states. Telegraphed news about the outbreak of the Civil War soon propelled Union Square into national prominence. When New Yorkers heard about the Confederate Army's attack on Fort Sumter in 1861, more than a hundred thousand demonstrators gathered in the square to voice support for the Union. During the next four years the square remained a major site of patriotic parades and meetings, including one marking the passage of President Abraham Lincoln's funeral cortège when the president's body was brought to New York after his assassination in Washington, D.C. Statues in the park commemorated national presidents and heroes: first, George Washington and then, in the effort to strengthen national identity after the Civil War, Abraham Lincoln and the Marquis de Lafayette, who had traveled from France to fight in the American Revolution. Protest demonstrations continued to rally in the square, especially during the economic crisis of 1873. The city's new Parks Department hired the architects who planned Central Park to freshen up Union Square's design; they removed the fence, planted trees, and created a small parade ground with a speaker's platform and viewing stand at the northern end "to meet the public requirement of mass-meetings." In 1910, in a new age of municipal reform, the city's parks commissioner declared that he would dedicate the north side of Union Square to "an open-air people's forum."[8]

Not surprisingly, then, mass meetings at Union Square drew thousands of the city's new factory workers, many of whom were Italian, Russian, Jewish, and Eastern European immigrants. In 1882 the country's first Labor Day parade was held there, in September, though, in deliberate contrast to the socialist-led May Day celebrations that immigrant workers had brought with them from Europe. Within a few years the date of this celebration evolved into a source of contention over use of Union Square. An international socialist call for a march in favor of reducing the workday to eight hours brought workers to the park on May 1 in 1889, and from then on the Socialist and Communist parties, joined by labor unions and anarchists, held an annual May Day rally there. Even after the U.S. government firmly placed the country's official Labor Day on the first Monday in September, workers continued to march to Union Square on the first of May. Years later, though, during the cold war, when the United States plunged into anticommunist persecution, a local merchants' group succeeded in pressuring the New York City Police Department to deny May Day parade permits to the Socialist and Communist parties. In 1954 the police allowed the local merchants' association to take over the park on May 1 for their own day of patriotic activities, when they renamed it "Union Square U.S.A."[9]

But there is another side of Union Square's history, one tied, again, to real estate development. While labor protesters used the square for mass meetings, the area around it acquired a name for luxury shopping. The "Ladies Mile," on Broadway, offered a large concentration of dressmakers, milliners, jewelers, and furniture stores, though around them, on the smaller streets, brothels and boardinghouses of questionable reputation flourished. By 1900 these bawdy establishments and the factory workers who were now coming to work in new loft buildings around the square drove away the luxury trade. As if to emphasize the area's low social status, a large women's discount clothing store, S. Klein "on the Square," opened across the street from the park during the 1920s, drawing crowds of factory workers and immigrants who grabbed bargains from the sales tables without any pretense of politeness. The humorist James Thurber described sale days at S. Klein as near-riots.[10]

From an elegant residential neighborhood and then a popular shopping and entertainment district, Union Square turned into a center of cheap stores for the working poor. This is how it remained until the 1970s, when, an architectural history of the city says, the square was "threatened...by a slow social decline that was turning it into a seedy and menacing corner of the city."[11]

Like the privatization of other responsibilities formerly carried out by government, the privatization of public space in New York City begins with this narrative of urban decline. But it also reflects conscious decisions by investors and shoppers to go elsewhere. Elite stores and families had been leaving U.S. cities since the time of the First World War. By the 1940s, after the Great Depression and World War II, downtown business districts looked shabby, old, and congested, especially in contrast to new shopping malls and office parks in the suburbs. When the pace of shopping mall construction sped up after 1950 and more city dwellers, thanks to federal home mortgage loans to military veterans, moved to new suburban homes, the old downtown shopping districts lost many middle-class customers. Department stores and small shops that remained catered to low-income shoppers, especially members of ethnic minorities who were not welcome in the suburbs.

Fourteenth Street became enormously popular in the 1960s and 1970s among these shoppers, who came from all parts of the city to hunt for bargains. What to them was a comfortable public space looked to others like a jumbled mass of "schlock shops" or a "third-world bazaar," where merchandise spilled out to the street, vendors shouted out to shoppers, and both merchants and customers were often African American, Latino, or Central Asian. Both ethnically and socially there was a marked contrast between the discount shoppers and neighborhood residents, who were generally richer and whiter and tended to avoid Fourteenth Street. The area wasn't dangerous, but middle-class people didn't care to shop there and they didn't like the throngs of shoppers who came by subway to the cheap stores. The remaining big businesses near Union Square—the utility company Consolidated Edison, which supplied New Yorkers with gas and electricity and was the biggest employer in the area, and the Guardian Life Insurance Company, whose headquarters had overlooked the square since 1909—as well as The New School, a private university, feared losing potential employees and students if Fourteenth Street's reputation got any worse.[12]

Newspaper headlines from the 1970s confirm their pessimistic view, trumpeting public authorities' loss of control over the park: "Bums Triumph; City Shuts Park," "War on Crime Declared in Union Square Park,"

"Man Slain in Union Square Pk as Hundreds Watch in Horror." Though drug dealers did consider the park their turf and carried on their business behind abundant bushes that hid the park's interior from sidewalk scrutiny, men who worked in the neighborhood at the time recall eating lunch on benches in the park on summer days. The city's image crisis didn't hit this area more heavily than others, but like the general sense of citywide decline, the image of decay in Union Square was subject to selective interpretation.[13]

For young artists and musicians who were drawn to downtown's gritty aesthetic, the neighborhood was a launching pad for punk culture, street art, and music clubs. Andy Warhol's Factory, with the eccentric actors, models, and flashy types who clustered around the Pop artist, rented space in a building on Union Square for several years; Max's Kansas City, a music club and restaurant on the next street, was a hangout for rock and punk musicians, artists, and writers. The low rents and shady characters that plagued building owners around the square enabled hipsters and rockers to anchor the downtown culture scene. Though Union Square was not the center of the action, it was close enough to SoHo and the East Village to count as "downtown."[14]

What made Union Square dangerous, though, as it did the East Village and Harlem, was the illegal drug trade, which grew throughout the city during the 1970s. This form of criminal activity made Union Square, like the traffic island on Upper Broadway depicted in the Hollywood movie *Panic in Needle Park* (1971), a tangible image of urban danger. The police department's inability to control the illegal drug trade, which worsened during the long reign of fiscal austerity that began in 1975, paved the way for more intensive policing and reliance on private security guards.

The Union Square Partnership's retelling of this narrative praises the police but dramatizes its own role in reversing Fourteenth Street's decline: "From blight to bloom" reads the subtitle on a recent account by Robert W. Walsh, who served as the Partnership's executive director in the 1990s and was later appointed commissioner of the New York City Department of Small Business Services, which oversees all of the city's BIDs, by Mayor Michael Bloomberg. "Union Square Park was a mess," Walsh writes about the Partnership's origins in the 1970s. "Drug dealers controlled the park, vacant storefronts littered the streetscape, and NYU students referred to their color-coded campus maps to see which streets they should avoid after dark." Walsh is not making up these stories. Farmers at the Greenmarket recall being robbed in the early morning by men whom they believed to be drug addicts. A retired police officer who patrolled these blocks declares, "If you stopped anyone who was on the street after midnight, in one of three cases you would find a weapon or drugs." The director of the Roundabout Theater Company, which moved to Union Square in 1983, says, "I distinctly remember having coffee and a bagel and seeing people openly selling drugs outside the window, and then someone tried to rob the coffee shop, and there were people screaming and jumping all over each other to get out."[15]

Other neighborhood residents did not have the same dreadful experience. But for those who were robbed and for commercial property owners and real estate developers, these stories testify to the problems of jump-starting new development in a downscale district. S. Klein shut its doors in 1975, leaving a block of empty, old-fashioned buildings on the east side of Union Square, an area zoned only for low-rises. A few designs were proposed for massive new buildings on the north side of the square, but they never found sponsors. Lofts to the west and south of the square began to be converted to residential and live-work use, and Fourteenth Street was crowded during the day. At night, though, when the steel gates were pulled down over the stores, the street was dark and forbidding.[16]

Two problems made matters worse. First, because the city government was required by a fiscal oversight commission to cut its budget and reduce its debt, the city could not pay for better public services. Second, because the political geography of Union Square was fragmented, no single government agency could deal with the area as a whole. Jurisdiction over the three-acre park and the surrounding blocks was divided among three different community boards and three police precincts; if something was broken, no one was responsible for fixing it. When Charles Luce, chairman of the board of Con Edison from the 1960s to the 1980s and one of the Partnership's founders, spoke of "bringing community and private resources together with coordinated delivery of city services," he was clearly casting the neighborhood's biggest private institutions in the role of a local czar, carrying out the duties elected officials could not perform. But Luce did not create this vision alone. As a prominent member of New York's corporate business community and a liberal Democrat, he no doubt participated in many discussions beginning in the 1960s about how to save the city's faltering reputation. These discussions led to the creation of public-private partnerships that supported public relations and tourism campaigns, including The Big Apple and I ♥ NY promotions, and also, within a few years, to the public-private arrangements of business improvement districts. Luce was a force behind forming the Fourteenth Street–Union Square Local Development Corporation in 1976 that led, in 1984, to the Fourteenth Street BID. Within a few years Union Square became a model for the formation of bigger, richer BIDs in Midtown Manhattan: the Bryant Park Corporation, the Thirty-Fourth Street Partnership, and the Grand Central Partnership around Grand Central Terminal.[17]

The BIDs carried on the tradition of business promotion that had been set by local merchants' associations in the nineteenth century. By the 1980s, though, they represented a way for big business, corporate employers such as Con Ed and large commercial building owners, to outflank small retail stores, especially local merchants who catered to low-income shoppers. Forming a BID required a majority vote by commercial building owners in the area, and these owners had to be able and willing to pay extra taxes to the BID to provide extra services. For these reasons BIDs appealed to the interests of the largest, most substantial property owners, who also had the greatest motivation to use their collective influence to push out cheap retail stores and find both retail and office tenants who would pay higher rents. Though Walsh argues that Con Ed and Guardian Life were just acting like good corporate citizens, with John Angle, a Guardian CEO, even living near Union Square, it is clear that the heads of these companies were motivated to upgrade the area around their headquarters for business reasons. Moreover, as members of the city's corporate leadership, they took charge of their neighborhood as part of a corporate consensus about dealing more directly with the city's most visible problems: crime and trash. They could also exert direct influence as a group on city government agencies, especially after the pro-growth mayor Edward I. Koch was elected to his second term in 1981. The Union Square Partnership demonstrated its ability to shape public policy almost immediately, in the 1985 upzoning of S. Klein's former home, the block front to the east of Union Square, against the opposition of "local merchants and area residents who did not want high-rise condominiums—largely in the name of resisting density and gentrification."[18]

The high-rise condos of Zeckendorf Towers that opened on this site in 1987, Walsh writes, brought a thousand new residents, "and [their] eyes, ears, and pocketbooks," to Union Square. New chain stores on the ground floor facing the park, including a supermarket that was impressive in its time, set a higher standard for retail shopping in the area. The Parks Department dedicated some of its scarce resources to developing a new design for Union Square Park and putting in new landscaping, aided by volunteers and funds mobilized by the Partnership. After the 1987 stock market crash, when the department's budget again declined to fiscal crisis levels, "the BID and LDC became increasingly responsible for the park's upkeep," hiring gardeners and buying equipment.

At this time Union Square began to develop attractions for foodies, with the media playing a big role in promoting the area's new identity. The weekly Dining section of the *New York Times,* the restaurant columns of *New York* magazine, and feature articles in other lifestyle media praised the Greenmarket's seasonal produce and the restaurant kitchens that sourced there, especially the Union Square Café, which opened near the park in 1985 and quickly earned reviewers' stars. The tastes of journalists, foodies, and chefs created a new consumption community whose ground zero was Union Square. Meanwhile, middle-class residents and residential developers were drawn by the area's still reasonable housing prices. With the growth of good jobs and high bonuses in the city's financial firms during the 1980s and the emergence of new media companies near Broadway, the entire district flourished. Neither the stock market crash of 1987 nor the weak real estate markets that followed it stopped Union Square from becoming a destination for the middle class and the young.

The expansion of The New School and, even more so, New York University also helped to anchor the area's revival. A private institution, NYU recovered from its own financial crisis during the late 1970s to mount an extensive growth strategy, buying properties throughout Greenwich Village and building new dormitories east of Union Square after Fourteenth Street was rezoned for high-rises. Dorms filled the gap when developers could not raise capital to build in the early 1990s, flooding Union Square with affluent college students 24/7. Despite the absence of hard data, it is clear that the two universities sparked a huge increase in the area's population of single, young adults who were primed to spend money on clothing and entertainment, and also attracted capital investment by wealthy parents who bought apartments for them.

The Union Square Partnership worked hard to expand this new public of investors and consumers. Like all BIDs they put a phalanx of street cleaners and security guards to work, even hiring a former NYPD officer as head of security to ensure the cooperation of local police precincts. Together with the Parks Department, they changed the park's landscaping and design, opening it to the street and removing trees and bushes to allow clear sight lines from all points. Like the Bryant Park Corporation, the Partnership adopted the ideas of William H. Whyte, a journalist turned urban anthropologist, who argued that the best way to control behavior in a public space is for everyone to keep everyone else under surveillance.[19]

The BID encouraged shopping at the Greenmarket, leased the front of the park to a crafts fair during the winter holiday season, and promoted a growing number of stores, take-out shops, and restaurants. The times were good for commercial development; with more middle-class residents in the neighborhood, more people using the square, and even hipsters coming by subway from Williamsburg to shop on Fourteenth Street, chain stores moved in. Barnes & Noble opened a superstore to the north, Kiddie City (now Babies 'R' Us) opened another to the east, and after several years of vacancy and thwarted negotiations with different kinds of firms, Whole Foods Market rented three floors of an empty five-story building to the south of the park, followed by two national discount chains. In 2008 the last remaining institution on the square affiliated with a labor union, Amalgamated Bank, sold its headquarters, which had been built by Tiffany & Co. during the era of the Ladies Mile, and moved to a smaller space around the corner. The building was turned into multimillion-dollar residential condos.

Local residents did not object to the area's commercial revival. Despite the influx of young people, or "studentification," longtime residents felt they benefited from this kind of upscaling. Neither did residents complain about residential gentrification. Because new apartment houses took the place of factories and other commercial buildings, some of which were already partly empty, few residents were displaced. Moreover the BID repeatedly evoked a narrative of narrow escape from urban decay, representing the area's earlier incarnation as unsafe despite its low crime rate compared to other districts of the city. For all these reasons most neighborhood residents and community organizations did not speak out against privatization. Instead, they credited the BID for Union Square's "dramatic turnaround."[20]

The issue that finally stirred protest was the BID's long-simmering plan to renovate a stone pavilion that had been part of the old speakers' platform at the north end of the park and transform it into a white-tablecloth restaurant.

For years the unused structure had been open to the elements, causing it to become dilapidated and require extensive repairs. It provided occasional shelter to pigeons and homeless men and women, but was avoided by every-one else. During the 1990s the Partnership leased the park land in front of the pavilion to an informal outdoor café that was open during the daytime in the summer, but when that closed the BID turned its attention to creating indoor space for a more permanent restaurant that would be open all year round. By this point, as we know from Harlem's experience, both the Giu-liani administration in New York and the Clinton administration in Wash-ington encouraged local governments to take an entrepreneurial approach to public resources. The city's Parks Department was open to new kinds of market-based arrangements to raise revenue and make up for continual budget cuts, much deeper cuts than those imposed on the essential services of police and firefighters. Not only did the department raise vendors' fees in parks all over the city, but they also leased more space to restaurants and cafés, sold signage rights (basically, billboards) to corporate sponsors, and encouraged rental of park land for special events. Critics charged that the Parks Department was violating its legal obligation not to sell, or alienate, public property without getting explicit permission to do so from the New York State Legislature. But BIDs and private parks conservancies took some of the heat off the department by managing these ventures.[21]

In Union Square, though, a vocal constituency formed against leasing space to a white-tablecloth restaurant, causing discussions to drag on for years. "The organization is imploding" over this issue, a board member of the Union Square Community Coalition said in 2005, almost a decade after the idea was first formed and shortly before that group sued the Parks Department over its plans for the pavilion. The project was, in fact, a bit more complex than just alienating public land. Though the point that stirred controversy was who could use the new restaurant, the project also included new water pipes and wiring for the open-air Greenmarket so the farmers could have access, for the first time, to electric generators and toi-lets, as well as improvements to the playgrounds and offices for the Parks Department. The department would pay twelve million dollars of the ren-ovation costs, with the Partnership raising the remaining eight million, five million of which was given in advance by an anonymous donor. Despite the lawsuit, work began in 2008.[22]

Rumors flew around the local blogosphere about the Parks Department's, and the Partnership's, betrayal of the public trust. The number of trees that truly needed to be cut down, the renovation's real consequences for the playgrounds and Greenmarket, and the possibility that the owner of the Union Square Café had donated the mysterious five million dollars in hopes of strengthening his chances of acquiring the lease on the pavilion—all of these issues, substantiated or not, were linked to criticism of privatization. A few months after the work began a state supreme court judge issued a partial injunction, permitting the electrical and plumbing work to go on but halting the renovation of the pavilion until further court action. This decision was followed by protests in the park led by "Reverend Billy," an activist whose frequent street theater performances around the city called attention to civil liberties issues. The protesters marched through the park, hung a big banner saying "Not for Sale" on the pavilion, and called for an end to privatization. Several months later another state supreme court judge ruled that leasing space in a public park to a restaurant is consistent with public purposes. She left the door open, however, to the plaintiffs' returning to court when specific plans for the restaurant were announced.[23]

Despite the checkered history of the pavilion's renovation, more burning national issues revived Union Square's reputation for protest rallies. Antiwar activists led demonstrations there before, during, and after the U.S. invasion of Iraq in 2003 and during the Republican Party's 2004 national convention; rallies for immigrants' rights met in the park in 2007 and 2008; and marches for Hillary Clinton and Barack Obama started at the park during the Democratic Party primary season in 2008. In a more routine way candidates for election to local office came to the Greenmarket to greet voters before Election Day each November; on Saturdays activists collected signatures on all sorts of petitions; and vendors who set up their stands outside the park every day sold T-shirts with political slogans and images. Union Square also became the gathering place for fun events such as New York's first silent rave and the annual Idiotarod, an ironic, New York–based adaptation of the famous Alaskan dogsled race, the Iditarod, in which participants race shopping carts through the streets of the city. Cyclists sometimes met there to join up with Critical Mass, a monthly evening bike ride to show support for environment-friendly transportation, a mobile demonstration that, like a rave, announced its gathering place by text message at the last minute and did not seek a permit from the New York Police Department.

The NYPD did not favor the flowering of political protest at the square. In the late nineteenth century the police were known to swing their clubs at labor protesters there and treated anti-Vietnam War protesters harshly during the 1960s and 1970s. So too during the Giuliani and Bloomberg administrations of the 1990s and early twenty-first century they issued fewer permits for political demonstrations, restricted demonstrators' freedom of movement by penning them within steel barriers, and increased arrests of demonstrators, often on flimsy grounds. The police stopped the antiwar activist Cindy Sheehan from speaking at a demonstration at Union Square and arrested the event's organizer for using a sound device without a permit; Sheehan had become a leading figure in antiwar demonstrations, even camping out at President George W. Bush's ranch in Texas, after her son died in the U.S. military in Iraq. The NYPD also arrested Reverend Billy at Union Square for harassing police officers by reciting the First Amendment during a protest against the new permit regulations imposed on the Critical Mass bike rallies. And the police stationed mobile command centers at the square, near the place where the Critical Mass bike riders gathered on Friday nights. Together with the surveillance exercised by the Partnership's security guards every day and frequent NYPD patrols, this clampdown on using the square for political dissent gave more support to critics of privatization.[24]

Eat. Shop. Visit.
Union Square.
—Promotional slogan, Union Square Partnership, 2008

Neither as visually coherent as a theme park nor as hard to access as a gated community, Union Square nonetheless forms a part of the "archipelago of enclaves" that the Dutch urbanists Maarten Hajer and Arnold Reijndorp describe as typical of the new public spaces that cities have constructed since the 1980s. Offering special events in pleasant surroundings, with a low risk of "worrisome encounters," these places set up islands of calm in a turbulent world, re-creating urban life as a civilized ideal. Even if they don't require paying an entry fee, and indeed, city parks do not, they use both explicit and subtle strategies to encourage the docility of a public that, by now, is used to paying for a quality experience. These places break with the past not just by passively relying on city dwellers' civic inattention when they calmly ignore the stranger sitting on the next bench, but by actively enabling them to avoid strangers whom they think of as "aliens":

the homeless, psychologically disoriented, borderline criminal, and merely loud and annoying.[25]

Business Improvement Districts direct a new kind of governance of public places by creating "discretely manicured spaces" as playgrounds for adult consumers who have internalized norms of proper behavior and keep watch over others to make sure they conform to the rules. In an implicit bargain for the power to exercise control, BIDs provide quality services that show users they are being catered to: cleanliness, safety, well-tended flower beds, poetry readings. Policy experts support this bargain for controlling crime and "return[ing] to an earlier set of values." It is not clear, though, what values they are referring to or whose those values are. A "return" implies nostalgia for the 1950s or early 1960s, just before the social movements for civil rights, women's rights, and gay rights made it possible to shed many historical inhibitions on public displays, before the Supreme Court held the police to more stringent standards of engagement with civilians, and before massive increases in major crimes reduced official attention to minor ones—a return, in other words, to when people behaved in "civil" ways. Of course, values of civility, such as politeness and mutual respect, are widely shared and are especially welcome to groups who are likely to be bullied. But norms of civility are also important to elite groups who seek to "civilize" others. In the nineteenth century the public museum was a place where exhibits set out the nation's moral history, lower classes were expected to learn proper rules of behavior from their social betters, and all visitors were held to a prescribed way of looking and walking, under the gaze of others. There are remarkable parallels with BID-managed public spaces today, shaped by Whyte's idea of mutual surveillance and Jacobs's "eyes on the street."[26]

The BIDs' enforcement of good behavior in public spaces turns the circumstantial case against them into a strong argument against privatization. Shifting control from ourselves and public employees such as the police to private groups of property owners and their employees places great power in their hands. Power to deny people the use of public space may take away their basic rights—freedom of speech and assembly—with no laws to hold the BID accountable. Critics connect privatization since the 1970s to the rise of neoliberal ideas and practices, with an increasingly repressive state enforcing market norms against unionized workers, the unemployed, and welfare recipients. In fact, since they began, the BIDs have hired nonunion workers at lower wages than for city government employees who perform the same tasks; they also provide jobs to participants in welfare-to-work programs who directly replace unionized government employees.

BIDs equally respond to other unwelcome trends: the fear of living in a more diverse society, which calls for uniformed authorities to keep groups apart, and the influence of consumer culture, which breeds an acceptance of public spaces that are organized around standardized shopping experiences. As Union Square suggests, BIDs translate these broad social and cultural changes into a set of market-driven strategies to reduce vacancies and increase rents, make up for the inadequate financial resources of city government agencies, and create a local "brand identity." Privatization through BIDs, in short, speaks through the goal of local economic development to a social, political, and moral crisis, in which the state gives up its responsibility to private groups. "There is something profoundly wrong," says Darren Walker, a vice-president of the Rockefeller Foundation, speaking at the panel discussion "Has New York Lost Its Soul?," "when government cannot deliver basic services and private individuals take it upon themselves to carve out communities that pay additional taxes and receive additional services."[27]

Though Mayor Rudolph Giuliani supported the idea of BIDs, he confronted their relation to the state in the 1990s when he charged the Grand Central Partnership with exceeding its authority and dissolved it. The Partnership had taken on more responsibility, and shown more hubris, than the city government had bargained for. It was issuing bonds to finance its extensive operations without government approval. It was paying the executive director, who also directed two other midtown BIDs, a higher salary than the mayor's. And, as accusations by advocates for the homeless showed, it was forcing homeless men who slept on streets and in building entrances in the district to accept low-paying jobs within the BID itself. These conditions stirred political controversy over BIDs that ended when the City Council tightened oversight of them by the city's Department of Small Business Services, and the executive director of the three BIDs in question was forced to resign from two of his positions.[28]

In the long term, though, the crisis was resolved in the BIDs' favor. When Mayor Bloomberg was elected in November 2001, he encouraged an expansion in the number of BIDs and permitted them to increase the amount of money they could raise by self-assessment. There was no way the public sector, led at this time by a billionaire mayor, would try to rein in the real estate industry or market norms. With the uncertainty about the city's economic future that followed 9/11, the city government would not challenge corporations and developers. And when the economic crisis that began in 2008 lowered both corporate and governmental revenues, the city government drastically cut the Parks Department's budget, making it even more dependent on BIDs for financing.[29]

For the most part, the public does not object to BIDs. The alternative to private control, at least in most New Yorkers' imagination, is a return to the bad old days when public spaces were overrun by homeless people, the least privileged, most "alien" group in the city. Many New Yorkers still remember with dismay the homeless encampments in Tompkins Square Park in the East Village from 1988 to 1991, political support for them by punks, squatters, and some other neighborhood residents, and the resulting police violence. It wasn't just Tompkins Square where New Yorkers felt embattled. In the summer of 1994, when homeless men and women built camps in public parks, BIDs cooperated with the NYPD in demolishing the shelters, closing the parks, and intensifying policing to make sure the homeless would not return in any organized form. Robert Walsh, who directed the Fourteenth Street–Union Square BID at that time, even provided barricades for nightly curfews. But he was responding to the domino effect, as the *New York Times* called it, of the homeless being pushed out of other nearby parks and then congregating in Union Square. "When I started seeing tents and a hundred people one night like an outdoor shelter, I became frightened," Walsh told the *Times*. "We're just trying to protect our own turf. With the other parks closed, you really have no choice." Residents may have felt sympathy for the homeless, but they supported clearing them out of public space to enable broader public use.[30]

Yet BIDs are, as early critics charged, "unequal partnerships." They are unequal, though, in different ways. On the one hand, they embody the private sector's growing role as both a moral and a practical authority, which many people believe to be more effective than government in every way. As Heather McDonald, a neoliberal policy expert, wrote about BIDs after the fall of communism in Eastern Europe, "They provide a vital and dynamic West Berlin to city governments' sclerotic East Berlin." On the other hand, BIDs are an oligarchy; they embody the norm that the rich should rule. First, because big corporations and landlords have more money than the public sector, they have been granted the responsibility of planning and paying for basic services. Second, because voting rights within each BID reflect the total taxable value of each member's land, owners of the most valuable properties have the most power. If there is a difference of opinion in a BID, for example, on whether property owners should rent to chains rather than to locally owned stores, the big landlords will prevail over those who own only one building, and landlords will overpower small retail tenants.[31]

There is also a serious inequality of resources among BIDs that reinforces other social and economic inequalities. Because self-assessments are based on commercial property values, BIDs in areas of the city with high values can raise more revenue and carry out more ambitious programs than BIDs in poor areas. Recent annual budgets vary, for example, from a low of $53,000 in the 180th Street shopping district in Jamaica, Queens, to a high of $11.25 million in the Lower Manhattan financial district near the World Trade Center site. Not surprisingly, this inequality of resources reflects social class and educational differences among BIDs, with corporate lawyers and executives predominating on the boards of directors of the richest BIDs, as well as income differences among residents, with the richest BIDs operating in areas where the richest households live.[32]

Besides maximizing benefits for the rich and minimizing benefits for the poor, the BIDs reinforce inequality in the exercise of social control. Homeless people are the tip of the iceberg. While the police make sure they cannot build permanent shelters for the night, the BIDs' security guards prevent them from stretching out on park benches during the day and rooting through trash cans for aluminum cans and glass bottles they can return for recycling deposits. At Union Square the police have arrested and chased away skateboarders who liked to practice on the park's wide front steps and in the open paved area on the north side. In truth these are crowded areas, where skaters risk crashing into pedestrians. Besides targeting the homeless and skaters, though, the selective exercise of control is not so easy to predict. In Madison Square Park one afternoon, a young woman in a two-piece gym outfit exercises around a decorative fountain, but Parks Department rangers and BID employees ask another woman who is sunbathing on the grass to pack up her towel and leave. In the evening at Bryant Park, despite Parks Department rules against consuming alcohol outside the restaurants and refreshment stands, the BID's security guards permit men and women waiting for the weekly movie presentation to drink cocktails while they picnic on the grass, an upscale image of leisured consumption. Meanwhile the police harass men and women drinking beer out of cans hidden in brown paper bags.[33]

Both Mayors Giuliani and Bloomberg ignored these forms of inequality, preferring to praise BIDs as a model of how business can serve local communities. In the Bloomberg years the number of BIDs increased to sixty-four, in poor as well as rich neighborhoods throughout the city. The BIDs remain attractive to political officials because they are mechanisms for not only privatizing responsibility for public space but also upscaling a neighborhood; they're a Starbucks for the streets. Moreover BIDs likely raise property values in economically marginal neighborhoods, as they already have done in the corporate office districts of Midtown and Lower Manhattan. Whether this drives out locally owned businesses and brings in chain stores, as it did in Harlem, is another matter.[34]

Like the Union Square Partnership and the 125th Street BID, all of the BIDs express pleasure with escaping the narrative of urban decline. The Bryant Park Corporation, located on Forty-Second Street in Midtown Manhattan, is probably the most successful example. According to the *New York Times,* Bryant Park in the 1970s was "so shunned and overrun by undesirables that it was considered a symbol of the city's fall." Today on summer days as many as five thousand visitors drop into the park for a noontime poetry reading or a sandwich on the grass, an evening movie, a free Wi-Fi connection, or the use of the recently renovated, $200,000 restroom. During the winter Citigroup sponsors a popular, free ice skating rink. So many people use the park—and so many have complained about its being closed to the public for the semiannual Fashion Week that was held in the park for years—that the BID insisted the fashion industry promotion move to another location and is seriously thinking about scaling back other activities. But they find it hard to argue with success. While total annual expenses for maintaining the park have risen from just over one million dollars in 1990 to more than six million dollars today, concessions and rental fees contribute a much greater part of the budget. In the neighborhood around the park, office rents have risen and high-income residents have moved into new apartments. The Bryant Park BID's entrepreneurial management of public space sets a high standard of collective consumption for the financially lean public sector to follow, in marked contrast to the continued deprivation of the public schools, subway system, and public parks not yet under private management.[35]

Despite the inequities of BIDs, their heavy load of surveillance, and the commercialization of public spaces under their control, Union Square emerged after September 11, 2001 as the city's most significant public space. Almost immediately after the attack on the World Trade Center, New Yorkers gathered in the park to mourn the dead. They also flocked there to *be* in public, to surround themselves with other people, to learn the latest news after most TV and radio stations' antennas had been destroyed with the Twin Towers, and to demonstrate what could only be called solidarity with other people around the world. They posted handwritten signs calling for peace and justice in different languages around the park, including a greeting that scrolled along an extremely long, white fabric in memory of the airplane crew that died on United Airlines Flight 93 under the hijackers' control. In the hours after the Twin Towers fell, the ground beneath George Washington's statue filled with the lighted candles, flowers, and penciled messages of an impromptu shrine; the flames burned for more than two weeks while more flowers and candles were piled high. Some messages were even scrawled on the base of the statue, looking remarkably like graffiti, but during these few weeks no one cleaned them off or arrested the writers. Police officers stood respectfully on the sidewalk before the park entrance, watching, chatting, but not trying to force people to move on. Time stopped. People strolled around the park, reading the signs, talking softly. It was a provisional community—spontaneous, temporary, mobile—but at a moment of crisis it created the sense of an "authentic" public. The authorities did not control the space; it was our agora, our forum, and our park.

Why did this happen at Union Square? To some degree it was a matter of geography. After the terrorist attack the police closed Lower Manhattan south of Canal Street to everyone except local residents. They permitted only rescue workers to get close to the World Trade Center site. As the largest public space near that location, though two miles to the north, and the most convenient to mass transit, Union Square was a logical gathering place for New Yorkers who could not go to ground zero. The park may also have been living up to its embedded tradition of political protest. Most important, however, was the persistent difference between New Yorkers' feeling that they were constructing "authenticity" at Union Square and that they were shut out of decisions about the World Trade Center site.

[The Lower Manhattan Development Corporation] will be the vehicle through which Governor Spitzer expresses his vision and articulates his voice in Lower Manhattan.... With new leadership and new direction,

a reinvigorated LMDC will help revitalize an area that is important not only to New Yorkers but to all Americans.
—Avi Schick, chairman, Lower Manhattan Development Corporation, 2007

The special circumstances of the terrorist attack on the World Trade Center in 2001—the shock of an aircraft attack on civilians in the United States, the targeting of one of the most recognizable symbols of U.S. power, and the location in New York, a global media capital—made the site a public space like no other in the city. Unlike Union Square, which even today could be described as a neighborhood park, the WTC site was immediately tied to national identity. Media commentators and elected officials from the president of the United States to the mayor of New York, as well as leaders in every town and county in the country, spoke of it in the same terms as people speak of the battlefield of Gettysburg and the naval base of Pearl Harbor: it was both ground zero as a military target and sacred and hallowed ground where heroes died to preserve the nation. The WTC site was treated with more reverence than the Pentagon, also attacked by terrorists on 9/11, and the field in Pennsylvania where Flight 93 came to a fiery end. In contrast to the Pentagon, few of the almost three thousand men and women who died at the WTC site worked for a U.S. government agency, a fact that dramatized the loss of innocent lives. Moreover, unlike rural Pennsylvania, the WTC's location in New York City guaranteed that it would become a major tourist attraction.

Despite many differences between Union Square and the World Trade Center site, some of the same trends shaped both as public spaces. First, even at the World Trade Center site, governance is fragmented between public ownership, private management, and public use. As at Union Square, public use is subject to strict controls in order to provide a general sense of security from an unnamed foe. Also like Union Square, the costs of building and maintaining the space exceed the government's means, requiring dependence on the private sector. In both cases, the site's program—the amenities that it offers, the narrative that it unfolds, and the public that it serves—reflects a continuous struggle among different groups of private sector stakeholders. These are all strong similarities.

Of course there are differences. Most important, the more or less commercial use of Union Square as a place of leisured consumption contrasts with the ideological uses of the World Trade Center site. Despite the social controls on behavior the BID imposes, its privatization is more benevolent than the state's authoritarian controls over the WTC site. In the case of the World Trade Center too, however, it is important to understand how public space is determined by a site's history, by changes in surrounding neighborhoods, and by broad cultural tensions.

The terrorist attack that brought down the Twin Towers focused worldwide attention on the origins of the sixteen-acre site. Planned in the 1950s as both an expression of New York's global economic role and an anchor of local economic redevelopment in a financial district that was beginning to lose bank headquarters and law firms to Midtown Manhattan, the World Trade Center took years to build and decades to fill. It was, in a way, a giant welfare scheme for the real estate operations of the financial sector, especially Chase Manhattan Bank, which built a new corporate headquarters in Lower Manhattan in the 1950s and was led by David Rockefeller, whose brother Nelson was governor of New York State when the trade center opened in 1973. Most New Yorkers, if they thought about the World Trade Center's architecture at all, did not find it appealing. The Twin Towers were impressively tall, though, even among the skyscrapers of Manhattan, and as an emblem of the city that was visible from many vantage points—crossing the bridges, flying into the airports, or just hiking in the asphalt canyons—they became familiar, respected, and eventually loved.[36]

Governor Rockefeller's involvement in building the World Trade Center did not just reflect his family's control of Chase or his own ego. It affirmed New York State's crucial role in all stages of the project, beginning with use of the state's power of eminent domain to seize property from reluctant property owners on the construction site and ownership of the new buildings by the Port Authority of New York and New Jersey, a regional public agency that already owned and controlled the crucial infrastructure of ports and airports. New York State also rented offices for state agencies at the Trade Center for many years, offsetting a lack of market demand for office space in the Wall Street area until the late 1990s, just before the complex was destroyed. From the outset, then, although the World Trade Center site was supported by public funds, it was controlled by a very narrow group of people: the governor himself and a public agency, the Port Authority, which was appointed by and accountable only to him.

But public ownership and control were combined with private management. As people around the world now know, the Port Authority leased the World Trade Center's office towers to Larry Silverstein, a local real estate developer, just weeks before 9/11. Because he was the lessee, Silverstein collected the insurance payments for the office complex after its destruction, but for the same reason he also bore sole responsibility for rebuilding it. Though the city government and local community board also had a great stake in rebuilding, only Silverstein and the Port Authority had the power to make decisions, demonstrating the rule, as the architecture critic Paul Goldberger has written, that in New York politics and money always shape big public projects. In its own way, then, the World Trade Center site, arguably the most prominent public space in America after 9/11, was as fragmented in its governance as Union Square.[37]

Fragmentation became dysfunctional as soon as people started to think of how, when, and in what form the World Trade Center site would be rebuilt. Both Larry Silverstein and an Australian property developer, Westfield America, which held the lease on the large, profitable underground shopping center at the WTC, pursued a plan to rebuild the commercial center as it had been before 9/11. Rapid rebuilding was also preferred by the Bloomberg administration, New York State Governor George Pataki, and other elected officials, in contrast to some members of the public—including, for a time, Mayor Giuliani—who believed that the best memorial for those who were killed in 2001 would be to leave the area an open void. But city officials aimed both to restore New York's image as a global financial center and to support property values in Lower Manhattan, which fell drastically after the attack. The mayor, though, disagreed with Larry Silverstein and the state about rebuilding the WTC as an office complex. Bloomberg's view reflected the reality that, since the 1980s, the residential population of Lower Manhattan had grown while demand for office space continued to decline, in contrast to Midtown and northern New Jersey. The community board, which represented more than thirty thousand neighborhood residents in the lofts of Tribeca, converted office buildings around Wall Street, and new apartment houses in Battery Park City, spoke up for building housing, cultural facilities, and stores. But they had a hard time making their voices heard. Incredibly, at first, neither the city government nor the local community board had a seat at the planning table.

New York State's control over the public space of the WTC was represented by the Republican governor George Pataki, the Port Authority, and members of a new state agency, the Lower Manhattan Development Corporation, whom the governor appointed soon after 9/11. Pataki hoped to pursue the Republican nomination for president in 2008 and saw a rapid rebuilding of the World Trade Center as a clear political advantage. For this reason, above all, he held tightly to the reins of control. Precedents set by earlier governors supported Pataki's role. Like the Port Authority, which had been founded in the 1920s, the LMDC was accountable only to the governor. Like the state's other public authorities, it could make decisions about land use and issue bonds for construction without the approval of either the voters or the state legislature. The LMDC was not only the face of New York State's authority in dealing with the city on rebuilding issues, it was, by the governor's decision, the single sovereign authority in dealing with everyone, from the U.S. government to victims' families.

But the LMDC had no legitimacy to represent the public. As first appointed by Governor Pataki, it was an all-male, all-white group with deep ties to the financial industry. Yielding to pressure by Mayor Bloomberg and other local elected officials, including the state assembly speaker, a Democrat who had represented Lower Manhattan for years, Governor Pataki increased the size of the LMDC, appointing a woman, who was the chair of the local community board, and several members who were proposed by Mayor Bloomberg. The governor's action slightly increased the corporation's ethnic diversity, making it more representative of the public at large, and created an official role in rebuilding for the local community. Even this provoked disagreement, though, for the LMDC lacked a representative from Chinatown, located to the northeast of the financial district, where businesses and residents continued to suffer because the area was cut off from traffic after 9/11. This issue was resolved by including Chinatown in the area of Lower Manhattan as far north as Canal Street that would be eligible for redevelopment benefits.

The public involved in the World Trade Center site was a diverse mix. Residents, financial firms, big commercial landlords, and, of course, developers lobbied the LMDC and the federal government along with elected city officials and Chinatown's representatives. Needless to say, these groups seldom shared the same interests. Two other important groups of stakeholders, moreover, formed in response to the specific circumstances of 9/11: first, families of the victims and survivors of the terrorist attack, a diverse group in itself, including Republicans and Democrats, supporters of the U.S. attacks on Afghanistan and Iraq and those who were against the war; highly paid professionals and investment analysts; technical and service workers, many of them immigrants; uniformed firefighters and police officers whose brothers- and sisters-in-arms had been killed; and second, architects, urban planners, and designers who pressed for inviting more teams of good architects to submit proposals for the site and inviting more public participation to decide between them. When the LMDC came up with a three-word slogan to express the consensus they hoped would emerge among all these groups, their best effort—"Reflect, restore, rebuild"—only turned conflicts of interest into prolonged disputes. Each element of this motto encapsulated a series of hard-core political and cultural struggles that unleashed a tumultuous sequence of controversies.

"Reflect" would take concrete form in the memorial to victims of the terrorist attack. From the first moment, though, conflict centered on whether any memorial should be built at all, or if, when built, it should cover over or leave bare the rectangular footprints of the Twin Towers, where most victims died. Because many remains of bodies were integrated into rubble and earth at the site, some victims' families pressed to leave the "sacred" place alone. Others wanted to preserve the visible imprint of where their loved ones had disappeared. After many long debates, carried out openly in the media as well as behind the closed doors of the LMDC, and a design competition, which provoked its own disagreements, a compromise was reached: the footprints would become reflecting pools of water, with a grove of trees planted around the edges. Another major battle then flared over how to organize the three thousand victims' names in an engraved part of the memorial. Should they be listed randomly or with the names of their workmates, since so many had died together at their workplace, or according to the floor and tower where they died? Should names of police and firefighters be grouped by their unit of command? Should the victims' names be arranged by rank, with fire chiefs, police captains, and executives who had died preceding lower-level employees? Or should everyone, as Mayor Bloomberg suggested, be listed alphabetically, showing that, in death, everyone is equal?

Another problem concerned the types of buildings that a memorial should include. By the end of the twentieth century many secular memorials included a museum of some sort that set out a narrative to shape historical memory. Holocaust museums commemorating the Jewish victims of the Nazis provided the most influential model, but governments in other countries, such as South Africa, also built museums that re-created past conditions of oppression by displaying their everyday artifacts—political tracts, identity cards, weapons, the chains of slaves—that connected individual lives to a larger story. Debate flared in New York over what sort of museum would convey the horror of the terrorist attack on 9/11 and suggest a high moral purpose for the victims' deaths. Would this be a purely national museum, presenting a narrative to serve the interests of the United States, or would it somehow serve universal values? The LMDC's less than artful compromise aimed to develop a "Museum of Freedom"; critics, though, including members of the victims' families, argued that it would be difficult to control such a museum's message. After all, they said, their loved ones died because of a fundamentalist Islamic intolerance of the West; "freedom" should not be offered to the attackers. But how could a Museum of Freedom limit one of the country's most basic rights, freedom of speech? The participants' inability to find a way around the controversy ended by their eliminating the museum from the memorial site.

And who would pay for the memorial? Here the federal government followed the model that was set in the 1980s for the renovation of the historical monument to immigration at Ellis Island. A key decision of the Reagan administration, privatization of Ellis Island shifted responsibility for managing an important symbol of national identity to a newly created private foundation. In this way the government would reap the glory of the site and provide park rangers as a visible public sector presence and private donors would pay a large part of the bill.

The conflict between national identity and universal values that caused the museum's demise also prevented agreement over another major component of the WTC site: the cultural center. Though local residents wanted art and performance facilities to serve the needs of their community, the LMDC sparked a competition among cultural groups for space on the site and encountered strong differences of opinion about which kinds of cultural activities would be most in keeping with the site's "sacred" character. As with the museum, troubling questions arose about whether and how the LMDC would limit freedom of speech to protect the U.S. government's interests and calm irate taxpayers, as well as cater to the sensitivities of victims' families. First the LMDC selected The Drawing Center, a well-regarded small museum in SoHo, but it was booted out of the plan in 2005 when some people argued that an earlier exhibition there had included an artwork that could be seen as critical of the U.S. government's policies during the Vietnam War. With the cultural center as with the other elements of the memorial, the goal of "reflection" failed to provide a framework for shaping diverse interests into a singular expression of cosmopolitanism, as had happened spontaneously in the first days after the attack at Union Square. "Reflection" failed to unify a contentious public.

Neither did "restore," the second part of the LMDC's motto, succeed in forming a consensus. On the one hand, practical issues made it difficult to settle questions of what would be rebuilt as it had been before 9/11 and what would be changed, how soon rebuilding would begin, and who would pay for it. On the other hand, emotional issues, especially the desires of the most vocal representatives of victims' families, prevented the LMDC from reaching agreement with Silverstein and Westfield, the private developers. The underground shopping center was a major bone of contention. Though victims' families did not want the banal commerce of shopping to pollute the sacred site where their loved ones died, community residents badly needed local shopping facilities. Meanwhile the architects, designers, and urban planners who had become actively engaged as public critics of the rebuilding process lobbied for using the rebuilding to restore the vitality of the streets, placing as many stores as possible above ground, on street level, and restoring the street grid erased by the superblock of the original World Trade Center design. These changes, they argued, would make the area lively and attractive, good for both residents and tourists. But the visibility of above-ground stores on "sacred" ground became a source of irritation for some victims' families.

Other issues concerned the amount of space devoted to offices. As Mayor Bloomberg argued, the increasing residential shift downtown suggested that there was less need for offices in a shrinking financial district. But the mayor could not win over downtown commercial property owners, represented by the Downtown Alliance, one of the richest BIDs in the city; the real estate industry, which wanted as many opportunities to build offices as the state would allow; and the state's two U.S. senators, especially Senator Charles Schumer, who defended the interests of financial institutions. Rebutting the mayor's position, they argued that diminishing the city's second largest business district—the third largest in the country and one of the best known in the world—would detract from New York's competitive image as a global financial center. The two lessees, Silverstein and Westfield America, introduced a legal argument about "restoration," claiming that their leases entitled them to rebuild exactly as many square feet of offices and stores as they had controlled before 9/11.

A related problem involved whether the height of the Twin Towers should be "restored." Though some boosters wanted New York to regain its reputation for hosting the world's tallest skyscrapers, there was no way to hide the widespread feeling that tall buildings were now more vulnerable than ever to destruction. The issue was blurred by the final design for Freedom Tower, the centerpiece of the rebuilt WTC site. Though its spire would make it one of the tallest buildings in the world, the upper floors would not be used for offices. Later the media broke the news that the Port Authority would not use the name "Freedom Tower" to market the office building, preferring the lower profile of its legal address: 1 World Trade Center.

"Rebuild," then, the third part of the LMDC's slogan, offered no way around the practical problems and political and cultural dilemmas of constructing a public space governed by *the state's* privatization. Rebuilding was determined, first and foremost, by the private interests of New York City real estate developers and of the ideologues and big oil and engineering corporations that supported President George W. Bush's expansion of executive power during his years in the White House. Governor George Pataki, followed by Governor Eliot Spitzer, put the personal interests of the governor above those of city residents. Both the federal and the state government overrode the interests of the local community and city government. Victims' families also took too big a role. Their private interests often took precedence over those of local residents and businesses, as well as over the constitutional right of free speech. The position of the victims' families as crucial stakeholders in the rebuilding process prevented the rest of the public from expressing different interests.

Because of its history, the WTC will always carry a greater burden of obtrusive security measures than most other public spaces. The bollards and barriers that protect all government buildings, and many corporate offices, from an errant crashing car will be a permanent feature, creating quite a different experience of public space from the lively mix urban planners and designers envisioned at the beginning of the rebuilding process. Already by 2008, 30 percent of public space in the financial district and around City Hall was off-limits to the public for security reasons. More than that, though, the NYPD, which won control of security at the WTC site over the Port Authority's own police department, plans an all-powerful network of security cameras, officers, and roadblocks modeled on the Ring of Steel developed in London during the 1990s to thwart terrorist attacks by the Irish Republican Army. Using more than a hundred cameras and license plate readers to monitor all cars entering Lower Manhattan south of

Canal Street, and coordinating three thousand public and private security cameras, the police have expanded their control not just over the WTC site but over a wide swath of the surrounding streets, parks, and sidewalks.

Such extreme security does not come cheap; costs are expected to reach nineteen million dollars to set up the system and eight million dollars each year to operate it. Though the U.S. Department of Homeland Security and the city government will each pay part of the bill, funding will have to be privatized. The entire security system promises to make life difficult for users of the site. "Security plan for WTC," a headline in the *Daily News* predicts, "means army of cops, barriers and traffic hell." As if this fortified territory were not enough, the NYPD proposed creating another ring of steel made up of license plate readers, armed police, and public and private surveillance cameras around Midtown Manhattan. Little by little, the open entry, free expression, and mobilization of dissent that produced the experience of "authentic" public space in modern cities is going to be erased.[38]

Something was brewing near Union Square on Wednesday afternoon. Witnesses said about 50 teenagers, congregating near a McDonald's, seemed to be waiting for something to start—and suddenly it did.
—*New York Times*, December 8, 2006

Despite the best efforts of either a Business Improvement District or the U.S. government, public spaces cannot escape their messy origins in confrontation. On a December afternoon in 2006 at Union Square, high school students from Brooklyn met up with students from nearby Washington Irving High School, and the two groups fought "with things like sticks, knives, belts and a cane." The fight was provoked by a dispute that had occurred the week before, between a girl who attended Washington Irving and a boy who hit her. Her brother and his friends came from Brooklyn to defend her honor and to seek revenge. A seventeen-year-old student was stabbed in the chest and died; two other teenagers were injured, the first casualties at Union Square in years.[39]

Incidents like this contrast with the area's recent pacification. Security and surveillance, on the one hand, and festivals and shopping, on the other, help to keep the square open to broad public use. But which are the most important factors that make Union Square, unlike the World Trade Center site, a truly public space? Is it the falling rate of crime throughout the city, or the BID's financial resources, or the ability of the park's users to keep an eye on others? Or is it perhaps a calming vision of social order in which a contentious public yields control to the benevolent power and authority of the private sector? The conflicts over the rebuilding of the World Trade Center site, the way the state shut the public out of the decision-making process, and the fortifications around the place do not suggest a better alternative.

The paradox of public space is that private control can make it more attractive, most of the time, to a broader public, but state control can make it more repressive, more narrowly ideological, and not representative at all. Our willingness to fight the violence of terrorism and crime with more violence takes us far beyond the capabilities of the urban village's microsocial order. The scale of public interactions today demands a degree of trust among strangers that we no longer command. One democratic alternative to both private control and control by the state would create different systems of stewardship. These would encourage collective responsibility for public space among ordinary city dwellers rather than corporations, and small businesses and stores rather than commercial property owners or city agencies. Improbably a model for this kind of stewardship comes not from powerful stakeholders in Manhattan but from the immigrant food vendors of Red Hook Park.

A Tale of Two Globals
Pupusas and IKEA in Red Hook

He had, he told me, been asked to write a story about the eating places of taxicab drivers. The theory, apparently, was that here you had a class of men familiar with alien foods who freely exercised their choices from a vast selection of establishments, and had no stake in the bourgeois dining enterprise: men supposedly driven by unfeigned primitive cravings, men hungering for a true taste of homeland and mother's cooking, men who would, in short, lead one to the so-called real thing.
—Joseph O'Neill, *Netherland* (2008)

It's a Saturday afternoon in mid-July and the city is swooning in 96-degree heat and fearsome humidity. You think it will be cooler out on the water than in the subway, so you line up at the Wall Street pier in Lower Manhattan to take the free water taxi across the East River to Red Hook, on the Brooklyn waterfront. The ride is sponsored by IKEA, the Swedish big-box chain that opened its first New York City outpost in Red Hook a few weeks earlier. Because the neighborhood is notoriously difficult to reach on public transportation and IKEA is hoping to lure shoppers whose apartments are starved for Scandinavian modern couches but who don't own cars, the store has decided to sponsor water taxis from Manhattan. They have a system to discourage free riders from Brooklyn. You get your hand stamped before you walk onto the ferry so the taxi company's employees, on IKEA's instructions, can refuse to carry any passenger on the return trip who didn't come to Brooklyn to make a purchase.

Sitting on the top deck of the ferry, you're caught up in an air of joyful anticipation. The small boat is full, with more than thirty passengers, some of them young children and their parents, all smiling and laughing from the unusual pleasure of being out on the water on a sunny afternoon, and from the pleasure of a shopping trip as well. The kids snap photos with cell phone cameras, everyone admires the Statue of Liberty on the other side of the harbor, and a few passengers point out the artificial waterfalls designed by the Scandinavian artist Olafur Eliasson that have been installed on the river for the summer as a public art project. Though the ride takes less than ten minutes, it's the kind of entertainment New Yorkers love: a chance to act like tourists on the town.

After the ferry crosses the river and enters the Buttermilk Channel, you start to see remains of an older New York on the Brooklyn shore. Rusted gantry cranes that once raised and lowered cargo from big boats stand like giant sentries, guarding the entrance to the basins where the city's port heaved and thrived for nearly a century, until, with water too shallow to service container ships, it shut down in the early 1960s. Fading redbrick warehouses built in the 1860s look like they're crumbling before your eyes, in contrast to the gleaming white cruise ship, a vertical city on the water, berthed at a modern dock that the city government recently built in hopes of attracting the kind of port business that seems more in keeping with today's tourist and service economy than yesterday's shipments of scrap iron, raw sugar, and rubber. Rounding a curve in the shoreline, the ferry approaches the Erie Basin. There, before your eyes, rising along the shore like a mirage, is a huge, new, shining, blue and yellow metal box under familiar flags: IKEA. You feel the other passengers letting out a happy sigh. We've arrived.

You file off the boat and walk past the newly landscaped waterfront park IKEA paid for, through the outdoor and indoor parking lots with spaces for more than a thousand cars, away from the giant blue and yellow box. All the other passengers go directly into the store, moving with a sense of purpose, like astronauts transferring from a space shuttle to the mother ship. But you're heading for the Red Hook ball fields.

You walk toward the big park you can see from the front of the store. You pass the Red Hook Community Farm, where neighborhood teen-agers raise the vegetables that they sell at a local farmers' market, and

Old and new on the Red Hook waterfront: IKEA, dock, and cranes. Photograph by Sharon Zukin.

turning right on Bay Street you find yourself surrounded on both sides of the street by large, green playing fields that belong to the city's Parks Department.

Now the air is so hot and heavy that the five teams out on the fields, outfitted in striped soccer jerseys and shorts, are just taking photos of each other and resting in the few spots of shade under small clumps of trees. Onlookers chat while families spread lunch on picnic tables nearby. Close to the sidewalk men and women in their twenties are sunbathing on the grass, and one young woman waits in line to buy food from a vendor's truck wearing only a two-piece polka-dot bathing suit.

The vendors are your real destination. Six metal carts and trucks with panels open on one side are lined up around the quiet intersection of Bay and Clinton Streets, the national flags of Mexico, Colombia, El Salvador, Ecuador, and Guatemala flying overhead, the whole setting of trucks and flags and people forming a multinational Latino food court for the soccer players and their families, and for foodies who don't know a word of Spanish. Mainly white with a small number of Asians, they make the journey to Red Hook every Saturday and Sunday afternoon for the "authentic" foods of Latin America—pupusas, huaraches, taquitos, elotes, marinated, stuffed, grilled, and fried—that immigrants have been cooking and selling at the Red Hook ball fields since the 1970s.

Today is the opening day of the 2008 season, after an almost three-month delay, during which the vendors rushed to comply with licensing and permit requirements that the New York City Health and Parks Departments imposed on them for the first time at the end of 2007. The severity and cost of these requirements sparked a fiery response from the vendors' many loyal customers, most prominently the authors of local food blogs such as Chowhound, Porkchop Express, and Serious Eats.com, as well as New York's senior U.S. senator Charles Schumer, a Park Slope resident, Brooklyn Borough President Marty Markowitz, and local City Council member Sara Gonzalez. They all feared the vendors would not be able to comply with the city agencies' new regulations. When the vendors folded their tents and closed for the winter in 2007, no one knew if they would ever come back.

Opening day starts slowly. At a little before 9 only one large vendors' truck and two carts are setting up. A team is playing soccer out on the field, the only game that will be played in the heat that day. Two reporters, notepads out and cameras ready, are interviewing the vendors and the handful of people milling around. When the game ends, several players, speaking Spanish, order cold tamarind and hibiscus drinks. More vendors' trucks arrive. Cesar Fuentes, the executive director of the vendors' association, who is also the stepson of one of the vendors, puts up a sign: "Welcome back, Red Hook food vendors."

Around 10:30 more people line up at the large truck that sells pupusas, stuffed corn tortillas from El Salvador, where the vendors are now ready to serve. Customers place their orders in Spanish. Cesar walks around greeting longtime customers and welcoming new ones, assuring everyone that business will build throughout the day. He talks with two men hired by the vendors, telling them to pick up the trash and keep the park clean. Music starts to play from a Guatemalan vendor's truck.

By noon, true to Cesar's prediction, more customers have arrived. Sixty people, who are now speaking English and do not seem Hispanic, wait in line to buy food. A low-key buzz of excitement builds while the lines grow longer.

By 3 two hundred people are waiting patiently for the attention of six vendors. The two largest trucks, parked on either side of the street corner, attract the longest lines. About thirty men and women wait to buy huara-ches (cornmeal parcels stuffed with black beans or grilled meat and salsa, made in an oblong shape, and then fried) at the Martinezes' truck, and an equal number are waiting for cold fruit drinks at the Vaqueros.' You walk past the lines that have formed at the other trucks and carts, going all the way down the block, until you come to the cart farthest from the street corner, where the Rojas family, she from Ecuador and he from Chile, sell plastic containers of Ecuadorean ceviche—raw, marinated seafood and fish—and Chilean empanadas filled with meat or cheese. Because the ven-dors now work inside trucks instead of outdoors under awnings, you can't see the piles of tortillas unless you're first in line and can look through the open window. In any case, each empanada is freshly filled, each tortilla specially folded as it is ordered.

"It's the first time I've come here," a young man who looks Chinese American says. He smiles. "It's great to taste different things without get-ting jet lag."

The "original" Salvadoran pupusas: Red Hook ball fields, 2008. Photograph by Sharon Zukin.

Though the trucks stand in the same places where the vendors have stood for the past thirty years, they no longer create the effect of a *mercado,* an open-air marketplace, as they did before. What Cesar feared and what he talked about in interviews with the media during the preceding weeks, while tensions grew that the vendors would miss the entire summer season, has come to pass: selling pupusas from mobile trucks rather than in the open air has destroyed the physical intimacy between the vendors and their customers that had turned ball fields in Brooklyn into a Little Latin America. Made famous by gringo food blogs, reined in by the Parks Department's regulations, and located a big schlep away from any other attraction besides IKEA, the Red Hook food vendors' claim to the public space of the ball fields depends on their catering to the tastes of both immigrants and foodies and to the rules of the city's bureaucracy.

Despite the *Red Hook* part of the vendors' label, they live in other Brooklyn neighborhoods: Bushwick, Flatbush, Sunset Park, the less gentrified areas of Park Slope. Like most street vendors, they come by day and disappear at night. The weather limits them to working here only on weekends from April through November. Moreover, unlike most residents of Red Hook, they are immigrants. This is why they are both praised by the media for their "authenticity" and vulnerable to the rigid enforcement of state regulations.

Their social distance from the city government also reflects Red Hook's physical isolation from other neighborhoods in Brooklyn, located between the waterfront and the Brooklyn-Queens Expressway, with no subway station to offer easy access. One edge of the neighborhood is still a working waterfront, though much smaller and quieter now than when many of its longtime residents, today's senior citizens, loaded and unloaded big boats or worked in warehouses, coffee roasters, and shipyards on the Red Hook piers. That's when the Erie Basin was the busiest cargo port in the country, according to the 1939 *WPA Guide to New York City*. Red Hook was considered a dangerous, polyglot place in the 1920s and 1930s. It was a good site for an H. P. Lovecraft horror story and the fear of foul play in Thomas Wolfe's "Only the Dead Know Brooklyn." In the 1950s the docks were the setting for the Oscar-winning movie *On the Waterfront* (1954), in which a young Marlon Brando mourns his failure to win a boxing career that would transport him out of the neighborhood with the immortal words "I coulda been a contender." That movie, though, was filmed in Hoboken,

New Jersey, and in many ways, over the past half-century Red Hook has also missed out on opportunities for the bright lights of either commercial or residential redevelopment.[1]

The city government has never seriously pursued new, green manufacturers that could locate here, and gentrification has been limited. The homes are too small, the area is too far from mass transit, there are environmental nasty spots like a waste transfer station, and also a large public housing project whose tenants are mainly black and Puerto Rican and that until recently had a reputation for gangs, drug dealers, and murder. These are "the projects" where Matty Rich's *Straight Out of Brooklyn* (1991) was filmed; built as high-end but low-cost housing for dockworkers, factory laborers, and their families during the Great Depression, in that movie they have become a dead-end for the unemployed and a killing field for ambitious youths.[2]

The stories of origin represented by IKEA and the Latino food vendors have little connection to the global trade that shaped the industrial waterfront in an earlier era or with the lives of longtime residents, either older white homeowners who worked at the port or black and Puerto Rican public housing tenants who were never hired on the docks. A Latino marketplace and a big-box store represent the city's new beginnings that shift power from older, poorer groups to the new, mobile, urban middle class. But between these two forms of today's global commerce lie great differences of scale and power: on one side, a small number of immigrants who are likely to be targeted, arrested, and deported by national security agencies and harassed by local cops; on the other, a transnational chain that is courted by local officials and developers and treated with respect by national states. During the past few years each side has developed a claim to be an "authentic" part of Red Hook, a claim that involves capital investment, state power, the media, and consumers' tastes, but not many longtime residents, whether they are white, brown, or black.[3]

Give IKEA credit. As much criticism as it has received for traffic, importing and labor practices, it appears poised to successfully open a big-box store in New York City, perhaps the environment most hostile to big-box stores in the United States, one where even Wal-Mart has thrown in the towel.
—*New York Times*, May 16, 2008

Four weeks before the vendors' opening day, in mid-June, IKEA opened this store, its first in New York City. The event sparked even more anticipation, fanned by IKEA's reputation for offering well-designed furniture at modest prices and by a long trail of community protests and lawsuits and a rising crescendo of articles in the local media, from the *New York Times* to Brooklyn blogs. A month before the opening IKEA declared that it would not allow customers to line up outside the store until forty-eight hours before the doors were officially unlocked at 9 A.M. "That may seem like a bizarre warning," the *Times* says, "except that a man showed up two and a half weeks before the opening of a West Sacramento Ikea store in California in 2006, and another person showed up two weeks early in Tempe, Ariz., in 2004"—all, apparently, hoping for giveaways of free merchandise. But IKEA openings have also brought tragedy. When a new store opened in Jeddah, Saudi Arabia, in 2004 three early shoppers were crushed to death by a stampede of eight thousand customers who rushed to claim credit vouchers for $150 of merchandise.[4]

Enthusiasm on the part of potential customers contrasted with ambivalence at best and outright hostility at worst on the part of Red Hook residents. Both criticism and acceptance centered on the nature of the big-box store and its implications for the neighborhood's future development. Though much smaller than Wal-Mart, with fewer than three hundred stores compared to the giant discount chain's seven thousand, IKEA employs more than a hundred thousand workers in thirty-six countries around the world, primarily in the economically developed countries of North America, Europe, and Asia. In 2008 alone, the year the Red Hook store opened, another nineteen IKEA clones were born in metropolitan areas from Paris to Shenzhen. All IKEA stores are big—the Red Hook store has almost 350,000 square feet—and each uses a warehouse design to cut labor costs and enhance shoppers' feeling of getting bargains. Like Wal-Mart and other big-box stores, IKEA depends on most customers providing their own transportation, usually by automobile, and driving their purchases home; for this reason IKEA branches, like other big-box stores, are surrounded by parking lots. The chain's claim to show corporate social responsibility by encouraging sustainable forestry and forbidding the hiring of child labor stands in marked contrast to the environmental evils of traffic congestion and air pollution they are often accused of producing around their stores. Whether these conditions really harm residents' quality of life or are just a screen for defending property values, they have sparked protests in many communities, including Red Hook, against IKEA's plans to open stores.

In the first years of the twenty-first century the chain began to build a ring of stores in suburbs around New York City. Because so many New Yorkers who own cars then drove to the nearest IKEA, in Elizabeth, New Jersey, to shop, Mayor Rudolph Giuliani complained that the city government lost millions of dollars in sales tax revenue for all the knock-down bookcases and Swedish meatballs sold there to city residents. But most big-box chains find it hard to open stores inside the city. First, New York's zoning laws prevent superstores from locating almost anywhere except in manufacturing zones along the waterfront. Second, it is difficult and expensive in a densely built city to acquire enough land to build a 300,000-plus-square-foot store and parking lot. And third, when stores add the cost of improvements to nearby streets, parks, and subway stations demanded by the city government, they often just give up. In some cases, though, the most serious problem is community resistance. While some New Yorkers object to the aesthetics of a big-box store sitting on the waterfront, and others dislike turning over what could be open public space to commercial uses, residents who live close to a projected site, even in a brownfields location like Red Hook, say they cannot accept the traffic congestion and air pollution of thousands of shoppers' cars passing through their neighborhood every day. Homeowners' organizations in Red Hook argued that the neighborhood's cobblestone streets were not suited to heavy traffic and emphasized the lack of public transit lines and highway exits near the proposed store's location.

In fact, IKEA was not completely successful in its efforts to open stores in or near New York City. In 2000 six hundred residents of New Rochelle, a near northern suburb, crowded into a public hearing to testify against the chain's plans to build a store there. Though some residents welcomed IKEA because of its potential to contribute to the town's revenues from sales and property taxes, most bitterly opposed it because of three contentious issues: a projected increase in traffic through the community's streets, a potential decrease in property values, and a planned demolition of twenty-six businesses, two churches, and 160 homes to build the store. After two years of controversy IKEA dropped its plan to open a branch in New Rochelle.[5]

At the same time, however, the chain was negotiating with a real estate developer to build a store in Brooklyn. The first site they chose, near the

Gowanus Canal, had housed a coal transfer station for a local utility company and was in the center of an area slated for redevelopment. Here too, though, community groups protested IKEA's plans. Building the store would not require displacing any homes or businesses, but local residents, who lived near an old industrial site, objected to the air pollution and traffic congestion that would be caused by car traffic. These residents preferred an alternative strategy that would produce entertainment facilities and new housing, and in this vision to upscale the Gowanus area they were joined by some local developers and community organizations. Defeated in Gowanus, IKEA shifted its sights to an unused piece of land on the Red Hook waterfront, a place with a dying shipyard, practically no residential neighbors, and few prospects for commercial redevelopment. Opening an IKEA on this site seemed to be a slam dunk.[6]

But redeveloping the Red Hook waterfront would not be easy. A community-based 197a plan, adopted in 1995, called for a mix of industry, housing, and retail stores and was at first supported but then overruled by the City Planning Commission. Individual projects could not overcome conflicts of interest between local businesses and developers, or between white homeowners and black and Puerto Rican housing project tenants. When a local real estate developer said he was trying to put together a plan to open a gourmet supermarket—a branch of Fairway, a popular Manhattan chain—in a vacant, city-owned warehouse nearby, community groups erupted in dissent. Local politicians admitted that a supermarket could offer jobs to unemployed neighborhood residents, especially public housing tenants, and bring access to inexpensive, fresh fruits and vegetables that residents sorely lacked. Homeowners, however, protested that prime waterfront land could find more socially valuable uses and objected to expected increases in car traffic. After more than two years of negotiations the City Council voted to approve the sale of the warehouse to the local developer, who would partner with Fairway to build the store. Red Hook's City Council member at the time, who had pressed to use the warehouse site for affordable housing, agreed to support the sale in return for the developer's pledge to add 33,000 square feet of free work space for local artists and nonprofit groups to market-rate rental apartments on the upper floors.[7]

The fight over Fairway reflected the lack of consensus between white homeowners who wanted to upscale the waterfront with new residential construction and black public housing tenants who wanted jobs, as well as between developers who wanted to build stores and housing and business owners who wanted to upgrade industrial facilities around the old port. These arguments prefigured the conflict that would take shape when IKEA appeared on the scene, with disagreements over traffic, access to decent shopping, and jobs. In general, though, when Fairway finally opened in 2006 its presence suggested that the upscale tastes of Brooklyn's gentrifiers and foodies had developed influence, if not power, over the area's redevelopment. After all, Fairway had "discovered" Red Hook fifteen years earlier by renting warehouse space there to store imported olive oil.

In contrast to the lengthy conflict over Fairway, IKEA's entry into Red Hook took only three years. Though claims about air pollution from automobiles arose again as a major issue, the company tried to deal with it at the outset by saying it would arrange for public ferry and bus transportation to the store; as a sweetener, IKEA threw in a lushly landscaped waterfront esplanade along the unused Erie Basin. The chain's executives shrewdly stressed the economic impact of their providing five or six hundred construction jobs on the site and an equal number of permanent jobs in the store. "They are high-paying jobs," the company's real estate director said, "and the benefits package of IKEA is fantastic." But opinion in the community was divided, with most of the four thousand white homeowners and gentrifiers arguing against IKEA and most of the seven thousand black and Latino public housing tenants arguing for it. Talk of traffic and jobs dominated the conflict as it raged through successive rounds of public hearings at the local community board, City Planning Commission, and City Council, with both sides claiming Mayor Michael Bloomberg as an ally. First he said he was a supporter of the project, then he said, "But I think if I lived there, I don't know whether I would be, quite honestly." Even IKEA's claim that it would provide meaningful jobs was attacked by the city comptroller, who objected to the store's plan to pave over an old graving dock, one of New York's few remaining ship-repair facilities, for a parking lot. Except for the comptroller, though, local officials expressed their admiration for IKEA's deep pockets. "There hasn't been an investment of this size since World War II," said Sara Gonzalez, the City Council member whose predecessor had supported Fairway before losing his seat on bribery charges. Though the property had sat fallow for decades, she said, "no one ever stepped forward and had a financial commitment for that site until IKEA put their proposal and their money on the table." The store could find an "authentic" place in Red Hook, in short, if it sparked economic development.[8]

On the day the store opened, ahead of schedule, in June 2008 thousands of customers arrived. Water ferries pulled in at the dock every twenty minutes, teams of reporters and TV crews swarmed around workers wearing yellow IKEA shirts, and by noon all fourteen hundred parking spaces were filled. Families, who seemed to be mostly black and Latino, shopped with their children, and many Muslim mothers wore the hijab. Though it was a weekday, when most adults go to work, so many customers appeared that it took thirty to forty minutes to get through the checkout line. Shoppers also crowded into the cafeteria, where they waited half an hour to make their way to IKEA'S famous Swedish meatballs and fries.

Who could have known that so many Brooklynites would succumb to the store's "Swedephilia"? That in Brooklyn as elsewhere, the appeal of Swedish design would touch emotions to a degree that Macy's or Kmart, which depend just as much as IKEA on products made in Asia and the Global South, do not? The answer was clear when shoppers flocked to Red Hook throughout opening day and continued to arrive three times an hour by ferry on the weekends, surely a sign of interest if not fascination. Because IKEA didn't issue an official statement, it was difficult to know how many local residents the store had hired, but many of the workers, and nearly all of the cashiers, were black, as were the West Indian delivery van drivers waiting in front of the store and the security guards provided by another outside firm. All in all, except for its huge size, the store looked very much like the face of Brooklyn. It did not, however, look like the food vendors' site just a few blocks away, at the Red Hook ball fields.[9]

This is "real street food" served by common folks who have undergone their share of discrimination, toughing out a living in a foreign land while giving something back to their peoples.
—"J. Slab," Porkchop-Express.com, August 22, 2006

Unlike IKEA's entry into Red Hook, which involves a fairly well-known narrative of real estate development, retail chain store expansion, and community resistance, the food vendors' arrival is shrouded in individual memory and family history, folded in turn within the longer narrative of contemporary migration. The earliest vendors came to the ball fields in the mid-1970s when family members, Central and South American immigrants like themselves, began to play soccer there. At first some of the women just brought food so their families could eat during the entire day they spent at the park. Gradually, though, they began to think about selling the food. "They were coming as a family trip, on a picnic," says Ana, the daughter of the vendor who has been at Red Hook longest, a woman from Colombia who has sold homemade food at the ball fields since 1974. "And her uncle had a lot of friends here. People would come over to her and ask about her food. She brought steaks and arepas [South American cornbread], you know? For the picnic. So many people started asking her, 'Do you sell it?' So she said yes, and she started bringing more and selling it."[10]

In those years weekend soccer players who came to New York from Latin America were beginning to form national leagues like the Liga de Futbol Guatemala, which has been playing at the Red Hook ball fields since 1973. Though the Liga Mexicana was established two years earlier and is now the biggest Latino soccer league in the city, it only began to take a major role at the ball fields in the past few years. It's not clear whether the early teams mixed players from different countries. Today the Red Hook ball fields attract not only Latino men, but also men and women soccer players from many different countries, with the Mexican League organizing activities on Saturdays and the Guatemalan League on Sundays.[11]

Both the popularity of soccer in New York and the dominance of Latinos on the Red Hook ball fields reflect huge and quickly growing increases in Latin American immigration since U.S. laws were changed in 1985. Among the nationalities represented by the vendors, the number of Salvadoran and Ecuadorean immigrants living in New York increased three times between 1980 and 2000; that of Colombians, four times; Guatemalans, eight times; and Mexicans, thirty-six times. In 1985 New York City had one store that sold tortillas; by 2001 six tortilla factories owned by Mexican immigrants produced ten million tortillas a week in a small area of Brooklyn between Bushwick and East Williamsburg called the "Tortilla Triangle." Between 2000 and 2007 the number of Mexicans increased by more than 100,000 to 289,755, and the Ecuadorean population grew by more than 50,000 to 201,708. Though the largest number of documented, or legal, immigrants continues to come to New York from the Dominican Republic (602,093 New Yorkers in 2007), Mexicans and Ecuadoreans are the fastest growing Latino groups.[12]

Pedro, a Mexican vendor who has been selling elotes (grilled ears of corn topped with mayonnaise and lime juice) and tropical fruit drinks at the ball fields since 1988, first came to Red Hook with his friends to watch soccer. "I saw that nobody was selling Mexican food," Pedro says. "I started to sell some things because there was nothing [no food stands] in the park, just people playing soccer."

Yolanda's family, who comes from El Salvador, has also sold food at the ball fields since the late 1980s. "My mother was coming with my uncle," Yolanda says. "And then my aunt. You know, it's a family thing.

"And then he [the uncle] kept telling us, you know, 'There's a lot of people from back home. I'm sure if you guys go and sell pupusas you're gonna make a lot of money…' and I was, like, 'I've never made pupusas *in my life!*'"

Yolanda's mother didn't know how to make pupusas either, but her aunt had the skills. "And then my aunt taught my cousin, her daughter. So I just started by taking the money; I was the cashier. [My cousin] was the one making the pupusas, and my mother was flipping them and serving them to the people. That's how we started.

"And then, little by little, I was, like, 'I want to learn too!' So I started, little by little."

José, the son of another vendor, a woman from Guatemala, began coming to the ball fields with friends to watch soccer in 1991. A friend already sold food there, "and after a while, they started telling me, you know, 'Why don't you bring your mom?' So I brought my mother, and they told you, you know, 'Do *something!*' And then [in 1996] she started. She started with fried tacos." Only one of the ten vendors at the ball fields today—Matilde, who comes from Ecuador and started selling ceviche in 2003—owned a restaurant in her home country. A few vendors, though, have used their experience at the ball fields to enter the restaurant business in New York. Marta, Ana's mother, left to start a small restaurant elsewhere in Brooklyn before returning to Red Hook a few years ago; two other former vendors, a Mexican and a Honduran, own restaurants in other Brooklyn neighborhoods.

From the outset selling food at the ball fields has been a family affair. As in other immigrant-owned businesses that are carried on indoors, family members supply their labor, hone new skills, and pool their often scarce capital. They prepare traditional foods from family recipes as they remember them with ingredients that are at hand, re-creating a taste of home along with innovative fusions. Selling traditional products in a market where sellers and buyers share the same ethnic background and language establishes a common cultural space where immigrants feel at home. Meanwhile non-Latinos feel as though they have stumbled onto a foreign enclave, an unexpected Little Latin America, in the midst of Brooklyn. But this is not a typical enclave economy. Unlike nearby Sunset Park, the neighborhood does not have a large population of recent Latino immigrants. None of the vendors who sell at the ball fields has ever lived there. Instead the Red Hook food vendors' story of origin is entirely connected to soccer, and though business enterprise connected to soccer, or with other sports such as cricket, as in the New York novel *Netherland,* may represent a new form of the American Dream, it is located in Red Hook only because of the neighborhood's earlier decline.

When the first food vendors arrived in the 1970s the neighborhood was still suffering from the closing of the port ten years earlier. Though some scrap metal dealers, food distributors, and junkyards remained, most warehouses and docks lay half-empty or abandoned; Todd Shipyards, the future IKEA site, was failing. The city government talked about building a container port, which would create jobs for unemployed homeowners and public housing tenants in Red Hook, but these plans faded when the city's fiscal crisis broke in 1975. At that point and for years to come, the city had no money either to broker economic development on the docks or to maintain the large amount of park space it owned in Red Hook. "Years ago," says Greg O'Connell, the local real estate developer who renovated the Red Hook Stores Warehouse for Fairway, "this was dumpy. You'd see packs of dogs down here. You'd see no one."[13]

"Back then, it was ugly," Pedro says about the late 1980s. "You know, they would find people who died over there," adds Carolina, his daughter. "Lots of drugs," Pedro says. "Prostitution." "No white people," Carolina continues. "No families, because that place…it's…no people. It was a very bad place."

"Oh, God, it was scary," Ana recalls. "I used to be scared. By eight o'clock at night, I was, like [she makes a frightened face]. It was very dangerous. A lot of fights breaking out. And there were no cops."

The immigrants' presence gradually began to improve the park. "Our friends came," Pedro says. "We took care of each other. We were, like, ten friends altogether, and we helped each other. We weren't scared; we supported each other. Over time, we made the place better."

An upturn in the city's fortunes and a small surge of new residents also helped. In the late 1980s the Parks Department received a donation from Sol Goldman, a real estate developer, to renovate the historic swimming pool across the street from the vendors' site. Designed in monumental style and built as a public works project during the Great Depression, the pool was one of Robert Moses's contributions to the city's landscape, but like the McCarren Park Pool in Williamsburg it was taken out of service because of the disastrous erosion of the city's budget and social and racial tensions in the neighborhood. In 1991 the Parks Department reopened the renovated pool and families began to come to the park again. Around that time artists and gentrifiers started to rent lofts and buy houses in Red Hook, leading to perpetual rumors of revitalization. During the next decade, with city revenues seeming more secure and BIDs and conservancies taking over some of their financial burden, the Parks Department cleaned up the ball fields as part of a program to improve parks throughout the city. Though Red Hook did not undergo a total renewal, partly because of unresolved conflict over whether there would be commercial or residential develop-ment of the waterfront, the neighborhood began to attract more positive notice in the media.

An early though still rare write-up of the Red Hook food vendors appeared in Eric Asimov's "$25 and Under" column of restaurant reviews in the *New York Times* in 1994. Assigned to sniff out cheap good eats in neigh-borhoods that were located under the radar of the city's cultural critics, Asimov begins by talking about the soccer games at the ball fields. "World Cup soccer stars grow up in places like this patch of dirt on a square block near Gowanus Bay," he writes, balancing a view of Red Hook between the grittiness of Brooklyn's decaying waterfront and the hopefulness of kids from the barrios.[14]

Asimov goes on to say that watching soccer is best enjoyed with food, and "around the field is some of the best and freshest street food in New York, sold by families who have simply set up a table and a grill." He admires their informality as much as their food, for the scene at the ball fields looks and sounds like a street market in El Salvador or Mexico, as "vendors walk around with cardboard boxes, hawking beer, soda and Chiclets." He strolls among "the families [who] grill huge steaks on sidewalk barbecues and fry pork and empanadas in big pots set atop ashcans," and describes how "young girls sit at tables mixing dough, passing on the finished products to older sisters and mothers for stuffing and grilling." Pausing to praise the pupusas, Asimov also recommends "sweet tamales," "crisp tacos," and "chicharrones," which he says "are simply deep-fried pork rinds, but more delicious than any out of a bag." Asimov's column is very favorable to the vendors, but it revels in the standard rhetoric of first-world reviewers who, when they encounter third-world food, are attracted to the exotic and play off the poverty. They find "authenticity," though Asimov doesn't use the word, in the humble foods prepared by women.[15]

Yet this was how the vendors really worked. Then as now, the women of the family prepared the food while the men chatted with customers and took the money. Only one man cooks among the vendors today, Luis, a Dominican married to Cecilia, a woman from Salvador, who sells Salvadoran food. Like the other vendors, Luis first came to the ball fields by circumstance. In his case, though, he did not come for the soccer; he was invited by his future wife "to have pupusas and meet her family," who already sold food there. Though Luis had worked at various jobs since the age of fourteen, he really liked to cook. When a member of Cecilia's family decided to stop working as a vendor at the ball fields, the family invited him to join them: "That same day, I remember, they were collecting the money to help buy the supplies, and I said, I remember, 'Sir, please, I don't have all of the money.' But it was OK, they said OK. . . . After the meeting, we went to have a cup of coffee, and I had no idea of the change my life had just taken."

Luis quickly adapted to Salvadoran food and became expert at cooking it. "It's an art," he says, "making pupusas is an art." He even taught the young women who work at the stand with him, a cousin and a family friend from another state who is spending the summer in New York, to fill and fold them. "But I don't make them," he says, "because in Central America you would never see a man making pupusas. It's a woman's job. In Salvador, the culture is very *machista*. There's a difference because in Santo Domingo—yes, [there] you would see a man cooking."

As they made the transition from bringing food for a family picnic to selling it, the vendors kept the informal atmosphere of a Central American plaza. They continued to cook in the open air and to sell their special dishes at tables they set up in the morning and took down at night, a setup that eventually attracted the attention of the New York City Department of Health. Today family members from both the first and second immigrant generations work at the stands while their small children play in the park nearby, under the watchful eye of relatives. Until four or five years ago Ana's parents worked the stand by themselves. "Now," she says, "[our mother] needs our help, so we come help her." At one of the Mexican stands Maria works with her aunt Rosa and her uncle Juan, who are the primary owners, and with another aunt and uncle as well.

Like most of the owners, Rosa and Juan work seven days a week on this business, with Rosa in charge of food preparation: washing the dirty dishes on Sunday night, assembling the ingredients for the next weekend's dishes, preparing the meat on Monday, and from Tuesday through Friday getting everything ready for Saturday morning. Other family members work at the stand only on the weekends. This is a typical division of labor among the men and women and parents and children in the vendors' families. For the first generation running the stand is a full-time job, though they may have another full-time job working for someone else and also take occasional jobs catering a wedding or a party. For the second generation working at the stand on weekends is a way to help their parents financially as well as a moral obligation. It may also offer a means of supplementing their own income while nurturing a family business that could eventually be so successful that they would have to hire other family members or even paid employees.

Though many vendors of the first generation do not speak English well, their grownup children, in both the 1.5 generation who came to the United States as children and the second generation who were born here, speak it fluently. They have at least a high school education, and some are college students or graduates, including a banker, a nurse, and a social worker who is studying for a master's degree. Some members of the second generation own different types of small businesses and have moved to suburbs outside of the city or to Staten Island, returning to Brooklyn on weekends to work at the stand. Not as highly educated as the children of, say, Korean or Russian immigrants, the food vendors' children are more likely to stay in the family business, at least part time, while pursuing their own careers. The money the family earns by selling food at the ball fields and the sense of initiative the children develop may give the second generation more of a boost, in both social and economic capital, than the children of Latino immigrants who work in factory or restaurant jobs and don't have an opportunity to develop entrepreneurial skills.

The children's contribution is crucial to the vendors' success. Besides working at the stand, the second generation act as intermediaries between their parents and the growing clientele of non-Latino customers, between their parents and the media, and, most important, between their parents and the state agencies that control street vendors in New York: the city's parks and health departments. These forces have been crucial to creating the vendors' "authentic" place, their right to do business, in Red Hook.

The number of non-Latinos descending upon the fields, ordering *huaraches* and *agua fresca* and asking about *masa* and *baleadas,* has noticeably ballooned over the summer. Add to this an eclectic assortment of folks—from law students to German filmmakers—who have come to both eat and [do] research, and you're left with a pretty dynamic scene.
—"J. Slab," Porkchop-Express.com, August 22, 2006

Since the 1970s the Red Hook vendors' clientele has changed in two important ways. First, as more immigrants arrive in New York from all the Latin American countries and come to play soccer at the ball fields, they encounter foods they don't know, prepared and sold by vendors who speak Spanish as they do but do not share other elements of their culture. Meanwhile, the growing non-Latino customer base interprets and promotes the vendors' products as "authentic" food. The result is that each vendor represents a national culture, but the marketplace as a whole becomes Latino.

"The Mexicans didn't know what a pupusa was, they were like, 'What's that?'" Yolanda says. "And we said, 'It's a pupusa.' And they said, 'What's inside it?' And we told them, 'Meat and cheese; we have different fillings.' And they're, like, 'OK, let me try one.'" For her part, Yolanda, a Salvadoran, has learned to like the Ecuadorean seafood ceviches that Matilde sells. By the same token, when José's mother displayed her Guatemalan fried tacos, the Mexicans recognized them as flautas.

In time, though, the presence of *different* Latin American specialties, sold *side by side* in Spanish at different tables, created an unusual, pan-Latino atmosphere. Most customers bought food from vendors from their homeland. But unlike at home, they also bought food from vendors of other nationalities, and some vendors began to prepare and sell the foods of other countries along with their own. The Red Hook vendors started something unique in New York City: an authentically Latino cultural space to sample authentic Latino food that was *not* sold in an authentically Mexican or Ecuadorean or Salvadoran way. It is not unknown for immigrants from different countries of the same region to reinvent authenticity in this manner; West Indian immigrants in New York, London, and Toronto have created pan-Caribbean carnivals, immigrant vendors in Harlem have opened an African market, and Korean-owned restaurants in New York sell dim sum and sushi. But the Red Hook vendors have established a rich, pan-Latino space, exploiting both their common cultures and differences.[16]

The second, even more important change in clientele is the increasing number of "American," or white, customers, as the vendors call them, who are neither Latinos nor immigrants and who don't speak Spanish. Vendors are hazy about when the majority of their customers shifted from Latino to white, but it could not have been before the early twenty-first century. By 2008, though, the vendors estimated that between 50 and 60 percent of their customers were not Hispanic, up to 80 percent during the weeks some of them sold at Brooklyn Flea, an outdoor swap meet held in a schoolyard in Fort Greene, before they passed the Health Department inspection and returned to their location at the ball fields.[17]

Some vendors think the growing number of white customers reflects the expanding gentrification of Brooklyn neighborhoods, including Red Hook. But it also reflects the vendors' growing media presence, especially in the food blogs and wikis that began to emerge around 2003. The two trends are related, for the demographic changes of gentrification are often expressed in the bloggers' language of cultural consumption, representing, in this case, the tastes of a new, mobile, urban middle class that seeks the experience of "authentic" food.

Anglos may claim to love pupusas, but in fact their somewhat different food preferences have influenced the vendors to tweak the menu. Rosa, a Mexican vendor, follows her mother's recipes from Pueblo but recently made some changes: "Since we work with different people, including more white people, we add different things. We add more vegetables. Here, people like to eat more vegetables than us. So there are small things like that we change." Yolanda's family went through the same experience: "We changed [the menu in 2006] because of the population change [among our customers]. We used to have [pupusas with] meat and cheese and plain cheese, because that's what we like. But when the population started changing, that's when we introduced beans and cheese."

Luis, the Dominican who cooks pupusas, claims not to have changed any of his Salvadoran wife's family recipes. But when a customer at the other pupusa stand, perhaps a more recent immigrant or one who comes from another region of their country, told Yolanda's family, "Back home, in El Salvador, they make shrimp pupusas," Yolanda recalls, "[we] said, 'Oh, really? I wonder how they taste.' So we went home [to our kitchens], and we tried them, we tested them out, and gave them to people, and said, 'What do you think?' And they were very good."

Some of Yolanda's willingness to experiment with ingredients comes as a response to competition from Luis's stand, for both vendors specialize in pupusas. The food vendors' association tries to regulate competition by limiting the number of new stands that would offer the same dishes, but it's not easy to tell vendors who have been there a long time what to cook. Yolanda's family, who started selling at the ball fields eight or ten years before Luis and Cecilia, has put up a sign, "The Original Pupusas," "to differentiate" their stand, as they say, from Luis's. They see themselves as the *authentic* Salvadoran vendors at the ball fields in both senses of the word: they were there first, and they create original products. "Back home, the cabbage [that accompanies the pupusas] is white," Yolanda declares. "But from the beginning, we decided to make it pink. If you buy [Luis's] pupusas now, the cabbage is pink as well. He just recently changed this from last year." The sense of competition must have grown sharper when Luis rose to be a finalist for the 2008 Vendy Award, an annual honor given to the vendor whose dishes are judged to be the best street food in the city.

If vendors struggle a bit to differentiate the identity of their stands, they must also contend with changes in the ebb and flow of tastes among soccer players, customers, and fellow vendors representing different nationalities. Marta, the Colombian vendor who has been selling food at the ball fields since 1974, recalls that when she first came, "they had more people, Puerto Ricans. It was more a mixture, the people playing [soccer] over in the other fields." At the same time, she remembers that there were more Colombians selling food: "[Today] we're the last ones left." José, a Guatemalan vendor who has been selling at the ball fields since 1996, says, "Not that many Spanish people [are] coming to this park. There's not that many players, teams. They have been saying that we need them [the soccer leagues]...but not anymore. *They* need *us*."

Luis, on the other hand, thinks, "[We vendors must promote ourselves to the] many, many people [who] come, even Americans, just for our products, even if there isn't soccer," but they must also make an effort to keep their Latino customer base: "We want to help the Guatemalan League so they get the publicity they need, so we can have more football matches. The Hispanic public can go to other places, to Flushing [Queens], or to other places.... We need to make sure the Red Hook games can yield good prizes. Otherwise, the best players and teams will go to other places like Flushing or wherever the prizes are bigger."

The mix of Latino customers from different homelands creates fewer problems for the vendors than the cultural differences between Latinos and whites. But accommodating Anglos' food tastes has been easier than adjusting to the times and rhythms of their meals. For Latinos, eating is only one part of the seamless experience of spending a day at the ball fields. They play or watch their friends play soccer, they cheer for their favorite teams, they chat with family members and catch up on news from their home countries, and they eat. In contrast, "the white people [come] for two hours," Rosa says. "They eat...they look around...and they leave! But the Latinos, no. Because with Latinos, you know [she and her niece Maria look at each other and laugh], they arrive, they eat breakfast, they eat some more, and they eat dinner there too."

Anglos mix and match foods on their plate to sample tastes, textures, and ingredients; they have developed the habit of grazing on all different foods at once. Latinos, however, have developed a cultural sense of which foods are appropriate to eat at different hours of the day. "In the morning," Rosa says, "they eat breakfast foods. In the middle of the day, they eat fruit. And later in the afternoon, they eat corn. The Latinos change what they're eating, but they keep eating."

These different patterns challenge the vendors' ability to pace production. Though an Anglo will line up to buy one or maybe two huaraches, "with Hispanics," Maria says, "sometimes they get ten huaraches at a time. There's one person, and they get ten. Everybody else with them is sitting down." But the Anglos' lack of familiarity with the Latino foods is good for business; not only are more Anglos buying from the vendors now, but some buy a large variety of different products just to taste them. "They doubled our sales," Pedro, another Mexican vendor, says. "The Spanish people," Carolina explains, "they make [this] food at home. For the white people, they don't make [this] stuff at home. They come [to eat]."

My wife and I were there yesterday and ate at several of the tents/stands lined up by the soccer field. As usual, I pointed and bought, but [I] don't have much of an idea exactly what each item was.
—Steve R., Chowhound.com, May 5, 2003

What brought the *blanquitos* to Red Hook—and brought them in droves, in the early twenty-first century—was the Internet, especially the food blogs and Brooklyn-based wikis that emerged then. "It was the web," Cesar Fuentes says. "It was a grassroots effort that came from the new patrons.... It was a blogger revolution."

The earliest post about the vendors appeared on October 1, 2000, on the Outer Boroughs board at Chowhound.com, a foodies' wiki. Though the post offers a very positive review, the writer does not show great familiarity with the dishes. What must be a pupusa is described as "something about tacco [sic] size, about 6" round. They form a pocket in the dough and fill it with ground meat and cheese, and then fold the dough over it, flatten it and fry." It's "worth the trip," the post ends, because it's "the kind of real food that readers of these boards seem to favor," and the Latino vendors are "cooking for people who know what it is supposed to be." In the words of the novel *Netherland,* this food is "the real thing" because it carries "a true taste of homeland and mother's cooking"; the food is good because it meets accepted standards of "authenticity."

This post elicits little response until, three years later, on May 5, 2003, another post about the vendors, this time by Steve R., says the food is "great," but again, the writer can't identify any dishes by name. "One was a 'pancake' which clearly had cheese and a meat inside, freshly griddled in front of us. Another was a flauta-like deep fried with chicken (?) thing that came with a red sauce poured over it. A third was at the taco stand but used very large flour tortillas to hold the fillings (burittos?). Any ideas? Thanks."

Later that day another post identifies the "pancake" as a Salvadoran pupusa. But it isn't until six weeks later that a lengthy post for the first time goes into rapturous and specific detail about the dishes. "This is chow heaven," Chuck declares,

an absolute must for Brooklyn hounds. Everything I sampled was super, with the pupusas being the single most exceptional treat. For the chow record, there were two pupusa tents set up the day I was there [Yolanda's and Luis's]. One featured a long line and three or four women with movie star looks, the other (the ones I sampled) an even longer line and also beautiful, in a more earthy way, women. And a patriarchal looking man who regrettably informed me that the atole had just run out—next time I'll get there earlier! Between the scene and the food, this is possibly the single most transportive spot I've encountered in my six years in the city.

In just a few lines Chuck not only sketches all the features of an "authentic" culinary experience, including the "beautiful," "earthy" women and "patriarchal" man, but he also connects this experience to the emotional bliss of gentrifiers and hipsters (it's "transportive"). Going farther than Eric Asimov's column of almost ten years earlier, this writer's combination of exoticism and primitivism speaks less of Red Hook than of an urban Shangri-La, a mythical place of unheard-of delights. As for Chuck, someone who seeks "authentic" places in the city, he is clearly not Latino.

During the next few years other local wikis and blogs emphasized how *good* the Red Hook vendors' foods taste and how *little* they cost. The explicit hook, by this time, is *authenticity*. Writing about the "authentic Mexican, Honduran, Colombian, Guatemalan, Dominican, *and* Salvadoran food" on the daily blog Gothamist.com, Allison Bojarski praises the vendors' willingness to "pat out pupusa patties by hand from 10am until their rations run out." In addition to the food, the authenticity of the neighborhood attracts her, this "out-of-the-way corner of Brooklyn" with its "hardscrabble housing projects" and artists. Bojarski establishes her street cred, and her credentials as a cultural consumer, by emphasizing that she has "ventured" to Red Hook "many times." Like many others in the new urban middle class, she establishes her *own* authenticity, her right to the city, by her hard-won local knowledge.[18]

"J. Slab," the pseudonym of the founder of the Brooklyn-based food blog Porkchop Express, takes a somewhat different view. Slab loves the vendors' food and is the first media person to conduct an extensive interview with Cesar Fuentes, by now the manager of the Red Hook Food Vendors' Association, but he reverses the usual framework that sees the vendors as authentic because they reproduce a distant, exotic locale. Instead he suggests that the vendors are authentic because they contest a rapidly gentrifying city. It's all about *respect,* Slab says. "Respect the fact that, in an area where the bells of gentrification have begun to toll loudly, where Fairway has arrived and Ikea is not far off, a scene like this refuses to be anything but what it is." He reinterprets authenticity in *New York* terms, as a way of life that resists gentrification, but it is a way of life that gentrifying bloggers, like white residents of Harlem, can consume.[19]

Cesar Fuentes, the vendors' spokesman, agrees with this point. He underlines "the paradigm shift that's happened from Latino to non-Latino [and] to a changing neighborhood." For Cesar, the media, especially Porkchop Express, are crucial players in expanding the food vendors' clientele to meet this demographic shift. But Cesar has his own take on the vendors' authenticity. He doesn't say the tastes are exotic, the women are earthy, or the *mercado* scene is a sensual evocation of a dusty Central American town. It's that the vendors are artisans, "*artisans* of their craft." Unlike ordinary street vendors who "will sell you a hot dog or an ice cream," the Red Hook food vendors "cook with the soul and with the heart, just as if they were cooking at home. This is how you get what you get over here: *fresh* authenticity."

The Red Hook ball fields, where Latino families put up makeshift restaurants serving real, honest food of their home countries, is one of the last bastions of real food to be found in New York City. If it's replaced by a series of dirty water [hot] dog carts, a sausage-and-pepper stand, or some generic high bidder, it would be a travesty.
—Ed Levine, Seriouseats.com, June 5, 2007

Despite, or because of, their growing celebrity, the Red Hook food vendors became the target of tightened regulation by the two city government agencies that control street food and public parks. In June 2007, after the vendors' summer season had already begun, the New York City Parks Department abruptly decided to "regularize" the temporary use authorizations they had granted to the vendors for years. Instead of continuing to issue four-week permits and renewing them throughout the season, the Parks Department would impose an open bidding process like the one in use at other public parks for vendors to buy longer-term licenses. Though the auction could have become an excruciating annual procedure, the Parks Department eventually decided to issue use permits that would be valid for six years. At the same time, though, the New York City Department of Health declared that the conditions in which the Red Hook vendors had worked for thirty years violated the city's health code, and threatened to shut them down if they did not qualify for a license.

No one knew for sure why the city government suddenly went on the attack. The Parks Department said that because the vendors wanted to use the ball fields for a longer season, they went beyond the limits of temporary use. Though the Health Department claimed they did not know that food was being prepared and sold at the Red Hook ball fields, most vendors vaguely recalled health inspectors visiting them eight or ten years earlier. Meanwhile Cesar Fuentes claimed that he "had receipts" to prove that the vendors had "registered" with the city's Department of Consumer Affairs. Cesar also suggested a financial reason the city government clamped down. He said the City Comptroller, New York's chief financial officer, discovered that the Parks Department was not extracting as much money from the vendors as they could do by auctioning use permits: "[The Comptroller's Office] was [now] coming down hard on us about these kinds of affairs." But what really may have motivated the city government's attack is Red Hook's gradual gentrification and the imminent opening of IKEA. "One of the interesting things about gentrification," Cesar says, "is...that once this change takes place, someone's going to get evicted. Sooner or later. It's happened in Harlem, in Williamsburg, it's happening here."

In fact the vendors had not had an easy time with city agencies since the 1990s. During the 1970s and 1980s, when the Parks Department lacked the staff and the desire to enforce their control over public parks in a troubled area of the city, they sold a use permit to the Guatemalan League and left the Liga to deal with the vendors. "It was just a very vague, very informal attraction," Cesar says. By the 1990s, though, with more Latino immigrants coming to the ball fields, the Parks Department formally required the Liga to apply for a permit. Though the food vendors still had an informal arrangement with the league, they gradually drifted apart. The reasons for the breakup aren't clear, but during the 1990s, with more vendors selling food and drink, problems arose over a continual pile-up of garbage and the illegal consumption of beer. Because of these two issues, by 2000 the vendors were in trouble with the Liga as well as with the local police precinct, the local community board, the city's Health Department, and the borough parks commissioner for Brooklyn, Julius Spiegel. At that point, when Cesar, a college student who spoke both English and Spanish, was frying plantains on weekends at his family's stand, the vendors asked him to negotiate on their behalf with the authorities. "And Julius Spiegel gave me a shot. Gave me two weeks. And in two weeks, change began happening."

Cesar developed a three-part strategy for defending the vendors' interests. First, he insisted that, like a Business Improvement District, the vendors should take responsibility for sanitation and security, hiring people to clean up all the garbage left in their area of the park, whether it was the vendors' own garbage or someone else's, and forbid the sale of alcohol. "Between 2000 and 2004, we really cleaned up our act," Cesar says. "I mean literally." He also met often with the head of the local police precinct: "Just so the cops [on the beat] would know that I know him." The biggest change, though, was that he organized the food vendors into a self-governing association so they could pool resources, coordinate actions, and speak with a single voice—Cesar's. Maybe because he studied sociology in college, Cesar saw the beauty of collective action.

The vendors' reputation grew not only with the Parks Department and the police, but also with local politicians, mainstream media, and bloggers. In 2006, at the peak of the media buzz, Cesar persuaded the vendors to incorporate their group as a not-for-profit association, a 501c6, according to a provision of the U.S. federal tax code. As he explains it, they formed a trade association "whose main vision is to preserve and maintain the thirty-four-year tradition that is the Red Hook Food Vendors." Cesar "may have had a premonition," as he says, that increasing publicity would motivate city agencies to look more closely at the vendors. At any rate, their new nonprofit status helped them the next year, when the Parks Department demanded that they bid for a use permit.

This demand aroused serious anxiety. The vendors had no idea how much competition they would face for a permit to sell food at the ball fields, or how much a winning bid would cost. They had heard that the hot-dog vendor with one of the most lucrative spots in the city, in front of the Metropolitan Museum of Art, paid one hundred thousand dollars a year just for the permit. (According to the Parks Department, the cost of a seasonal permit for a hot-dog stand in Central Park at that time varied from six hundred dollars to three hundred thousand dollars, depending on location.)[20] In Red Hook the food vendors were paying a total of $10,500 a season for a series of renewable, four-week permits, and an additional $30,000 for cleanup. If other groups or individual entrepreneurs put in higher bids for a new use permit, the vendors would lose the location they had developed for thirty-four years and lose a major share of their livelihood as well. They were also disturbed about the time it took for the Parks Department to issue the application form and rules for completing it— from June, when the department told the vendors they had to enter an auction to bid for the permit, to the following January, when the vendors finally got the application form. Moreover the Parks Department set the deadline for filing the form only four weeks later, giving Cesar, who, as the executive director of the Food Vendors Association, was responsible for completing the application but also held a day job as a social worker, "a lot of sleepless nights."

Just at this moment, tensions within the vendors' association exploded. Several members accused Cesar of not giving a full accounting of the money he collected from them, a few hundred dollars a month, and of paying himself too big a salary. Cesar replied by resigning from his position as executive director and threatened to stop representing the vendors in negotiations with city agencies. Three weeks later, after all the vendors had signed a petition asking him to return and pledged him their "total support," Cesar resumed his position.[21]

The contacts Cesar had cultivated, as well as his premonition that he should incorporate the vendors' group as a nonprofit organization, worked out well in the permit crisis. A staff member of a local development corporation helped Cesar complete the forty-page permit application, which he did on behalf of the nonprofit organization rather than for the individual vendors. "When a nonprofit applies for something," Cesar says, "it's something that the city really needs to consider very strongly. Because it's not greed, it's *for* something." During the months of waiting for the Parks Department to issue the application, and waiting again for their decision, the vendors also benefited from the support of local elected officials and the media, support that Cesar actively solicited. "I decided right off the bat," he says, "I decided to go public. First, I decided to advise our intimate friends, our supporters, the news writers.... Then we tapped into politicians, who were very proactive because the news on the web blogs went like wildfire."

As a result the Red Hook Food Vendors Association had no competition in their bid for the use permit, which the Parks Department granted at the same price the vendors were already paying: $10,500 for the season. The new permit is good for six years; it covers the entire year rather than just the summer months, and it carries only 5 percent increases for inflation each year after the first. Cesar credits the vendors' triumph to the media that supported them, but more grandly he also sees it as a triumph for democracy: "Even if there were very big forces at work," he says, "there's nothing bigger than the force of people coming together. It wasn't just about the vendors—twelve people and their representative. It was about a whole city fighting for something. It became symbolic."

This is a sad update for me to write. The government agencies whom WE are supposed to be in control of have taken their toll on yet one more of our fun and particular to NYC gems and reduced what was once one

of the most unique and rewarding experiences in NYC to just another generic, watered down, lowest common denominator of any other bureaucratically regulated version of their kind of fun they think we should be having that there could be. Welcome the end of an era that had successfully prospered and pleased the populace of NYC for three decades without problem nor incident.
—Steve M., Yelp.com, August 17, 2008

Though the vendors' unity worked to great effect in gaining the group a permit from the Parks Department, each family was on its own to bring its stand into compliance with the city's health code. This was an expensive and time-consuming process. Every vendor had to find an enclosed, mobile truck or cart of the kind the Health Department required for hygienic food preparation, scrape together the money to buy it, and then renovate or retrofit it for immediate use. Buying a used truck is expensive—it could cost fifteen thousand to thirty thousand dollars—and equipping it to pass the health code inspection adds another twenty thousand to thirty thousand dollars to the bill. Vendors' families pooled their savings to meet these costs, with some of the grownup children taking out loans on their houses and other families seeking loans from relatives in their home countries— an unusual reverse remittance. Family members drove down the East Coast to pursue leads on used trucks that might be suitable, but some vendors, even after spending thousands of dollars to install new equipment, failed to pass the health code inspection on their first try. Moreover, because the Parks Department did not issue a full permit until the end of March 2008, several vendors waited until then to buy their equipment. That is why, on opening day in mid-July, only six of the twelve vendors in the association, the first to get their licenses from the Health Department, were ready to do business at the ball fields.[22]

Equipment was only one part of the problem. The Health Department demanded that every person working at the stands, from the owner to each assistant, get a food vendor's license. This required each vendor and worker to take a course on sanitary food preparation; passing a four-hour course entitled them to a two-year mobile food vendor's permit, while passing a fifteen-hour course qualified them for a lifetime. Another problem involved putting all workers at each stand on the books. Licensed street vendors must pay taxes; this requires them to incorporate their business or file tax forms as a sole proprietorship, which opens their bookkeeping to all state agencies, including the U.S. Immigration and Naturalization Service and the Department of Homeland Security as well as the federal, state, and city tax bureaucracies. Finally, food vendors pay two hundred dollars each for the Health Department permit that enables them to have their truck inspected and also rent space in a commissary where they store their truck during the week.

After months of drama over the permit crisis, including last-minute charges and countercharges when a city agency lost the paperwork, the Red Hook food vendors prepared for their return to the ball fields. In March, when the news came that they had won the Parks Department permit, a headline in the weekly *Brooklyn Paper* set the joyful tone: "The Red Hook vendors are back!" For the next three months food bloggers, radio stations, and the city's leading newspapers kept up a constant stream of anxious reports and hopeful speculation. By early June Cesar was being interviewed everywhere and sending out email bulletins about when the vendors would likely return. Supporters, including professional journalists and chefs, posted video clips of the previous season online. The city seemed collectively to lick its lips and hold its breath in antici-pation of the vendors' opening day, though some people, joking about IKEA's imminent arrival, predicted a culture clash between tacos and Swedish meatballs.

Striking a somber note, Cesar cautioned the vendors' many fans that meeting the Health Department's requirements might alter their appeal. "Our victory was bittersweet," he told Porkchop Express. "The physical, unique aesthetic—weather-beaten tarps, an Old World food bazaar and unique '*mercado*' feel—couldn't be kept despite our appeals." This ear-lier "character," he said in a later radio interview, "was very rustic, very *authentic*."[23]

Though most of the vendors' fans remained loyal, everyone noted the changes. A few bloggers even posted negative reviews. New customers com-plained about the long wait to buy food, rude treatment by vendors, and exhaust fumes from the trucks. For old customers there was an even more serious problem: the intimacy was gone. Of course it wasn't surprising for the vendors to feel on edge and maybe give that impression to custom-ers when the uncertainty over their situation had delayed the season from opening on time and shortened the number of days when they could try to recoup their investment. Working in a truck may be more hygienic, but the whole process of preparing and selling food at the ball fields was no longer as informal as it had been before. Moreover dealing with the large number of non-Latino customers did not enable even the most generous-spirited vendors to pretend they were cooking for neighbors and friends. Instead vending at the ball fields had become, as Steve M. and others suggested on Yelp.com, a bureaucratically controlled situation. Seeing the vendors as a counterweight to Brooklyn's rapid redevelopment was much harder than it had been in the 1990s and early 2000s—and was surely very different from when the first vendors came to Red Hook in the 1970s. Looking into the future it seemed unlikely that immigrant food vendors could coexist with the alternative form of global commerce practiced by IKEA just a few blocks away.[24]

"THE REAL WORLD: BROOKLYN" (MTV, 10 P.M.) ... Anyone who watches a show about eight 20-somethings set loose in a house with a manufactured beach and a mini Crunch gym, and then makes fun of them because they're not living an authentic Brooklyn lifestyle, is seriously missing the point. Even if the house is in Red Hook.
—*New York Times,* January 4, 2009

The consensus among Brooklyn's resident cultural critics before the store opened was that IKEA did not conform to the borough's "authentic" lifestyle. Too spare for the working-class traditionalists, too conformist for the hipsters: IKEA's aesthetic would appeal to no one, they said, and would betray the monumental ruins of the waterfront as well. Red Hook residents who opposed IKEA made a different point. They argued that the store would draw such heavy traffic that the area was "going to be a madhouse," as one neighbor said. Within a few weeks of the store's opening, though, the media reported a new consensus: the real effects were not so bad. IKEA's free water ferries and shuttle buses "made the hard-to-reach neighborhood without a subway stop a little less remote," said the *New York Times,* and an unanticipated large number of visitors, many walking around the neighborhood on foot, confirmed that Red Hook now appeared *interesting.* "It's transformative," the architecture critic Philip Nobel wrote in *Metropolis* magazine, unconsciously evoking Chuck's earlier Chowhound post ("it's transportive") about the food vendors. In one way or another, through pupusas or Swedish meatballs, consumer culture was going to change the neighborhood from an urban wasteland into a destination: "Red Hook is now, for the first time, on the way to other places."[25]

Surely it had been unrealistic to think that IKEA shoppers and fans of the Red Hook food vendors were separate tribes, each with its own tastes and customs. Despite the criticism of mass consumption that IKEA fed— see the scene in the movie *Fight Club* (1999) where Edward Norton's character says, "I had become a slave to the IKEA nesting instinct.... What kind of dining set defines me as a person?"—vaguely creative twenty-some-things and would-be nonconformists really like IKEA products. It isn't all about modern design. In a post on Mark Bittman's food blog on New York Times.com, Daniel Meyer confesses that he alternates between trips to Red Hook for quesadillas at the ball fields and trips to IKEA for Swedish meat-balls. This provokes posts from other readers, who admit that they love the Swedish meatballs too. Does this mean that tastes have shifted *from* the vendors *to* IKEA, or that there is a chance for peaceful coexistence?[26]

Cesar's fears about the food vendors' vulnerability to gentrification appear to be well founded. But the vendors have been willing to court non-Latinos as a new clientele, not only tweaking their menu at the ball fields but pursuing new customers in other places. According to a recent Chowhound post, two of the ten Red Hook food vendors park their trucks late at night in front of a music club near the Gowanus Canal and sell dishes to patrons coming out of the shows. Paradoxically the trucks that the vendors bought in order to stay at the ball fields really make them more mobile. But this may be an involuntary mobility, thrust upon the vendors by several factors: changing expectations about Red Hook inspired by new chain stores; foodies' changing tastes in ethnic foods, compounded by less discretionary income in the economic crisis; and competition from the city's growing number of Mexican restaurants and food trucks, some of which are not owned by Latinos.

When Luis competed for the 2008 Vendy Award, he lost to the Vendley brothers, three white guys from southern California who sell tacos and carne asada at Calexico, a "chainlet" of two food carts that they park on the street in Manhattan; in 2009 they opened an indoor restaurant on the waterfront near Red Hook. This doesn't mean that Luis's pupusas aren't great, but it does demonstrate that the vendors face sharp competition in a city of eaters where cosmopolitanism is a way of life, and that authenticity is always subject to new interpretations.[27]

Luis's loss to the Vendley brothers also suggests that after all the ven-dors' efforts to meet the city agencies' requirements, after all the political support they won, and after all the media buzz, they still haven't achieved a permanent right to the city. Many street vendors are hounded by the police and the enforcement agencies, pushed out of central locations and neighborhood shopping streets by planters and other street furniture and local "anti-vendor" rules. Like Luis, about 90 percent of New York's street vendors are immigrants. Most don't speak fluent English. They find it hard to defend themselves against unpredictable coercive action by the state's security organizations. In 2008, when the City Council held hearings on bills intended to lighten the vendors' burden and increase the number of full-time food-vending permits from thirty-one hundred to twenty-five thousand, the Bloomberg administration proposed fingerprinting people arrested for unlawful vending, a serious step against immigrants trying to earn a living by selling tacos without a license or in an illegal location.[28]

Red Hook's future is bound to take more twists and turns as the city government tries to figure out how to deal with the demands of different forms of globalization. Some think the best strategy for future growth would renew Red Hook's industrial roots. Just before IKEA opened, the Port Authority of New York and New Jersey signed a lease that permits a cargo port to continue operating on four piers for the next decade. And a new study criticized the mayor for allowing IKEA to turn the old graving dock into a parking lot because this made it hard for the shipping industry to have repairs done in New York City.[29]

But this is not the only plan under way, and Cesar is right to fear that the vendors cannot outlast Red Hook's gentrification. The permit and license crisis of 2007—occurring, perhaps not coincidentally, on the eve of IKEA's arrival—nearly drove the vendors out of the location in the ball fields that they had held for more than thirty years. If the space that they created is, in its own way, an urban village, it is threatened by the corporate city of chain stores that is gradually forming along the waterfront.

Yet the vendors' supporters are trying to imagine another model. At the end of the vendors' 2008 season, the New York chapter of Architecture for Humanity, a nonprofit group that designs and builds social service projects in Africa and South Asia as well as in New Orleans after Hurricane Katrina, organized a competition for ideas about designing a permanent marketplace at the ball fields. This marketplace would reproduce the informal *mercado* the vendors had created before the Health Department imposed its new regulations. While keeping conditions sanitary and up to code, it would restore the immediacy of vendors cooking for their customers under canvas canopies in the open air. Thirty-one entries were submitted to two juries, one consisting of five of the Red Hook vendors; the other, more specialized, including Cesar Fuentes, "J. Slab" of Porkchop-Express.com, four well-regarded architects and designers, and a high-level staff member of the Parks Department. The designers of the winning entries were asked to work together with Architecture for Humanity, the Vendors' Association, and the Parks Department to build a permanent home for the food vendors. This would be a new public space sponsored by a different sort of public-private partnership, an urban village "for the public realm."[30]

Unlike the traditional urban village, this marketplace is a consumption space to bring ethnic groups and social classes together—not too different from the farmers' market at Union Square but certainly different from the corporate food court in a shopping mall. Though the *mercado* would be a victory for Brooklyn's foodies, it would also be a triumph for a vulnerable group of immigrant vendors who until recently operated in the shadow of the law. Unlike most groups with only an informal claim to a place in the city, the Red Hook food vendors will have won recognition of their right to put down roots.

The struggle for the right to the city at both Union Square and the Red Hook ball fields underlines the growing importance of food consumption in defining an "authentic" urban experience. In a different way, food production is beginning to define another kind of common space, community gardens, where land is publicly owned but not classified as park land. Here, unexpectedly, another group of stakeholders with little money or power has also won the right to put down roots.

The Billboard and the Garden

A Struggle for Roots

The New York I lived in [during the 1970s]...was rapidly
regressing. It was a ruin in the making, and my friends and
I were camped out amid its potsherds and tumuli....If you
walked east on Houston Street from the Bowery on a summer
night, the jungle growth of vacant blocks gave a foretaste
of the impending wilderness, when lianas would engird the
skyscrapers and mushrooms would cover Times Square.
—Luc Santé, "My Lost City," *New York Review of Books*,
November 6, 2003

The weather is unusually warm for a Saturday morning in mid-October,
and the clear horizon of the sky stretches blue and wide above this distant
patch of Brooklyn. To the southeast, high above the elevated subway tracks,
a jet plane climbs on the first part of its journey, away from Kennedy Airport in Queens, its real point of departure, but also far away from the two-
story, redbrick houses and vacant lots of East New York, long known as
one of the poorest neighborhoods in New York City. When you get out of
the subway train at Van Siclen Avenue and walk down the stairs from the
elevated tracks, you feel a bit lost in the shadows and the absence of shops,
except for a small corner bodega, on the quiet street. But a short, smiling

Community garden, East New York: urban agriculture under elevated subway tracks. Photograph by Sharon Zukin.

woman in her sixties, who gets off the train with you, sees that you don't look black or Hispanic and senses that you don't live in the neighborhood; she invites you to walk with her.

Improbably, on the next block, almost directly under the tracks, three lush, green gardens, carefully tended and fenced, come into view. Inside, planted in neat rows, green beans and mint wait to be picked. Small onions peek through the earth, ready to be dug before the first frost. A few peppers flash slivers of bright red through the leaves of tomato and squash plants that have already seen the last harvest of the year. These oases represent the time and effort of a small number of community gardeners who live in the neighborhood. Since the 1990s they have been created and maintained by the gardeners' hard work and earnest planning, both subsidized and jeopardized by the city and state governments; like the Red Hook food vendors, they are a tangible symbol of the constant struggle to put down roots in the city, especially if you don't have much money. The helpful woman whom you have just met invites you to visit one of the gardens, a small lot of about one-third of an acre. "New Visions

Garden," says the dark green and white sign on the fence; another sign says, "Everyone welcome."

Inside the fence three scarecrows stuffed with straw and dressed in old plaid shirts and jeans sit on a weathered wooden bench. Scarecrows are not a common sight in East New York, but they help to create an image of rural peace and plenty. A wheelbarrow rests nearby, grape arbors line up neatly against one wall, and brightly painted murals of farm scenes can be glimpsed through trees at the back of the garden. The first person you see, giving instructions in a quiet but commanding voice to about a dozen teen-agers who are working in the garden, is Marian Johnson, a retired school-teacher and one of New Visions' founders. A straw hat perches on her head; though she wears overalls and a sweater, she looks elegant, and she is clearly in charge. You're surprised that most of the teens she's talking to are of Asian descent, and one girl in the group wears a burkha. They are weeding, turn-ing the soil, moving things around—cheerfully doing the tasks Ms. John-son assigns them. They tell you they're members of the Community Service Club of Stuyvesant High School, one of the city's most selective public schools, where students come from all over the city. For the past three years the club has sent volunteers to work in the garden on Saturdays.[1]

Ms. Johnson lives in one of the neatly tended, single-family homes down the block, modern, redbrick houses with small front yards and a parking space for the family car. Except for the fact that they're attached to each other, the houses look like homes in the suburbs rather than like the neighborhood's old tenements and small frame dwellings. Black iron gates surround some of the yards, the fence posts adorned with small, white plaster lions, a sign of house pride in many Brooklyn neighborhoods where migrants first from Italy and then from the South, the Caribbean, and Africa have settled in successive waves since the mid-twentieth century. These houses near the garden were built in the 1980s, when a community organization called East Brooklyn Congregations won scarce public funds and dug deep into church members' pockets to build desperately needed new homes for low- and moderate-income residents. In 1992 Ms. Johnson and twelve of her neighbors founded New Visions Garden on a vacant lot owned by the city government; as they have got older or moved away, only three of the original gardeners still work there.

But Ms. Johnson talked so much about the garden to her colleagues at the public school where she taught for years that Sarah Harris, the woman who invited you to come in, had to take the subway out here to see it herself.

Now, having also retired from teaching, she makes the trip from her home in downtown Brooklyn every Saturday morning to work on her plot. This is a good place to socialize, to eat a burrito in the autumn sun at noon, and to admire the work that you have done all summer before spreading mulch for next year. While Ms. Johnson shows you the rose bushes and tells you how she will change the plantings by next summer, Ms. Harris, who hears you have a cherry tomato plant growing in a flower pot on your windowsill, presses you to take some bean pods and onion bulbs home to plant "for next year." It's not hard to see this garden, or the smaller herb garden around the corner or the larger vegetable garden and farmers' market across the street, as providing new beginnings for an old urban village.

Marian Johnson and her neighbors are not the only New Yorkers to grasp community gardens as a lifeline. But this neighborhood is important, for East New York contains eighty-eight of Brooklyn's 316 community gardens, while the borough has almost half of the city's current total of more than seven hundred gardens. Though the first, and most politically active, of New York's community gardens are located in Manhattan's East Village, East New York is more typical of the neighborhoods where the gardens now thrive. Residents of these neighborhoods are mainly black and Latino, and a large number are immigrants or older migrants from the South, many with rural roots. Unlike Ms. Johnson, they tend to rent apartments rather than own homes, and both their rents and incomes are low. Not surprisingly, neighborhoods with the densest concentration of community gardens have the fewest public parks. These are in northern and central Brooklyn; the Lower East Side (including the East Village), Harlem, and Washington Heights in Manhattan; and the South Bronx.[2]

The growth of community gardens in these areas has reversed the expectations of business and political leaders. During the crisis years of the 1970s city officials quietly accepted an idea of "planned shrinkage"—or to put it more crudely, "urban triage"—that would have permitted low-income neighborhoods like these to become abandoned and overgrown with weeds and turn into jungle or farm land. Promoted in New York by the housing commissioner Roger Starr and carried out by default by local officials in increasingly poor cities like Detroit, Baltimore, Newark, and Gary, Indiana, planned shrinkage gave up neighborhoods in the face of capital disinvestment and severe physical and social decline. Instead of fighting the disastrous effects of decline on the overall standard of living and residents' morale, city officials allowed poor neighborhoods to lose businesses and residents, pulled back on public services, and watched the neighborhoods fall apart in arson, drug dealing, and crime. The only productive use of abandoned houses and vacant lots that politicians and business leaders could foresee in the 1970s was to turn these spaces into farm land or parks.[3]

This did not happen in New York the way those leaders planned. Against all odds, between the 1970s and the 1990s community residents and their outside supporters transformed nearly a thousand vacant lots into havens for their neighborhoods' survival. Community gardens gave them the means and opportunity to put down roots. Roots were as important for new immigrants from Latin America and Asia who arrived with little English and minimal education as for the low- and middle-income African Americans and Puerto Ricans who remained tied to the city by jobs and family. But few people would have predicted that this form of roots could survive. Like the Red Hook food vendors, community gardeners were, and still are, a vulnerable social group. They confront the powerful forces of city government and the equally powerful drive of real estate developers. They had, and still have, no legal claim to ownership. Like the food vendors, they won the land they claimed for gardens only by mobilizing supporters outside of their communities, especially in the media, and through them, reaching a broader public.

Community gardens won support because of their "authenticity." But the specific form this authenticity takes has changed over time, as the gardens shifted from being a grassroots social movement challenging the state to an embodiment of ethnic identity, then an expression of secular cultural identity in tune with gentrifiers' values, and finally a form of urban food production consistent with the tastes of middle-class locavores and strategies for sustainable development. Unlike most other urban spaces, community gardens are literally a *terroir*. Gardeners work with earth, sun, and water to grow flowers and foods, struggling to coax new life from the hostile forces of nature and culture. In the city, though, they also contend with the no less brutal forces of politics and the floods and droughts of capital investment.

New York City would have no community gardens today if during the 1970s landlords, banks, and the city government had not walked away from working-class and lower-middle-class neighborhoods. During the 1990s, when prospects of gentrification made these neighborhoods more interesting to investors, the Giuliani administration pushed to replace the gardens with new housing development. Developers were coming up with new sources of financing—though as we know now, much of it depended on shaky credit and risky speculation—and city officials were eager to put

Farmers' market, East New York: community gardener selling local produce.
Photograph by Sharon Zukin.

New York's image of decline behind them. Mobility was the order of the day: capital mobility reflecting investment "flows" and human mobility reflecting both gentrifiers' movement in and old residents' movement out. If residents' desire to stay in place was represented by community gardens, pressure for mobility was represented by new entrepreneurial spaces like cafés and boutiques and new entrepreneurial signs like giant vinyl billboards. Both a form of mass persuasion and a visual entertainment, these gargantuan advertisements overwhelmed busy commercial streets and were even hung on private residential buildings, turning much of the city into a promotion of the free-market economy.

This is a free-market economy; welcome to the era after communism.
—Mayor Rudolph Giuliani, 1999

Like many of their neighborhoods, community gardens have a tortuous history. When they were first formed in the 1970s they reflected the social movements of the time, when young people who wanted to work for social justice became antiwar activists and community organizers in poor neighborhoods. In New York and other big cities these activists joined low-income tenants in rent strikes against landlords who wouldn't provide heat and hot water or make necessary repairs and protests against the terrifying spectacle of arson-for-hire that relieved these landlords of their responsibility but provoked little response from a negligent city government, which had enough power nonetheless to deny these neighborhoods the new public schools, sanitation, and social services they needed. It was a time, as current histories describe it, when the South Bronx and many other neighborhoods where poor people, many of color, lived were literally burning. Looking back on those years white writers who had lived in buildings near Harlem or slummed on the Lower East Side recall dystopic ruins, harsh streets bleeding into wastelands. "By 1980," the writer Luc Santé says, "Avenue C [in the East Village] was a lunar landscape of vacant blocks and hollow tenement shells. Over there, commerce—in food or clothing, say— was often conducted out of car trunks, but the most thriving industry was junk, and it alone made use of marginally viable specimens of the building stock. The charred stairwells, the gaping floorboards, the lack of lighting, the entryways consisting of holes torn in ground-floor walls—all served the psychological imperatives of the heroin trade."[4]

Beginning in the 1970s residents of these neighborhoods took control of vacant lots where the rubble of tenement houses abandoned by landlords and scavenged by drug addicts lay amid rotting garbage, used heroin needles, and discarded furniture of unknown origin. In an audacious act of civil disobedience and hope they cleared away this urban detritus and planted gardens, ignoring questions of legal ownership. Like houses in Harlem that were also abandoned at this time, ownership of these lots was taken by the city government *in rem,* in place of the owners' unpaid taxes. Neighbors who claimed this space for community use were both joined and led by more highly educated activists who brought the values and tactics of the environmental movement from virgin forests to the more sordid wildness of the city. A group that called itself the Green Guerillas threw "seed-bombs" and "green-aids" over cyclone fences onto vacant lots they couldn't enter. They made common cause with the Puerto Rican activist group the Young Lords, who enlisted community residents to sweep the streets in East Harlem to dramatize the failure of the city's sanitation department to pick up garbage, and the newly hatched environmental movement that was brought to life by U.S. Senator Gaylord Nelson, President Richard Nixon, and the first national Earth Day demonstration in Washington, D.C., in 1970.[5]

New York's first community garden was set up in 1973 on several adjacent rubble-strewn, city-owned lots at the corner of the Bowery and Houston Street, which in those years was a kind of DMZ between the East Village and the Lower East Side. "'You could not have picked a more unlikely place to start a garden,' recalls Bill Brunson, an early Green Guerilla. 'At the time, there were still all these men lined up along the Bowery drinking wine and panhandling. To put a garden there—in what was probably the ultimate slime spot in the city—that was unheard of.'" Reclaiming this territory for common use, the Liz Christy Community Garden, named in the 1980s to honor the memory of one of its founders, created a model that spread throughout New York City, mainly through the efforts of the Green Guerillas.[6]

City agencies did not want to help them. Though the gardeners applied for and got official permission to clear the Houston Street lots, the city government accused them of trespassing on private property and threatened to throw them out. After Christy invited television crews to document how she and her colleagues had cleaned the lots, fenced them in, and spread donated topsoil for a garden, the Department of Housing Preservation and Development (HPD) offered them a lease on the space for a nominal rent: one dollar a month. The lots, though, did not look like a good site for a garden. Black-and-white photographs taken after the debris was cleared show parched, sandy soil. Gaping windows in the old brick factory in the background suggest that it was also abandoned. Like other buildings throughout the city in the 1970s and 1980s, it may have been inhabited by squatters, who, like the gardeners, risked arrest for trespassing.[7]

Despite their lack of power, the Green Guerillas had some influential friends. Artists who lived in SoHo lofts illegally in the early 1970s lobbied allies in the city administration to support their right to live in a manufacturing zone; years later the Red Hook food vendors asked supporters to lobby the Parks Department to grant them a permit to use the ball fields. For their part, the Green Guerillas knew people in universities and the U.S. Congress. While they ran training sessions for community residents and gave away free plants and trees, Representative Fred Richmond of Brooklyn sponsored legislation to establish a federal program to support urban gardens. A demonstration project was set up in Brooklyn with the help of

Cornell University's Cooperative Extension Service, and its success fueled a three-million-dollar program that soon spread to fifteen other cities. In 1977, after newly elected President Jimmy Carter made a historic visit to the devastated lots of Charlotte Street in the South Bronx, his administration proposed a ten-million-dollar grant to aid the area's renewal, of which they earmarked half a million dollars for new parks and recreation facilities. This amount was doubled to more than one million dollars by the federal and state governments, but they required local institutions, both public and private, to contribute matching funds. When the city government counted tree planting and sidewalk improvements in their share of the contribution, volunteer gardeners calculated all the hours of sweat equity they had spent clearing vacant lots, spreading topsoil, and planting, as well as the economic value of the debris they had recycled and the compost they had made. A new concept among social activists in the 1970s, sweat equity suggested that the "authenticity" of community roots and labor could offset legal ownership of land.[8]

Not wanting to be outflanked by activists who had only a moral claim to the land they planted, and fearing a further erosion of government's authority during the city's fiscal crisis, Mayor Edward I. Koch tried to centralize control over the gardeners' efforts in a new program, Operation Green Thumb, run by the Parks Department. Though Koch had represented the liberal district of Greenwich Village in Congress, he was elected mayor in 1977 with the support of the city's business leaders, who expected him to restore law and order and help the real estate industry. Green Thumb took over part of the Green Guerillas' leadership role, distributing topsoil, compost, and other resources. More important, the Green Thumb program controlled legal access to city-owned vacant lots. In return for gardeners setting up a formal operating structure and opening their garden to the public at least ten hours each week, Green Thumb issued them leases for only one dollar a year. But Operation Green Thumb conferred no permanent right to the land; gardeners had to agree to vacate the space within thirty days if the city government, or a private entrepreneur, decided to develop it. This provision guaranteed there would be conflict over the gardens in the future, when the investment climate changed. Within a few years the Parks Department agreed to grant some five- and ten-year leases, except for gardens occupying land valued at more than twenty thousand dollars. Nonetheless the Koch administration made it clear that community gardeners had only "interim" use of the land.

Still, during the 1980s hundreds of community gardens were formed on city-owned lots. Most were in areas with low-income, minority populations, far from Lower and Midtown Manhattan, and with little likelihood of attracting private development. In the East Village, though, a constant stream of college students, recent graduates, and young, single workers on Wall Street and in the arts encouraged landlords to raise rents, which in turn raised the threat of gentrification. New construction of market-rent housing near community gardens began to look feasible, at least in the East Village. By the same token, in Harlem and Bushwick, black and Latino neighborhoods where houses lay vacant and falling apart, the city government began to work with community-based organizations to finance construction, renovation, and ownership of low- and moderate-income housing. East Brooklyn Congregations built more than a thousand Nehemiah Houses, first in Brownsville, then in East New York at this time. In 1986 the Koch administration started to transfer management of some community gardens from the Parks Department to HPD. This was clearly a first step toward reclaiming the land for housing, which would be built by either public-private partnerships to aid the low-income population or private developers who preferred market-rate apartments.

The Koch administration's decision to destroy the widely admired Garden of Eden, built in concentric circles on five vacant lots on the Lower East Side during the 1970s by an eccentric environmentalist and local social critic who went by the name Adam Purple, aroused concern about the gardens' future, especially among young artists and activists. This was one of the reasons—along with the administration's use of repressive police action against homeless people, housing squatters, and assorted anarchists and punks who gathered in the East Village—behind the protests in Tompkins Square Park in 1988.[9]

During the single four-year term of Mayor David Dinkins, community gardeners took heart from the city government's adoption of community-based planning and environmental justice goals. But when Mayor Rudolph Giuliani took over in 1994, after ethnic riots in Brooklyn, increases in street crime citywide, and perceived threats to voters' safe and secure "quality of life," he felt he had won a mandate, like Koch, both to restore the city government's authority and encourage private-sector housing development. City-owned "vacant" lots, whether or not they had been put to productive use as gardens, became the mayor's tool for meeting both goals. In 1977, when Koch was elected mayor, the city owned around twenty-five thousand of these lots; twenty years later, in Giuliani's administration, the number had fallen to eleven thousand, which was still a huge amount of land to control. Soon after taking office Mayor Giuliani directed the Department of General Services (DGS) to make an inventory of the lots. All requests to create new gardens were denied. As Koch had tried to do in the mid-1980s, Giuliani began to transfer management of the community gardens from the Parks Department to other city agencies, especially HPD. As Koch had also tried to do with city-owned housing in Harlem, Giuliani moved toward auctioning off hundreds of lots occupied by community gardens to the highest bidder, without informing the bidders about the gardens or informing the gardeners about the impending sales. Neither did the mayor consult with local community boards, which was legally required by the city's Uniform Land Use Review Procedure. In 1996 Giuliani gave DGS five years to sell off all the vacant lots in its inventory and justified the loss of community gardens by the potential gain in housing.[10]

By that time some community gardeners were savvy enough to protest. Their City Council member or borough president, usually a Democrat, often supported them against the Republican mayor. This was enough to get a garden temporarily removed from the auction list. By this time also the environmental movement had spawned activist urban organizations such as the Neighborhood Open Space Coalition as well as private foundations that sprang into action to protest the sale of gardens. Moreover official institutions connected with the city government, including the Green Thumb program and the Brooklyn Botanic Garden, encouraged and legitimized thousands of community gardeners. With critical coverage by reporters at the *New York Times,* who clearly supported the gardens, the auctions provided a target for attacking Giuliani, who was already disliked for his rough approach to civil liberties, confrontations with liberal opponents, and support of gentrification.[11]

College-educated social and environmental activists used the creative tactics of street theater to dramatize their defense of the gardens. In 1997 two hundred protesters held a rally at City Hall Park. "Accompanied by 12-foot puppets that towered over toddlers clasping stalks of celery in their strollers," according to the *New York Times,* "they delivered gifts of vegetables and flowers and hundreds of letters from their supporters to Fran Reiter, who was then the Deputy Mayor for economic development and planning, and other city officials." These tactics escalated when the Giuliani administration refused to stop the sale of city-owned lots. Protesters quietly infiltrated an auction held at the Police Headquarters in 1998 and released ten thousand crickets into the room. "The result," said the *Times,* "was bedlam." The next year, at the climax of a two-day conference, "Standing Our Ground," sponsored by the New York City Community Garden Coalition, the New York City Environmental Justice Alliance, and the New York chapter of the Sierra Club, five hundred protesters, many of whom came from out of town, rallied in Midtown at Bryant Park, chanting "Stop the Auction!"[12]

Giuliani did not shy away from taking on the protesters. When they enlarged their "spaces of engagement" with the mayor's policies, he escalated his rhetoric, calling those who wanted to stop the auctions socialists and accusing them of being stuck "in the era of communism." Because the 1990s were the first decade after the fall of communism and the emergence of market economies in Eastern Europe and the former Soviet Union, Giuliani hoped his name-calling would have some traction. "This is a free-market economy," the mayor was widely reported to have said. "Welcome to the era after communism."[13]

The phrase "free-market economy" also applied to the Giuliani administration's efforts to dismantle the social welfare programs that the city had developed since the Great Depression. Though this reorientation of public policy began during the Koch administration in the late 1970s and became a national strategy during the presidency of Ronald Reagan, Giuliani gave it his personal stamp. Between 1984, when Koch was mayor, to 2000, near the end of Giuliani's two terms in office, ninety community gardens were destroyed. Most were bulldozed and turned over to developers during the Giuliani years. But the end to this policy came in 1999, when newly elected New York State Attorney General Eliot Spitzer developed an interest in stopping the mayor.

Whether it was true or not, Spitzer said that he was convinced to support the gardens because of lobbying by Green Guerillas, particularly by one Green Guerilla dressed, in another example of street theater, as a sunflower, though he already had a record of favoring environmental causes. It was also clear by this time that the Democrat attorney general wanted to distinguish himself from the Republican governor, George Pataki, who promoted his own reputation as an environmentalist. On behalf of the state, Spitzer sued the Giuliani administration for violating New York's environmental laws, notably laws requiring environmental review of land-use changes through the sale of public properties. Spitzer also argued that, because the lots used for years as community gardens constituted de facto parklands, selling each lot would require the state legislature's approval. Though environmental organizations had already filed four different lawsuits against the city government to stop the sale of community gardens, the state's legal argument and pressure had great force.[14]

Just a few months earlier the Giuliani administration had rejected a two-million-dollar offer by the Trust for Public Land to buy seventy gardens from the city. After Spitzer filed suit the administration showed greater willingness to talk. The Trust, working with the New York Restoration Project, private foundations, and individual donors, made a new offer of three million dollars for sixty-two gardens. But the Giuliani administration demanded as a condition of the sale that all private and nonprofit organizations drop their lawsuits against the city concerning the gardens, a demand that the plaintiffs refused. Only one day before the auction was to be held the New York State Supreme Court ruled on the attorney general's suit, deciding that the sale of parkland could not go on until the city government proved it would cause no environmental harm. This judicial decision in Spitzer's favor broke the mayor's resolve, though it came too late to stop the bulldozing of Esperanza Garden in the East Village, where protesters had chained themselves to the fence in a futile effort to stop the garden's destruction. Prominently featured in the media, the bulldozing of the Puerto Rican–themed garden and the arrest of the protesters became a symbol of the city government's disdain for both environmental and social justice.[15]

Shortly after Giuliani left office the Bloomberg administration began negotiations with the state attorney general's office to settle the lawsuit. Unlike Giuliani, Mayor Michael Bloomberg accepted the requirement to carry out an environmental review before changing the use of the land, and he was willing to agree to preserve most of the gardens. In the compromise Bloomberg struck, five hundred community gardens would remain in the portfolio of the Parks Department and other city agencies, and another hundred would be bulldozed to build housing, including affordable apartments, under the sponsorship of HPD. The remaining hundred or so gardens were either owned already by private foundations such as the Trust for Public Land and the New York Restoration Project or left under the control of a handful of other city agencies.[16]

Though the final settlement won praise for its fairness, with the city government recognizing the gardeners' claim to space and promoting affordable housing as well, it left several important issues unresolved. Like the Williamsburg waterfront, which became attractive to developers after new, hip entrepreneurs created a lively commercial district around Bedford Avenue, the area around community gardens had increased in economic value, even in the poorest neighborhoods. This sharpened developers' interest in building market-rate rather than affordable housing there, and the Bloomberg administration was not likely to push against them on this point. Development meant that low-income gardeners, especially renters, could be displaced from their homes; the lack of control over which gardens would be selected for development increased their pain. A third issue concerned the role of the private foundations and nonprofit organizations that had bought hundreds of gardens and would donate more money to maintain them in years to come. Their financial contributions gave these organizations a great deal of influence over the gardens' use and design— despite potential opposition by some of the community gardeners. The most serious issue, however, was the lack of a permanent, legal resolution of the gardeners' right to the land. Though it was not emphasized publicly, the settlement between the Bloomberg administration and the state attorney general's office would expire in 2010. Granting the community gardens a permanent right to the city's parkland would require action by the New York State Legislature.[17]

In the meantime the Bloomberg administration expanded its support of the gardeners. The Parks Department, which most people consider the gardens' logical administrative home, granted municipal insurance coverage to the gardens in its portfolio; paying expensive premiums for required liability insurance had imposed a huge financial burden on community gardeners. Green Thumb continued to provide topsoil and compost, some from the Bronx Zoo, as well as expert advice, workers to carry out some tasks, and lawnmowers and other equipment that most gardens couldn't afford to buy. Community gardens continued to be razed and their lots developed for housing, especially in Harlem, where the federal, state, and city governments were all committed to extensive new construction; however, other gardens set up training programs for urban farmers and opened farmers' markets with the help of the state Department of Agriculture and nonprofit organizations such as Just Foods. The Manhattan Borough President's Office issued a report, *Food in the Public Interest,* that proposed creating a regional "foodshed" and developing new zoning laws and other incentives to expand community gardens. Far from the 1970s idea of "urban triage," in the twenty-first century growing food in low-income neighborhoods represented a strategy for fighting the lack of healthy food alternatives, a public policy that would eliminate "food poverty" and obesity and improve residents' quality of life. Connecting to sustainable development, "food justice," and "green" jobs offered community gardens a lifeline to the future.[18]

What we're working on right now is keeping gardens sustainable for many generations into the future. They're permanent, so we have to make sure there is somebody to care for them forever.
—Edie Stone, Operation Green Thumb, quoted in GothamGazette.com, July 17, 2006

Traditional *terroirs* in the countryside that produce specific kinds of wine and food, such as Bordeaux wines or Camembert cheese, don't have to justify their existence. Their connection with the land is organic; it goes back a long time. Over years, decades, and even centuries farmers develop ways of dealing with their region's soil quality, rainfall, and native animals, as well as with distant markets and state controls. Though they may succeed or fail at these tasks, especially when they try to protect sales of their products from outside competition, regional producers develop an identification with the land that almost seems, on its own, to be a force of nature. In the United States, though, and in all regions where industrialized agriculture dominates food production, the development of *terroir* requires a formidable amount of work. Restaurant chefs and home cooks who seek local products encourage small farmers to grow them, food writers praise their taste, schools and governments gradually begin to educate a broader public about the environmental and nutritional benefits of locavore diets. The resulting networks of producers and consumers are quite visibly a deliberate social construction. Like community gardens, these new *terroirs* depend on a wide range of outside supporters, including the media and the state, as well as on social bonds of community and trust.[19]

Community gardens show both the strengths and the strains of mobilizing these forces. First, many gardens face a serious labor shortage. Like New Visions in East New York, a large number of gardens are run by senior citizens, and many of their founders have aged, moved, or passed away. Middle-aged community residents are too busy working and caring for their families to tend garden plots, and local teenagers and college students are either working to earn money or not interested in doing garden chores. At least one-fifth of 650 gardens that were recently surveyed have fewer than ten members, and about the same number have between ten and twenty; only fifteen gardens, 2 percent, have more than one hundred members. The need for active gardeners has encouraged informal partnerships with the city's schools and universities, such as the high school that sends students to New Visions on Saturdays.

The gardens also contend with a shortage of capital. About one-third of them collect membership dues of ten to thirty dollars a household; more than two-thirds, however, collect no dues at all. Their modest means keep them dependent on the state, private foundations, and, indirectly, corporate sponsors. To stay active gardeners must know about and apply for external funding. Since the 1980s the New York State Department of Agriculture and nonprofit organizations that are dedicated to urban farming have paid for internships for local teens; planning how to get access to these funds, as well as coordinating a production network of compost suppliers, interns, and produce sellers, requires community gardeners to organize more intensively than when they only plant ornamental flowers or grow vegetables for individual use. Farming in community gardens requires the efforts and skills, and often the networking abilities, of professional activists and full-time managers. When the gardens establish more ambitious job-training programs, connecting teenagers to future green jobs, as Red Hook's community farm Added Value does, and to jobs in the digital economy, organizational skills become even more important.[20]

Activists who cleared lots to create the early gardens did not imagine that one day they would have to write grant proposals or manage a local labor force. Most of those gardens built on solidarity created by either family and ethnic bonds or radical political activism. In the East Village, where bohemian artists lived alongside old and new immigrants in an ethnic mix, alliances formed across boundaries of social class and culture—but not in all gardens, and not without conflict. Puerto Ricans, who until the 1980s were a significant presence in Loisaida, as they called the Lower East Side, often formed gardens on their own and were suspicious of making alliances with either newcomers or outsiders. After clearing lots and putting in a few plants they hung Puerto Rican flags and built little shacks, or *casitas,* where the men socialized with music and games of dominos or cards. Many didn't actively garden so much as use the space for leisure and to express an ethnic identity, a tangible memory of home, that had few outlets in other public spaces. Though some gardens were headed by women and had plants as well as murals and sculptures representing Latino themes—like the large statue of a *coquí,* or Puerto Rican frog, that symbolized Esperanza Garden, which was demolished by the Giuliani administration in 2000—they didn't always translate their feeling of home for non-Latino neighbors.[21]

But in times of crisis Puerto Rican and working-class gardeners often looked outside for help. When a garden was listed for auction it was crucial to take quick action, drawing on the contacts of college-educated, non-Latino activists with officials and private foundations. Internet access was another resource that emphasized the difference between longtime local residents and environmental activists from outside the ethnic community. Before 2000 few Latino and working-class New Yorkers were connected to the World Wide Web. By contrast, outside activists and non-Latino residents used listservs and websites to publicize protests and mobilize support. They felt freer, moreover, to use the tactics of cultural guerrillas: street theater, loud demonstrations in Midtown and city government offices, festivals that attracted media attention. Some of these tactics embarrassed more culturally conservative Puerto Ricans and immigrants, especially when artists came to an annual Rites of Spring celebration in the East Village as "earth spirits," in a state of undress, to the disapproving stares of African Latino spiritual leaders. Rituals of community, in other words, both separated different groups of gardeners and drew them together.[22]

These differences challenged a common ideal of authenticity. If Puerto Ricans defended their right to a community garden as a place to exercise their ethnic identity, their new neighbors called on a different kind of authenticity, one based on artistic expression and environmental values. The *casitas* represented nostalgia for an agrarian and also an ethnic utopia; solar panels and symbols of Gaia, the earth mother, represented nostalgia for a different utopia, one not tied to a specific homeland. As time went by, though, and gentrification expanded, the numbers of Puerto Rican gardeners declined. Gentrifiers' social and aesthetic values gradually became more pronounced in the gardens' use and design; *casitas* disappeared in favor of more formal landscaping, and entertainment shifted from dominos and traditional Puerto Rican music to film, concert, and poetry programs. Not surprisingly these changes were more in tune with the preferences of the Parks Department and private foundations.[23]

Other disputes between Puerto Rican and non-Latino gardeners arose over farming practices. Chief among these, though at first glance not an "urban" issue, was how to raise chickens. Under New York City's Health

Code, raising animals, birds, and insects requires keeping the livestock penned in and preventing their reproduction. In some community gardens Puerto Rican members let the chickens run free, as they might have done in their homeland or as fans of free-range chickens might prefer, but non-Latino gardeners complained—complaints that led on occasion to fist fights. On the other hand, non-Latino newcomers wanted to remove the cages around vegetable plants that Puerto Rican gardeners had installed to prevent the produce being eaten by rats. Each group strongly believed that some of the other's farming practices were unpleasant to look at or just wrong. Community gardens did not find it easy to develop the unified local knowledge of an authentic *terroir*.[24]

Ethnic differences have not been the only source of problems. If gardens claim a moral right to space, they must speak "authentically" for the surrounding community. But because ethnic gardens often rely on small family groups or several neighbors living in the same building nearby, they cannot claim to represent an entire community. Changing demographics also create problems, not just with gentrification but with new immigrants arriving from other regions of the world with different traditions. In East New York African American and Caribbean community gardeners now have to work with Pakistanis, which poses problems of reaching out to them and then of deciding what to plant and making sure everyone is included in making decisions. Different rhetorical styles and work practices, compounded by age and gender distinctions, make it hard for community gardens to sustain a unified story of origin.

All community gardens must deal with problems of coordinating different individuals with their own interests and motivations, very much like the interpersonal problems of any cooperative group.[25] Agricultural gardens, though, add layers of complexity. With a general shortage of plots and local food production gaining in esteem, many community gardens have waiting lists for membership. Knowing that there are others waiting to take their place puts pressure on gardeners to go along with what the majority want, though nearly all work on individual plots. Although about 75 percent of community gardens grow fruit and vegetables, the most popular and well-established organizations are the large, multipurpose gardens that combine individual plots for produce with high-value aesthetic features: fish ponds for meditation, grape arbors for shade, solar panels and rain-collection barrels for sustainability, benches and picnic tables for comfort. These gardens require a lot of coordination. Their greatest strength is not their size or aesthetic variety, however; it is the ability of their middle-class, more highly educated members, or their professional managers, to get grants from outside organizations. This kind of social capital, rather than their origins in a residential community or an ethnic group, enables them to thrive.[26]

Though they are not the socialist experiments Mayor Giuliani derided, community gardens do take land out of the market economy and "decommodify" it. Social and environmental stewardship gives the gardeners a de facto communal ownership that differs from both the private entrepreneurial uses of public space supported by Business Improvement Districts and the public entrepreneurial control of city government agencies such as the Parks Department. Community gardeners' striving for roots represents a model of common space different from the market model geared to city dwellers' mobility. Typical as this was in the recent era of neoliberal economics, it is even truer in the current economic crisis.

Cabs and buses are wrapped in advertising. Well, why shouldn't garbage trucks and street cleaners also be wrapped in advertising?
—City Council President Christine Quinn, quoted in *New York Daily News*, October 15, 2008

Beginning in the 1970s just when community gardens were emerging, the city's chronic need for funds drove New York's elected officials to embrace an entrepreneurial approach. Not only did Mayors Koch and Giuliani welcome gentrification as an important step toward private sector reinvestment in formerly "blighted" neighborhoods, but they also offered up the public space of streets and parks as money-making assets. The Parks Department, with so much land to maintain, was especially pressed to find "creative" ways to use its resources. Not only did they shift managerial duties to private conservancies and BIDs and auction licenses to hot dog vendors, they also required new parks to include commercial features such as restaurants and hotels. While creative financing led to socially useful places where people gathered, such as the Greenmarket at Union Square and the food vendors' trucks at the Red Hook ball fields, it also encouraged elected officials to rent every surface of public space for advertising, turning the city into a giant billboard.[27]

This is hardly a new development. At least since the eighteenth century London, Paris, New York, and other great cities where throngs of people

Giant vinyl billboards, Lafayette and Houston Streets. Photograph by Richard Rosen.

are constantly on the move have thrived on the shop signs, show windows, newsstands, and advertising posters of commercial culture. These visual displays provide a large portion of urban public art, promoting a specific kind of consumer literacy and stimulating the senses as well. Commercial promotions make city streets the primal scene of promiscuous stimulation described so well by the social theorists of early twentieth-century urbanism Georg Simmel and Walter Benjamin, a jangling streetscape that is expanding even now in Mumbai, Tokyo, and Shanghai. This massive onslaught of sights and sounds dramatizes a great city's urbanness, its aesthetic difference from small towns, and its tolerance, even encouragement, of individual expression. In a basic sense the media messages in the city center create a space of freedom. But commercial promotions, if left unchecked, reach a point of overdevelopment and become *too* intrusive.[28]

In the artisanal economy of preindustrial times, most men and women, especially women, made many goods at home, and stores depended on custom trade rather than casual customers. During this era commercial signs were well within the limits of human scale and visual decorum. But when mass production began to demand equally massive promotion to persuade shoppers to buy, stores and manufacturers engaged in more aggressive intrusions, advertising by every available technology and in every possible channel. When the novelist Henry James returned to New York on a visit in 1904, a high point in the city's growth, he was appalled by the crassness of the money economy he saw in the streetscape. The sky was blocked by tall buildings, "all new and crude and commercial and over-windowed"; department stores shamelessly copied the white-marble majesty of "Palladian pile[s]"; and, in what to him was another unacceptable intrusion into the calm beauty of public space, immigrant sweatshop workers swarmed over the sidewalks in a dense mass of humanity.[29]

Some of these issues also bothered the civic-minded, upper-class members of the Municipal Art Society. From 1902 to World War I this group led a campaign against advertising billboards, which were built higher than ever before, were more densely posted, and were even found underground in the city's new subway system. The campaign looked as though it would lose, for it was opposed by a widespread, pro-business alliance, beginning with the still privately owned subway companies that profited from ads, the advertising agencies that placed them, and the *New York Times,* and including Tammany Hall, the Democratic Party Machine of the time, as well as the Board of Aldermen (city council). In 1918, however, the Municipal Art Society found a way of using the city's new zoning laws to outlaw advertising billboards in residential neighborhoods. Two years later, after much lobbying and protest, the city government agreed to take the billboards out of one of New York's most sacred public spaces: Central Park.[30]

Despite the efforts of the Municipal Art Society, public spaces continued to spawn more advertising billboards, and these were even larger than before. Most advertised new movies, foods, alcohol, and cigarettes, confirming the central role of consumer culture in both the urban economy and popular images. Shopping, beginning with window shopping, became one of the city's main amusements, and retail stores provided growing numbers of jobs and revenue as well. The first great age of Times Square, where commercial theaters, fancy restaurants, newspaper offices, and stores clustered under multiple levels of spectacular neon signage, represented the city's dependence on media, shopping, and entertainment. From the 1920s to the 1950s, even during the Great Depression, brightly lighted theater marquees jostled for attention with a huge billboard for Camel cigarettes that blew smoke rings into the air and a giant whiskey bottle that really "poured." This was the constantly photographed scene that became a symbol of American culture around the world and, before the television or Internet age, the place where the public learned that World War II had ended, in headlines scrolling around the electric Motogram on the outside of the Times Tower.[31]

During the postwar economic expansion advertisers made ever more aggressive efforts to capture the attention of an increasingly mobile public. Not just in Times Square, but throughout the United States billboards became brasher, more pervasive, and more spectacular. In New York and Los Angeles, the biggest cities, and along new interstate highways, outdoor advertisements mushroomed. Meanwhile the companies that controlled outdoor advertising space lobbied city, state, and federal lawmakers for the right to put up even bigger, bolder signs.[32]

In the 1960s, as in the early 1900s, billboards reached a saturation point and suffered two apparently fatal blows. First, critics attacked them for aesthetic reasons, arguing that they ruined the pure beauty of public spaces, especially the natural beauty of woods and fields in the visual corridors alongside highways. These arguments found an articulate champion in Lady Bird Johnson, the president's wife, and Congress passed a law in 1965 removing billboards from the interstate highway system and other highways receiving federal funds. The second blow against billboards, this time in cities, came from the public's gradual withdrawal from public places of mass entertainment. Prosperity after World War II enabled Americans to buy automobiles, TVs, and air conditioners, all of which led them to spend more time indoors. But many Americans also withdrew from public spaces that they would have to share with different ethnic groups and social classes: amusement parks, public swimming pools, and shopping and entertainment districts such as Times Square. When the controlled public space of Disneyland and suburban shopping malls exercised allure, these open urban districts, and their giant billboards, began to seem tacky.[33]

The ground shifted back to billboards' favor, certainly in New York, during the 1980s. A lackluster design to build tall corporate office towers in Times Square was proposed and aroused fiery opposition among architects, urban planners, and civic groups. Ironically it was the Municipal Art Society that now led a campaign to preserve Times Square's aesthetic vitality, its unique experience of urban "authenticity," by requiring every new building there to sport a giant electronic billboard. This change of heart, leading to the creation of a special billboard-emblazoned district in Times Square, coincided with a shift in corporate strategy toward more aggressive branding. Building public knowledge of a brand encouraged companies to do more advertising, open their own stores, and rent billboards in urban centers with a lot of foot traffic—centers such as Times Square. New York City began to *look* revitalized because advertising billboards placed it at the visible forefront of consumer culture; the billboards became a symbol of the city's "brand." In another ironic twist, officially sanctioned billboards rose to prominence just when the city government was fighting against unofficial, personally styled graffiti that lay like a neon-colored plague on park benches, subway cars, and the walls of nearly every public building. The "style wars" between city authorities and graffiti taggers to control public space were even fiercer than the struggles between city agencies and community gardeners, though the graffiti writers often came from the same devastated neighborhoods that the gardeners called home.[34]

Around this time, in the early 1990s, an Israeli artist invented a way to make even bigger billboards than had been possible through centuries of hand-painted signs. Udi Aloni used new digital technology to make prints on large panels of lightweight plastic mesh; he brought this process to New York, where it was used to create giant vinyl advertising billboards. These giant billboards were quickly installed in the newly trendy districts that attracted young, affluent visitors, who were, and still are, the marketers' desired demographic target. During the 1990s hipster Williamsburg, emerging art gallery center Chelsea, and SoHo, which was just then becoming a popular shopping district of chain stores, all developed major concentrations of giant vinyl billboards. In fact the remains of these billboards, when they outlived their rental contract and were discarded for scrap, gave Vahap Avsar and Lexy Funk the raw material to start Brooklyn Industries. The availability of digital technology and its cheapness, compared to labor-intensive hand painting or pasting signs, made companies want to put up more vinyl billboards and to change them more often, which encouraged building owners to sell outdoor advertising space on every possible surface, including—to residential tenants' dismay—on the outside walls of apartment buildings where they covered tenants' windows. Consumers' mobility, as they moved from neighborhood to neighborhood from night to day, worked against residents' desire for roots.

At the very moment when community gardeners were struggling to decommodify their lots, the city was being overrun by more and bigger billboards, a visible sign of commodity culture. Many billboards were even owned by city government agencies, whose need for money stirred them to become ever more entrepreneurial. Beginning in 1992 the Metropolitan Transit Authority (MTA) permitted city buses to be wrapped in advertisements. In 2005 the MTA made a deal to build bus shelters that would be covered in ads; the same model was then applied by the Department of Transportation, which controls the sidewalks, to build outdoor public toilets. Moreover, the MTA turned every surface of the city's vast transportation system into a billboard, from the floors of the subway station at Union Square to the windows of subway cars on the Times Square shuttle, and even the great passageways above ground in Grand Central Terminal. Between 1997 and 2008 the MTA's revenue from selling public space for ads jumped from $38 million to $125 million. Meanwhile on the city's streets the sheds around construction sites, which are privately owned but licensed by the Buildings Department, became pervasive billboard locations.[35]

The Parks Department, also facing budget shortfalls, took the same path as the MTA. They discussed the sale of naming rights, a move that sports stadiums and commercial theaters had already taken, and considered restoring outdoor advertising to parks, a practice that had ended when they removed billboards from Central Park in 1920. When these ideas aroused the public's scorn, the Parks Department, often working through BIDs and private conservancies, instead expanded the rental of public space for private use. The most striking example occurred just before the economic crisis broke in 2008, when the department rented a field in Central Park to Chanel for a mobile art exhibition featuring the luxury brand's products.[36]

Accelerating use of billboards in public space made New Yorkers sad and angry. "It has changed a city of neighborhoods into just a drive-through advertising extravaganza," said a state senator from Lower Manhattan. What he meant was that the pursuit of mobility, especially on the part of public agencies, annihilated city dwellers' desire for roots.[37]

If you ask a hundred people about the meaning of terroir, they'll
give you a hundred definitions, which can be as literal
as tasting limestone or as metaphorical as a feeling.
—Harold McGee and Daniel Patterson, "Talk Dirt to Me,"
New York Times, May 6, 2007

A yearning for roots goes beyond the interests of any single group, but community gardeners express both the literal and metaphorical processes of growing roots in the city. Since the 1970s community gardens have evolved through different forms of stewardship in a continuous adaptation to a harsh political environment. Regardless of their politics, ethnicity, or social class, the harshest factor the gardeners confront is their lack of a legal right to the property they care for. Though they have used "authenticity" to claim this land, the authenticity community gardeners represent has changed over time.

In the early days the Green Guerillas exercised one kind of authenticity in their efforts to take possession of vacant land for community gardens. They were environmental stewards—an argument worked out in more detail in the 1990s, when the Giuliani administration tried to revoke their leases—and community organizers, doing what the government should have been doing if it were truly serious about stabilizing communities and reversing urban decline; this was also what Jane Jacobs implied when she urged that communities be allowed to determine their own fate. The Green Guerillas and their allies enabled low-income community residents to become empowered, an aspirational political discourse that has grown even stronger and broader since the 1970s, with the state's greater willingness to deal with and rely on community-based organizations. When stakeholders, including those with no legal ownership rights and few social resources, assert their interests and desires, they create an authenticity related to the authentic self of Rousseau and Marx, the romantic roots of both "getting loose" and democracy. Community gardens in this sense create roots for socially conscious civic actors who can take control of their community's well-being and take responsibility for their own lives as well.[38]

Because many Puerto Ricans, African Americans, and Caribbean Americans have taken a leadership role in community gardens, ethnic identity emerged as another important kind of authenticity. The strong ties of the gardeners' common origins gave their gardens life and opened the way to using public space to express ethnic identity. But with immigration and gentrification continuing to change local demographics, this form of authenticity is hard to maintain. Community gardens need to create roots for all newcomers and develop an organizational structure that survives any single group.

If community gardens can get funding from the state and foundations and build an organization that connects to public policies of sustainable development, they will have a good chance of survival. To do this, though, they must develop yet another kind of authenticity that goes beyond ethnic identity, environmental stewardship, and sweat equity to create permanent legal roots: a new form of collective entitlement between public and private ownership. The gardeners could learn from community-based organizations such as Harlem's Abyssinian Development Corporation and East Brooklyn Congregations, which develop housing in low- and middle-income neighborhoods in partnership with state agencies and private developers; Business Improvement Districts such as the Union Square Partnership, which manage shopping streets and public parks; and nonprofit trade associations, such as the Red Hook Food Vendors Association, a group of small business owners who formed a partnership of sorts with a city government agency. Each of these models uses the legal form of a nonprofit organization to carry out public duties in common space; no organization legally owns the space it manages, but each represents the public interests of a community. In any case, keeping the gardens "sustainable for many generations into the future," as Edie Stone of Green Thumb says, requires the government to favor the yearning for roots of the urban village over the corporate city's pressures for mobility.

In the present political climate elected officials try to balance the "sustainability" of the urban village and the visible signs of growth represented by the corporate city. On one side, growing healthy food in community gardens and making it available in local farmers' markets nurtures the people who live in the urban village. On the other side, electronic signs, chain stores, sidewalk cafés, and giant billboards dramatize the corporate city's allure. It's not clear, though, whether this balance will work. The continued urge to build a "destination culture" destroys city dwellers' ability to put down roots—and fails to restore the city's soul.

Conclusion

Destination Culture and the
Crisis of Authenticity

Do the dedicated yearners who would roll back this tide
look fondly on the charred South Bronx of the eighties?
Would they stick by the most depressed and derelict expanses
of Brooklyn, or the cracked-out squats around Tompkins
Square Park, or the blocks of boarded-up windows in
Harlem? *That* New York was not authentic or quaint; it was
miserable and dangerous.
—Justin Davidson, *New York* magazine, September 7, 2008

When Jane Jacobs wrote *The Death and Life of Great American Cities* in
1960, death was all too evident around her. New York City's port was shut-
ting down, factories and neighborhoods hadn't altered their look since
the beginning of the century, and middle-class families were fleeing from
declining public services and expanding dark ghettos to the suburbs. The
city, it was clear, lay in the grip of two malevolent forces, government and
developers, though Jacobs directed her ire at architects and bureaucrats,
whose plans, she said, destroyed lively neighborhoods and extinguished
all sparks of social life. In Jacobs's view the monolithic office towers, large

public housing projects, intrusive highways, and monumental cultural centers that marked postwar cities brought on a "great blight of dullness" and reduced residents to passive pawns. Followed to a logical extreme, these were not plans for growth; they were a design for catastrophe. The city's life, on the other hand, required preserving the old streets, buildings, and blocks that seemed so old-fashioned, for these sustained the delicate fabric of social uses and cultural meanings that wove people together. On this authenticity the city's future would depend.[1]

"Authenticity" was not a word in Jacobs's vocabulary. She talked instead about density and diversity, about "character and liveliness," and how to "avoid the ravages of apathetic and helpless neighborhoods." For the most part, she advocated resisting overscale development and permitting good design of urban spaces to encourage community involvement. It is not clear that following her suggestions would have allowed cities to avoid the lack of investment in public institutions and the miscarriage of racial and social equality that depressed so many neighborhoods in the next generation. By now, though, we have enough critical distance from those neighborhoods to see them as "authentic," and we can use our Jacobs-influenced vision to transform their authenticity into equity for all. We already use the streets and buildings to create a physical fiction of our common origins; now we need to tap deeper into the aesthetic of new beginnings that inspires our emotions. Authenticity refers to the *look* and *feel* of a place as well as the social connectedness that place inspires. But the sense that a neighborhood is true to its origins and allows a real community to form reflects more about us and our sensibilities than about any city block.

Yearning for authenticity reflects the separation between our experience of space and our sense of self that is so much a part of modern mentalities. Though we think authenticity refers to a neighborhood's innate qualities, it really expresses our own anxieties about how places change. The idea of authenticity is important because it connects our individual yearning to root ourselves in a singular time and place to a cosmic grasp of larger social forces that remake our world from many small and often invisible actions. To speak of authenticity means that we are aware of a changing technology of power that erodes one landscape of meaning and feeling and replaces it with another.

When the cultural theorist Walter Benjamin wrote in the 1930s about "the work of art in an age of mechanical reproduction," he pointed to a dramatic change in visual technologies of power that took place during his lifetime. Benjamin asked how we can make sense of unique and original creations when we also have them available in the photographs of glossy magazines, on postcards, and in movies. Does the new technology of Hollywood destroy the aura of the *Winged Venus* and *Mona Lisa?* What meaning can an original have when we see it outside of the culture that made it? A century later, in a world filled with copies, clones, and outright fakes, his questions about the authentic work of art are even more important. And they apply not only to art but to all other forms of culture, including cities.[2]

If we feel that cities have changed in the renewal and revitalization since Jane Jacobs's time, and in these processes have lost their authenticity, we are reacting to more than just a measurable change in the built environment: a larger than usual number of buildings torn down, replaced, and renovated beyond recognition. Quantitative has morphed into qualitative change, for both our visual and our emotional experience of the city have been altered. This isn't just a structural shift from an industrial to a postindustrial society or the result of a periodic boom in investment and construction. We are eyewitnesses to a paradigm shift from a city of production to a city of consumption, and from a resigned acceptance of decline to a surprising disillusionment with growth. We see skyscrapers in which work becomes invisible despite transparent glass façades; districts such as SoHo or the Northside in Williamsburg, where the city's business of media, tourism, and entertainment takes place; and chain stores and boutiques where squat factories and abandoned houses once stood. We also see the upscaling of areas like the East Village and Harlem that had become poorer, been abandoned, and lain derelict for years, reflecting a return of capital investment to the dark ghetto, from one point of view, and forced removal of the poor or ethnic succession in reverse, from another.

Calling these changes "gentrification" minimizes and oversimplifies the collective investment that is at stake. A lot of organized effort has gone into shaping the transformations we see. Real estate developers, joint partnerships between the public and private sectors, and community organizations have turned gritty streets, old loft buildings, and former docklands to gold. But this shining city is so rich it stirs our unease. "I couldn't keep up with the rate of change," the writer and director Woody Allen says about New York from the 1970s to the present, echoing a common view about the city that he has often portrayed in films, "and the change was always the progression, really, of opulence." On a deeper level, though, to say that the city is no longer authentic reflects our inability to grasp the shifting meanings of space and time. If this is not the end of history, at least it is the end of place-bound cultures and local identities that we thought, mistakenly, would last forever.[3]

Intimations of change, and pressures for it, build up over many years. Though most American cities trace their origins to the industrial econ-omy and massive European immigration of the late nineteenth and early twentieth centuries, the new beginnings that we see today crept into view in the 1920s, were repressed by the Great Depression and World War II, and reemerged in force in the 1950s, in the last days of the urban village and the first days of the corporate city and the new urban middle class. This threshold period of the 1950s and 1960s was marked by both mas-sive urban renewal projects that tore the guts out of the "original" city of the early 1900s and stirrings of resistance to that forced march to progress by both old and new city dwellers. Not until the 1980s did these changes reach a tipping point, when hipsters, gentrifiers, creative retail entrepre-neurs, community gardeners, and new immigrants established niches that reshaped the urban experience in many ways, making the city as a whole cleaner, safer, more interesting, and more modern. Their actions, limited to the small scale of individual neighborhoods and blocks, were fleshed out by journalists and politicians who gave voice and image to their efforts and spread them first citywide and then around the world. Local trans-formations were shaped by different kinds of social and cultural capital that greased the wheels of larger political and economic forces: the rise of lifestyle media and blogs; zoning changes, policing strategies, and govern-ment subsidies; officials,' developers,' and investors' interest in supporting new construction.

Eventually the city as we knew it was gone. It became the corporate city of transnational headquarters, big-box stores, and Business Improvement Districts—the "business-class" city, as the architecture critic Herbert Mus-champ writes, that no longer "recognizes the difference between creating and consuming." Somehow, in the illusion of smoothing the jagged edges of uneven development, the city also lost its moral authority.[4]

In this process one group's interests and desires often opposed another's. Land, after all, is a finite resource, and the developer's mantra—*Location, location, location*—expresses the eternal competition to control it. Oppos-ing groups found common ground, though, in reinventing the city, turn-ing its pervasive image of decay into an emotionally and aesthetically satisfying, and sometimes even cool and glamorous, lifestyle. What drove a wedge between them was the material means and symbolic language that made this new image possible, a wave of capital investment that bid up rents and the rapid growth of consumer culture. Each of these, in its own way, embodied the neoliberal thrust of the market economy since the 1980s and its global coordination by transnational investors, developers, and marketers. Together capital investment and consumer culture encouraged both city governments and city dwellers to think they could have it all: a postindustrial revolution with no human costs, both a corporate city and a new urban village.

We experience the conflict between the corporate city and the urban village as a crisis of authenticity. To understand the loss of the city that matters it is important that we take a close look at both historical origins in economic and demographic changes and new beginnings in cultural representations, especially media images and elected officials' rhetoric of growth. It is also crucial to look at the tastes and lifestyles of the upper middle class, for these dominate the cultural representations of cities today.

At the start of the threshold period, in the 1950s, the economic base of the old urban village was dying. Most manufacturers of heavy goods were migrating to the West Coast, lured by tax laws and federal government support for national highways as well as by an emerging market of new consumers who were themselves migrating from the East and Midwest. Smaller manufacturers were moving to the suburbs or rural areas, where land was for sale at reasonable prices, wages for even skilled workers were lower than in the city, and employees tended to be more obedient to authority. Factory owners and investors were also tired of dealing with city government's bureaucracy and political Machine, aging streets and buildings, and traffic congestion. Moreover voters outside the city often subsidized the costs of opening plants and changed zoning laws to suit them. New industries didn't think about locating inside cities because they needed large amounts of open floor space; they formed their own new clusters, sometimes around the transportation hubs of airports or highway interchanges or around universities. With jobs already gone or drying up, the urban village of white, Latino, and African American workers lost its livelihood.

Its culture survived in the streets where people continued to live and shop and in popular dramas, television shows, and movies. Even today the urban village is familiar to anyone who has watched Jackie Gleason and Art Carney in old episodes of *The Honeymooners* (1950s–1960s) or seen Spike Lee's films *Do the Right Thing* (1989) and *Crooklyn* (1994). This is a vibrant culture. When the theaters of social life are the home and the block, passions run deep over who owns every crack in the sidewalk. Housing—mostly in small tenement apartments and modest, single-family homes—is poor, but everyone is well fed, and married children tend to settle down close to their parents. The strong ties between people are both a form of repression and a source of pride, half *Goodfellas* and half *Everybody Loves Raymond*. Without new jobs, though, and without fresh investment in housing, these working-class neighborhoods become rundown and are stigmatized as "blighted." Powerful people in the city see them as a deviant space, looking down on their mean streets as on a slum. The strong web of reciprocity among residents is regarded as a trap even by those who grow up there and now yearn for respectability. Outsiders often blame the bad reputation of such a neighborhood on residents' lack of organization, but its "problem," says the sociologist William Foote Whyte, who studied the Italian working-class North End of Boston at the end of the 1930s, is not that the neighborhood is disorganized, but that its own kind of organization—intensely family-oriented, suspicious of outsiders, and distrustful of achievement—fails "to mesh with the structure of the society around it."[5]

Redeveloping these old neighborhoods in the 1950s was only a small part of the nearly worldwide campaign to modernize cities by driving out factories, ports, and wholesale food markets and expanding financial and government districts. Though cities with the biggest financial players and strongest base of national elites—New York, London, and Paris—created redevelopment projects on the largest scale, smaller cities also eagerly tore down and remade their centers. "Visionary" urban planners who knew how to juggle the demands of federal bureaucracies and local business leaders removed the bars and low-rent rooming houses of each city's Skid Row and nearby working-class neighborhoods, replacing them with office towers, hotels, apartment houses for the middle class, and other prestige-bearing projects. They built urban extensions—and the ubiquitous interchange—to the expanding national highway system. Some urban renewal money even paid for renovating "historic" tenements for tenants who would pay higher rents and built new housing for the teaching staffs of private universities.

Elected officials in different cities marched to the same drum. Though they didn't admit it, the urban sociologist Herbert Gans, who studied the demise of Boston's Italian West End in the 1950s, suggests that they were chiefly motivated by the desire to attract affluent residents who would pay higher rents and spend more money in downtown stores. Partly officials wanted to clear out the ethnic neighborhoods that had grown so close to downtown financial districts that they threatened to overrun them. But officials were also desperate to compensate for the city's declining tax base, which reflected in Boston, as elsewhere, decades of movement out of the city by both old manufacturing firms and high-income residents and the gradual loss of appeal of shopping in the downtown core. Politicians wanted to please local real estate developers by subsidizing the cost of acquiring inner-city land and providing incentives to start new construction. Caught up in the universal desire for growth, for visible signs of progress that would attract new investment, and for money to finance the police and firefighters, public schools, streets, and all the other things that local governments provide, mayors and city council members sealed the old neighborhoods' doom. The urban village had few powerful defenders, certainly not among mayors and urban planning czars such as Robert Moses, who proved to be adept at bridging the needs of federal government agencies and local real estate developers.[6]

Jane Jacobs saw the urban village on the cusp of these changes. By the time she moved to the West Village, though, many of the old Irish and Italian families had moved on, and the port that had provided them with a livelihood was finished. She also witnessed the changing of the political guard with the election, first, of a reformist mayor who ran against the Machine and got rid of Robert Moses, and then of another reformist mayor who opened the era of New York as "Fun City" and personified the ideal of New York as both a corporate and a cultural capital. In *Death and Life* Jacobs described cities on the threshold of these momentous changes, though she was unaware of both the influence she herself would have on responses to them and the impact of an intensified market economy.

The world has changed since Jacobs praised the small shopkeepers and stay-at-home housewives of Hudson Street and denounced Robert Moses for ruining neighborhoods with highways and big construction projects. Cities are different now. The decay—or "blight," as Moses and others called it— which seemed so overwhelming from the 1940s to the 1980s has itself been overwhelmed by new buildings, revitalized centers, and preservation and reuse of historic landmarks. The word "slum" and its close relations, "inner city" and "ghetto," have vanished or been transformed either into brand names or into low-income or gentrified communities, terms with fewer negative connotations. Most surprising, the people who live in cities have changed. Though not all of them are suburbanites "returning" to the city, as some journalists predicted in the 1980s, and though not all cities have benefited from this reverse migration, many more young people, especially those with college, professional, and art school degrees, are moving into cities now, and new immigrants from every region of the world are shoring up their economic and cultural base. To the city's origins in the uneven development of rich and poor neighborhoods, with longtime conflicts between power holders and urban villagers, the recent changes have added unexpected new beginnings. They have turned the city's image from a fearful place that many fled in Jacobs's and Moses's time into a destination culture.[7]

Only one of New York's "best neighborhoods," according to a recent issue of *Time Out New York,* a magazine that reaches out to readers in their twenties and thirties, gets good scores because of its affordability, while the others rate high because of their aesthetics: architecture, design, shopping, food, bar scene, arts community, and new immigrant diversity.[8] This palette of urban highlights reflects the new beginnings of old neighborhoods such as Williamsburg, Harlem, and the East Village, as well as the new attractions of consumer culture along Houston Street, in Red Hook, and at Union Square. The idea of what makes a good neighborhood also reflects Jane Jacobs's influence on the way we see the physical landscape. Mixing old and new buildings, limiting the scale of many streets, assuring a diversity of uses that attracts people 24/7: these are the building blocks of the vibrant city that Jacobs proposed. Most of all, though, Jacobs's elegant description of interdependence and social control, the ballet of the street, created an ideal to which many new city dwellers aspire.

But Jacobs romanticized social conditions that were already becoming obsolete when she wrote about them in 1960. In the years that followed, second-generation immigrant shopkeepers were replaced by chain stores; housewives who had time to look out the window to see what was happening in the street entered or returned to the workforce. A mix of machine shops and small factories, butcher shops and dry cleaners, and homeowners and tenants was crushed first by old residents moving out, businesses failing to meet competition, and landlords abandoning low-rent properties, and then by new waves of boutiques, condos, high-rise development, and gentrifiers. Underneath it all, the rootedness that connects people to place was made weak by new forms of mobility: police officers who had walked a daily beat would occasionally drive by in a patrol car; children who had walked to neighborhood public schools would disperse to charter schools and private schools outside the district or take the school bus and avoid the street altogether. Giant billboards and pervasive advertisements urged passersby to drop their old buying habits in neighborhood shops and choose new products of giant corporations that they could find in branded stores. Local roots would finally be destroyed when the state eliminated the social safety net of rent controls, and real estate investors and developers replaced low-cost housing with expensive luxury apartments.

Though Jacobs blamed urban planners for making neighborhoods into slums and building high-rise business centers and public housing projects that alienated their users, she was too smart a journalist, and too experienced a community activist, to ignore the forces that structured, and structure still, what is built and how: the force of money and state power. Jacobs preferred "gradual" to "cataclysmic" money, believing that small amounts of residents' savings invested in individual houses will save a neighborhood from decline; dramatic infusions of capital investment, especially in state-funded urban renewal projects, will destroy both residents' homes and the fine-grained texture of neighborhood life. She didn't realize then, or acknowledge later, that gradual investments by highly educated, higher income people like herself might, over time, grease the wheels of developers' high-stakes, large-scale projects, even without concerted planning by the state. Neither did she blame developers, except for Robert Moses, the public sector entrepreneur, when it is they rather than the planners who work for them whose financial priorities move investment capital around. The sociologists John Logan and Harvey Molotch said it best: city dwellers want to enjoy the use-values of their communities and homes, but developers are interested in maximizing exchange values—in making money.[9]

Despite her good intentions, Jacobs's ideal vision of urban life has shaped two important vehicles that enable developers to pursue their goals: elected officials' rhetoric of growth and media representations of cultural consumption. Skeptics may scoff that these are only words and images; both together and alone, they lack the power to make material changes in the city's built environment. These words and images, though, create a language that embodies our desire for a good place to live. In time this language persuades us, or just confirms our belief, that the good life depends on building more cultural attractions to draw tourists to the city, opening more new cafés and boutiques, and restoring more old houses to elegance. These images of the urban good life camouflage a basic conflict. Dependent on both private developers to invest and build and voters to keep them in office, officials walk a fine line between promising support for affordable housing that will help to preserve communities and redevelopment projects that will change them.

For the past thirty years many big-city mayors have taken their cue from market-oriented administrations in national government and the unanticipated success of gentrification. Their priority was "making markets," as the entrepreneurial slogan puts it, rather than helping poor people and small businesses to stay in place or permitting local communities to veto developers' plans. If developers could build in a way that is environmentally sustainable and preserve the aesthetic qualities of old neighborhoods that still attract interest, so much the better, for both green construction and historic preservation have a high market value. Nonetheless these strategies leave little room for examining who gains and who loses from upscale redevelopment.

Media representations both drive and reflect this vision. In the old days of print media, when local newspapers and magazines thrived on paid subscriptions and advertisements, they needed a growing population. In our time, the age of multiple lifestyle magazines and countless websites and blogs, the media's hunger for content leads them to support the generic goal of growth as well as specific processes of revitalization. More often than not they support replacing poorer residents with richer ones who renovate houses and gardens, hiring famous architects to design spectacular buildings and opening more stores, restaurants, art museums, and themed districts, all of which provide them with things to write about. The media don't cause neighborhoods to be upscaled, but they capitalize on it. Alternately mourning, glorifying, and dramatizing the city's gritty past, the media help that image to recede into social obsolescence while recycling it into the aesthetic code of a new urban lifestyle. Loft dwellers and historic townhouse owners, hipsters and gentrifiers lay claim to the bricks and mortar of the historic city, while the media either romanticize or form a collective amnesia about who, and what, has been displaced. Both mainstream print media such as magazines and nontraditional new media such as blogs stimulate our appetite for consuming the local, the past, the edgy, the different—the cultural tastes for authenticity that take spatial form in loft living, hipster neighborhoods, and the new Harlem Renaissance but also support farmers' markets, community gardens, and the Latino food vendors of Red Hook.[10]

These tastes would not be so important if they did not exert pressure for changes in both the physical landscape and the social community. New owners who restore houses to architectural glory usually kick longtime tenants out of their small, low-rent apartments. Superwealthy homeowners replace middle-class gentrifiers. New boutiques displace cheap, often ethnic stores, disrupting longtime residents' means and sites of social interaction. Overall the tastes of new, mobile, upper-income and highly educated residents—including editors, writers, and bloggers—create a cultural climate where older, poorer residents feel unwelcome, if not downright threatened.

The media do not cause people to take these actions. Gentrifiers and new retail entrepreneurs respond to both their own needs and their perception of needs in their community. They would not become agents of change without necessary actions by the city government, starting with more dynamic—or more repressive—policing. They also require capital: high salaries in finance, media, and culture industries; bank loans, some provided by overseas institutions; and occasionally, as in Harlem, loans from publicly funded programs and charitable donations from the same investment banks that fell so swiftly in the recent global financial crisis. During the past thirty years, though, media images of cities and neighborhoods have forged an increasingly important connection between capital, state, and the new urban middle class, between the interests of investors, officials, and consumers. The sociologist Leslie Sklair calls culture the "glue" that connects state power and financial capital; it's clear that media images and consumer tastes anchor today's technology of power in our individual yearnings, persuading us that consuming the authentic city has everything to do with aesthetics and nothing to do with power.[11]

The new urban middle class has led the way to a form of consumption that is both motivational and aspirational and feeds into the political and economic motors of urban change. The motivational desire for a looser lifestyle of the late 1960s and 1970s, which we can picture as thrift-shop chic, joined dialectically with the aspirational desire for "authentic" goods of the 1980s and 1990s, such as brownstone townhouses and lofts, to produce a widespread model of how to consume the city's authenticity. Call it the New York model, for this city's neighborhoods and institutions, starting with SoHo and BIDs, have created some of the world's most influential examples.

Consumption is the key element. Consumer culture has helped many men and women to make their peace with the city, and it has pacified spaces in the city to prepare them for growth. The cultural synthesis of the early twenty-first century offers boutique gourmet cheese stores side by side with mom-and-pop bodegas, farmers' markets and community gardens across the street from branches of Whole Foods, Latino food vendors and IKEA in the same neighborhood. If postwar mayors thought their cities could have it all, so too does the urban middle class. And in a curious way, this is where Jane Jacobs and Robert Moses find common ground: the journalist who saw the city through middle-class eyes and the autocrat who tried to rebuild the city for middle-class tastes and incomes. Their opposing views converge in the desire to have both the high-rise and the interesting neighborhood, both origins and new beginnings; both Moses's desire to build a corporate city and Jacobs's desire to preserve the urban village.

The conflict between the combined legacies of Jane Jacobs and Robert Moses brings its own contradictions. While some who yearn for the urban village work in the corporate sector—and these include most gentrifiers— others, like the hipsters, see themselves as fleeing corporate conformity. This contradiction took geographic form in the split identity of the West and East Village during Jacobs's time: gentrifiers living on the West Side, near Jacobs, and Beat poets and bohemians, such as Allan Ginsberg, living on the East Side. Today conflict comes when groups representing the opposing visions claim the *same* space, not only in the conflict between housing and community gardens, but also in the conflict over authentic representations of neighborhoods like Red Hook, between old working-class homeowners, public housing project tenants, and gentrifiers between immigrant food vendors and big-box stores.

The technology of power that cities have put in place since the 1980s combines consumption and repression. The iron fist in the velvet glove—or the velvet fist in the iron glove—nourishes our desire for cultural goods while making places safe enough to consume them. Just as control over public spaces depends on both security guards and festivals, so the power of private organizations like Business Improvement Districts to remake the urban landscape is deeply entrenched in the city's consumer culture. The clean, safe spaces BIDs provide make it easier for us to go about our business as consumers while making it less risky to operate a company, raising commercial rents, and polishing the image of cities and neighborhoods. In recent years image has become an important part of the city branding process. Just as image helps to market individual buildings and places, so it also markets cities as, if not productive, at least creative, interesting, and attractive. The process of branding always merges developers' interests and consumers' desires with officials' rhetoric of growth; branding tries to make each city appear different from and better than the competition.

The result, though, when all cities pursue the same modern, creative image is not authenticity; it is an overbearing sameness, not too different—in a global view—from the "great blight of dullness" that Jacobs despised. New York City and Sydney, Australia, both have an iconic structure—a statue and an opera house—in their harbor. New York had the skyscrapers of the World Trade Center and will have Freedom Tower; a half-dozen Asian cities have already built or are building taller towers. In the 1960s France created the Centre Pompidou for modern art in the rundown Beaubourg area of Paris partly in response to the postwar success of the Museum of Modern Art in New York City; twenty years later the Basque regional government in Spain built another museum of modern art, Guggenheim Bilbao, in a rundown industrial district in the city of Bilbao, partly because of the Beaubourg's success in restoring a glow to the image of Paris as a cultural capital. Many cities copy the look and name of trendy New York neighborhoods—with SoHo in Lower Manhattan spawning SoMa in San Francisco, SoWa in Boston, NoMa in Washington, D.C., and SoHo in Hong Kong—and New York–style lofts gracing downtowns from Manhattan to Moscow.

These elements of sameness do not just speak to a universal yearning for cappuccino culture, the status symbols of the new urban middle class. They embody consumers' strivings for the good life as well as cities' conscious use of culture to polish their image and jump-start investment. Cultural strategies of renewal make up an industrial policy for a new economic age, with city officials running on a fast-paced treadmill of global competition. New York competes with London not only to be the biggest global financial capital, but also, as former New York mayor Rudolph Giuliani once said, to be "the cultural capital of the world."

Competition at this level involves complex and largely unrelated procedures, beginning with decades of government deregulation of finance and moving on to art auctions that fetch record-breaking prices, nontraditional performances, and innovative bars. Smaller cities do not want to be excluded from these global games. If they can't build world-class museums or draw the action of big auctions, they all compete for a place on the global cultural circuit by developing art fairs, film festivals, and even parades in which painted fiberglass cows or bison or moose, depending on a city's chosen symbol, are installed on the streets as public art. Other repetitive events promote the creativity of local cultural industries. More than 150 cities, from New York to Rio de Janeiro, hold annual or semiannual fashion weeks, and design festivals for the furniture trade stretch from London to Ljubljana. Every city wants a "McGuggenheim." Keeping ahead of the competition is expensive, though, and officials complain when they realize that they can never do enough to maintain their city's lead. "We see ourselves as being in a competitive race with other cities from around the world," says Daniel Doctoroff, the former New York City deputy mayor for economic development, speaking to a meeting of high-level cultural administrators and CEOs. "Many of [them] are trying to copy us, whether deliberately, or in some cases, unintentionally.... They're stealing our cultural institutions. There's a Guggenheim all over the world now."[12]

Cultural competition is not the only way to explain the overwhelming force of homogenization in cities today. Jane Jacobs blamed the twentieth-century modernizers who worshipped progress and planned to rebuild the city with right angles and straight lines. Architects and urban planners developed the intellectual tools and aesthetic styles that resulted in homogenized superblocks and high-rise towers. From an economic point of view, the geographer David Harvey sees the homogenization of cities resulting from the actions of investors, who tend to withdraw capital from one area or type of investment and shift it to another in a concerted effort to maximize profits. If developers can make more money and have less political interference by building ranch homes in the suburbs, they'll do so, but when that becomes too difficult or costly, they'll switch to building loft apartments downtown. Concerted, for-profit development strategies were intensified by the overexpansion of global financial markets that began in the 1980s. The Asian economic crisis of 1997 and the subprime mortgage crisis of 2008 showed that this kind of financial homogenization can bring disaster, and the movement of private investment capital into New York City housing markets at that time inflicted unexpected pain. During the 1990s and the following decade private equity funds did not just target penthouse apartments and "trophy" buildings in Manhattan, pressing prices of less costly apartments to rise, but also purchased low-rent apartment houses in Brooklyn, the Bronx, and Queens. Many of these apartments were rent-stabilized, but, according to residents and housing advocates, the new owners tried to drive longtime tenants from their homes so they could increase rents on empty apartments to market rates. Between 1990 and 2007 New York City lost 30 percent of nearly 120,000 state-subsidized apartments, and in just four years, from 2003 to 2007, private funds bought 90,000 affordable apartments. This kind of ownership has homogenized the city in favor of what Woody Allen calls opulence.[13]

Like everyone else, investors, developers, and officials are also influenced by the flow of trendy strategies or "traveling ideas," as the urban planning researchers Malcolm Tait and Ole Jensen call them. These ideas may respond to investors' demands or specific conditions on the ground, or they may stir people's interest. When they are applied in one city after another, though, even with local variations, they lead to McGuggenization. Often developers choose a competitive response that copies what others are doing if that has proven to get media attention, politicians' support, or higher sale prices for the finished product, such as hiring Richard Meier or another star architect to design a new apartment house in a poor location, or asking Frank Gehry to design a sports stadium and then replacing his design with a cheaper building when financing disappears. Competitive strategies also travel because they are noticed by the media and promoted by business and professional groups that lobby for them in meetings with colleagues around the world. Responding to this blitz, groups in other cities take the same approach: building a Beaubourg or a Guggenheim Museum and using a Business Improvement District to revitalize—a traveling term in itself—the downtown. The net result is homogenization. Because it is notoriously difficult to come up with new ideas, the treadmill of competition condemns cities to keep on using the same strategies to outdo each other's achievements. It's aspirational production, with cities producing more modern art museums, arts festivals, hipster districts, and cafés because they want to look *different*.[14]

Like the market value of a rent-destabilized apartment, the value of these outposts of difference is nearly always calculated in financial terms. When the artists Christo and Jeanne-Claude installed hundreds of bright orange flags in Central Park in the middle of winter in 2005, New York City tourism officials estimated that four million visitors came to see *The Gates* and bought so many souvenirs to benefit local nonprofit arts and environmental organizations that they poured $250 million into the city's economy. For this reason the officials and the media judged the event to be a great success, though Central Park was already attracting more visitors than any other city park in the country. As colorful as the installation was, *The Gates* did not confirm New York's uniqueness. It was only one of many projects the artists have created around the world since the 1970s, wrapping huge swathes of fabric around notable sites such as Berlin's Reichstag and Sydney's Little Bay: their own transnational luxury brand. *The Gates* was a high-class variation on the Cow Parade, a temporary version of Guggenheim Bilbao, a way to place the Christo brand for a few weeks in New York City.

In a countercyclical offensive, the economic crisis that began with subprime mortgage lending has not deterred public officials from the dream of presenting these installations to tourists and residents as a means of confirming the city's distinction. "We've always understood that we have to encourage big, bold projects that set our city apart," said Mayor Michael Bloomberg, when he announced that another large-scale public art work, Olafur Eliasson's *New York City Waterfalls,* had created an inflow of $69 million in the summer of 2008. "This will be increasingly important while areas of our economy are struggling from the turmoil on Wall Street."[15]

These cultural strategies do bring one big benefit to elected officials: they suggest that all cities can be winners. Unlike old smokestacks and docks, they're clean. Like shopping centers and Business Improvement Districts, they make people feel safe. They create a sense of belonging. *The Gates,* the Guggenheim, and the Cow Parade, as Jean Baudrillard once wrote about the "Beaubourg effect," are a part of the "hypermarket of culture" that keeps people enthralled, "in a state of integrated mass." As a result, public art installations, modern art museums, and festivals have become a pervasive part of cities' toolkit to encourage entrepreneurial innovation and creativity, cleanse public spaces of visible signs of moral decay, and compete with other capitals of the symbolic economy of finance, media, and tourism. Together with hipster districts, ethnic tourist zones, and other cultural spaces, this toolkit of cultural strategies aims to reinvent authenticity.[16]

Reinventing authenticity begins with creating an image to connect an aesthetic view of origins and a social view of new beginnings. The new Harlem Renaissance connects the upscaling of an impoverished area of the city, long stigmatized by poverty and racial segregation, to a glorious cultural legacy. Hipster districts, on the other hand, connect trendy new cultural consumption to former netherworlds of tradition and transgression.

This image appeals to a mobile middle class in Europe as well
at least in areas of the city that are no longer seen as dange'
day a workers' quarter and red-light district, today a hap'
declares a large caption under a photograph of Vesterbro, a
in Copenhagen that seems a lot like Williamsburg, that was pu.
a recent issue of a Scandinavian airline's in-flight magazine. The article
presents Vesterbro's shift from gritty to trendy as the natural result of a
looser lifestyle: the neighborhood is "creative, laid back…with nothing
artificial about it." Residents are a diverse, multicultural mix, but familiar and family-friendly: "students, creative types, bohemians, immigrants,
returned expatriates and kids riding in bicycle wagons pulled by their
fathers." In a reversal of the old division of labor between women and men,
fathers take care of children while mothers manage trendy shops, and all
suggest an impression of leisure, "sit[ting] at cafés that sprawl out onto
the sidewalks, or brows[ing] through boutiques," though the immigrants
are likely cooking in the café's kitchen while the returned expatriates are
sitting at sidewalk tables drinking cappuccinos. These "creative types" are
guides to and role models of a new urban lifestyle, "providing a sneak preview of tomorrow's trends." In fact a sneak preview had already been provided by the travel and design magazine *Wallpaper,* a Discovery channel
for the global hipster set, which three years earlier declared Vesterbro to be
Copenhagen's hippest quarter.[17]

While these magazines carry Vesterbro's image into the discourse of
global culture, local cultural institutions connect the neighborhood's new
beginnings with its origins on the ground. The Copenhagen City Museum
offers walking tours of the area, with six different itineraries narrated by
"young writers and artists," available from the museum on individual
MP-3 players. "Get to know a local from Vesterbro," the official website of
the city's tourist bureau invites us. "With the 'sound-literary' storytelling
as your guide it feels like walking hand-in-hand with a local, showing the
way around." Each doorway on the route is a doorway into the past; each
house offers an overlay of individual lives and local character. "You can
easily imagine how people in the old days walked around in high hats,
that there was [a take-out sandwich shop] where today a bike workshop is
located, and that the storyteller's great-grandmother used to look out the
window that you are standing across from." For visitors who are too hip
to take the museum's walking tour, a two-day Vesterbro Festival features
eighty bands.[18]

A hundred years ago Vesterbro's biggest employer was the Carlsberg brewery. Today this redbrick urban fortress houses a museum of beer production. This is not so different from the transformation of old breweries, dairies, and warehouses into cultural centers in London, Amsterdam, Berlin, and Williamsburg. The Carlsberg *corporation* still makes beer. But since the 1960s, with beer consumption declining in Europe and growing in other areas of the world, the company has shut down breweries in its homeland and opened them in Africa and Asia. Carlsberg also pays for naming rights on the tallest observation tower on Sentosa Island, a new shopping, hotel, and entertainment development, in Singapore. Though the Carlsberg name, then, is a symbol of origins in Copenhagen, it's a symbol of Asia's new beginnings. It connects the globalization of cultural consumption in Vesterbro with the globalization of production elsewhere.

Neighborhoods that offer opportunities for cultural consumption also play an important role in cultural production. The interplay of production and consumption creates a distinctive *terroir* that nurtures specific forms of originality and innovation, which become a marketable brand for the district, its residents, and their products. The products are not necessarily manufactured there; the crucial fact is that they are conceived or designed there and identified with the lifestyle of the new middle class.

Despite the media buzz about these districts, the idea of urban *terroirs* is not really new. Just as the Latin Quarter of Paris and New York's Greenwich Village have served as models of creative districts for several centuries, so the new Bohemias of Williamsburg in Brooklyn, Hoxton in London, and central Shanghai near the Suzhou River are industrial districts for today's new economy. Not only are these neighborhoods incubators of new cultural products, styles, and trends, but they are also serious workplaces for graphic artists, fine artists, fashion designers, software designers, music producers, jewelry makers, metalworkers, and furniture builders. Artists and craftspeople seek spaces in these districts because they are built large and sturdy; their old wooden floors, solid walls, and lack of residential neighbors can take paint spatters, banging, and all-night work sessions. Local laws permit the noise of welding and smell of artists' paint and silkscreen printers' chemicals. Like more traditional forms of manufacturing, creative work leads to and benefits from clustering in special districts, whether or not these are recognized by a legal designation such as "artists' district." Creative clusters mobilize the social networks that are needed at every stage of the production process: getting commissions from firms in the mainstream economy, finding workers with specific skills for different projects, getting the work done, and forging collaborations for future jobs. Like SoHo in the 1970s, the East Village in the 1980s, and Williamsburg in the 1990s, a neighborhood's social networks support the local concentration of skills and talent. From an economic point of view, the bars, cafés, and boutiques that emerge in creative districts are important to production. They're like the office water cooler or coffee machine where colleagues and work mates gather, but unlike in an office, cafés and boutiques can so reinvent the character of a neighborhood that it becomes too expensive for the locals to live and work there.[19]

Unlike factory owners who in the early days of industry built workers' housing near the mill, media firms that hire creative producers have no interest in whether they can afford to live in the trendy neighborhoods where they have set up shop. They often hire artists, musicians, media producers, and fashion models as freelancers or for specific projects. Lacking a steady job and looking for their next gig, cultural workers are the "creative types" whom we see eating brunch in Vesterbro at 1 P.M. or tending bar in Williamsburg at 1 A.M. Their life as flexible workers creates a production of leisure and an image of idleness that stage authenticity, helping to make these neighborhoods a cultural destination.[20]

For the past few decades Destination Culture has offered a general model of a city's new beginnings in postindustrial production and leisure consumption. It suits real estate developers who seek to encourage the high value of urban land, especially in the center, by converting it to high-rent uses and appeals to a younger generation who trend toward an aesthetic rather than a political view of social life. Cities invest in different forms of Destination Culture, most often building spaces of consumption for shopping, museum hopping, or entertainment, but also building spaces of production such as artists' studios, live-work lofts, and cultural hubs. With media buzz and rising rents, these spaces shift the city, one neighborhood at a time, from traditional manufacturing to arts and crafts production, and then to cultural display, design, and consumption, testing the market for higher rents and creating "new" space for more intensive uses. Like *The Gates*, all forms of Destination Culture are judged according to their financial results. In the end upscale development triumphs over authenticity, whether that is the authenticity of origins or of new beginnings.

Destination Culture: SoHo, Greene Street, luxury chain stores in landmark district. Photograph by Richard Rosen.

SoHo's recent transformation illustrates the process. In the 1970s the legalization of loft living for artists in SoHo created a space of city-sponsored, though not publicly financed, cultural production. At that time nearly all street-level spaces, the neighborhood's storefronts and first-floor lofts, were used by small manufacturers and suppliers that catered to them. By 1980, a few years after the artists' district was formed, most of these spaces were still used by factories or factory suppliers, but almost as many housed art galleries. The district attracted an enormous amount of media attention in lifestyle magazines and art world journals and in "New York" movies as well. Foot traffic swelled. By 1990 art galleries dominated the storefronts, joined by new, individually owned boutiques and professional services, while manufacturing visibly waned. SoHo was now known as an artists' district, but it was also becoming an interesting place to shop for new art, trendy clothing, and fine imported cheese. By 2000 art galleries began to be outnumbered by boutiques, and chain stores of every sort planted themselves on Broadway, near the subway stations, as well as on the side streets. Only five years later, with rents dramatically rising, chain stores outnumbered boutiques two to one, a small number of art galleries remained, and factories had all but disappeared. An elderly landlord who bought a building on Broadway in 1966 and is now replacing one of his longtime tenants, a well-known modern dance company, with an expansion of Banana Republic, says of the rents that chain stores are willing to pay, "The sky's the limit, what they offer me."[21]

By 2005 SoHo was no longer an artists' district; it was an urban shopping mall. There were the low-price quasi-discount clothing stores such as H&M, the high-end designer fashion stores such as Chanel, and almost everything in between. For that matter, SoHo offered few brands of clothing, jewelry, or shoes that could not be found Uptown on Fifth or Madison Avenue or in most other big cities around the world. Though the city government's historic preservation laws prevented developers from destroying the physical fabric of the old cast-iron loft buildings, the local character that New Yorkers took to be "authentic"—the distinctive cultural meaning the neighborhood derived from use of the space for either manufacturing or art—was overwhelmed by the homogenizing force of new chain stores and multimillion-dollar lofts. It isn't possible to sustain this model through a long economic recession: manufacturers and artists produce things, chain stores do not.

In the 1970s no one expected artists' lofts in old factory buildings to become the "wienie," as Walt Disney called the attraction that lures customers to an amusement park, that would make SoHo a cultural destination. So compelling a vision of renewal did the artists' district become, though, that the same sequence of events—the conversion of unused or underpriced industrial buildings into live-work spaces for artists, with local government support, followed by the emergence of a market for cafés, boutiques, and bars developed by new cultural entrepreneurs, leading in turn to higher rents, chain stores, and luxury housing—became a model of Destination Culture, a model that soon spread to cities around the world. Hoxton, in the East End of London, offers another example, which is quickly summarized: "In the late 1980s," says *The Times* of London, Hoxton "was a derelict place, unaffected by the property boom. Artists marked it as their own and after a few years a community had developed and the area was slowly rejuvenated. There was a thriving creative scene incorporating a trendy nightlife, which attracted an influx of people, dramatically pushing up property prices and finally driving the impoverished art community out."[22]

By now the idea of the cultural hub has traveled from New York and London, to rapidly growing Shanghai. Some conditions in all three cities are similar. With Chinese political and business leaders supporting a market economy, rents in the urban center, coupled with lower wages for less skilled workers in distant regions, have driven factories out of the city, leaving their old buildings empty. Most have been torn down and replaced by expensive housing and offices for foreign corporations, overseas entrepreneurs, and wealthy business people. Local officials reflect pride in this sort of development, their rhetoric of growth expressing a nationalism and urban boosterism that even displaced low-income residents cannot resist. The officials aim to develop a global financial center that will successfully compete with the city's closest rivals, Beijing and Hong Kong, using projects constructed for World Expo 2010 and the skyline of the city itself, where seventy-story skyscrapers spring like mythical dragon's teeth. This doesn't sound so different from the rhetoric of growth in New York City. In China, though, local officials are directly involved in real estate development. They don't just change zoning laws; they direct development as planners, investors, and partners with private firms. In the 1990s Shanghai's local officials worked with a Hong Kong developer and his American architect in developing Xintiandi, a modern, upscale shopping district installed partly in old houses that, at the architect's instigation, had been saved from demolition by a historic district designation. Keeping a watchful eye on interest in the commercial reuse of old buildings, as well as on the cultural ambitions of their Asian rivals, Shanghai officials then encouraged the conversion of an old textile factory complex at 50 Moganshan Lu into artists' studios and galleries. Following British practice, the Shanghainese called the old factory a cultural hub.[23]

The hub began in an unplanned way, like artists' lofts in SoHo in the 1970s. In the first years of the twenty-first century the artist Xue Song moved into studio space in the vacant 1930s-era factory complex at 50 Moganshan Lu, near the Suzhou River, in central Shanghai. The factory was owned by Shangtex, a large textile and apparel holding company, which had recently moved to a new development zone on the Pudong side of the city, near the airport. The empty factory buildings that Shangtex left behind appealed to Xue Song and other artists, who not only knew about SoHo and Hoxton but also had heard of Factory 798, a complex of artists' studios and galleries that recently opened in Beijing. But local political officials and business leaders also knew about cultural districts and creative hubs, and they saw the site's potential for both creative production and upscale real estate development. Indeed, in Beijing Factory 798 was already generating media buzz and spurring the development of a hip district of galleries, cafés, and boutiques. Like artists, cultural entrepreneurs were eager to take advantage of the cheap rents and central location of the empty Shangtex plant.

Within a couple of years 50 Moganshan Lu drew artists from other parts of Asia as well as cultural entrepreneurs from Europe and the United States who opened galleries of contemporary Chinese art. In these raw, cement buildings people began to produce and display not only traditional landscape paintings and sculptures, but also self-conscious, avant-garde art that pictured Mao, the Red Guards, or a fat, communist bourgeoisie: images that until recently had been not only discouraged but banned by government and party leaders. This work was now a "wienie," a positive attraction, for foreign tourists and investors, who were prepared by the experience of SoHo to come to a gritty industrial district in Shanghai to "discover" new Chinese artists. The high prices paid for new Chinese art at auctions in Europe and the United States encouraged investors and officials to support the idea of artists' hubs, a traveling idea that joined art and power in any would-be global city.

As the hub's landlord, Shangtex became an eager patron of the arts. An image of creativity fit the company's branding strategy, which promotes Shangtex as an innovator for combining technology and fashion to produce new synthetic fibers for the clothing industry. The fledgling cultural hub also enjoyed the support of local party and government officials. In 2002 Shanghai's Municipal Economic Committee named the complex of twenty-one buildings an official industrial park; two years later this title was changed to "*art* industrial park."[24]

Spaces at 50 Moganshan Lu are occupied by a variety of creative concerns, from art galleries and graphic arts and design studios to architects' offices and facilities for TV and film production. The hub's own branding strategy explicitly borrows from New York, with the slogan "Suzhou creek/Soho/loft." Its website explains this slogan in the familiar terms of authenticity, for Suzhou, SoHo, and loft "embody that M50 [50 Moganshan Lu] is an integration of history, culture, art, vogue [fashion], and originality." This combination represents not just the appearance but the *experience* of authenticity: "The shabby factory buildings contain certain value, because the naked steel structure as well as the old brick walls and the mottled concrete make people feel the trueness and perfection of being existent." The cultural hub couldn't make a better connection between gritty origins and shiny new beginnings—the very basis of reinventing authentic urban places.[25]

As SoHo and Hoxton demonstrate, however, reinventing authenticity as Destination Culture destroys the original aura of the place. Supporting a cultural hub at 50 Moganshan Lu starts out well. It suits the ambition of local officials to preside over a financial and cultural capital, but it prevents them from doing there what they have done all over town: aggressively demolishing old buildings and districts and removing businesses and residents to make a cleaner, more modern, conspicuously global city. They have accomplished great things, including cleansing the Suzhou River of years of industrial pollution. But continued redevelopment around Moganshan Lu creates a financial hardship for artists even if the city government permits them to stay in the center. Rents are already too high; few artists can afford to live there, and some have moved their studios to the outskirts of the city, leaving the cultural hub to galleries and other commercial facilities. This suggests that, in Shanghai as in New York and London, reinventing a neighborhood's authenticity serves mainly to establish the market value of its buildings and location, even at the cost of preventing artists, residents, and small business owners from putting down roots. When an influential leader of the movement to make SoHo a historic landmark district in the 1970s was asked, years later, how she felt about the area's morphing into an urban shopping mall, she said, "That's the price of getting something saved. There's got to be money in it for someone."[26]

We still have this yearning kind of element, this urban feeling of being in the city and trying to survive.
—Lizzi Bougatsos, lead singer of Gang Gang Dance, quoted in *New York Times,* October 21, 2008

Changes in the city's habitus, its social and cultural environment, reflect the massive changes in ownership that have slowly built a corporate city around the core of an urban village. It's not just in artists' districts like SoHo or hipster districts like Williamsburg where you see these changes. Walk down any neighborhood shopping street: chain stores are filling prescriptions and selling groceries, bank branches are dispensing cash from ATMs, the multiplex is a giant black box, and the greasy-spoon diner has either been transformed into a cocktail bar or replaced by Starbucks. The comic writer Amy Sedaris is right to fear "that New York is turning into everywhere else and street names will eventually be replaced with corporations' names: Meet me on the corner of Johnson and Johnson, west of Procter and Gamble, take the Costco 1 train, switch at Bell South. I'll be in front of Mega Wal-Mart next to the Pfizer Museum." Since the 1990s the commerce of most neighborhoods has flowed through transnational firms instead of mom-and-pop stores, and though this has given some customers a better deal than they used to get from longtime landlords and merchants, it has changed the scale and character of urban life.[27]

This process has moved fastest in the original, *ur*-neighborhoods in the centers of cities, where the old urban village has been restored or rehabbed to conform to an "interesting" aesthetic vision, while losing the low-key, low-income, and low-status residents who gave it an authentic character. Walk around the remaining cobblestone streets; they are ghostly reminders of an *ur*-neighborhood's modest origins. It is hard not to sound nostalgic about these traces of the past when so many of them have been replaced by redbrick pavements and high-rise apartment houses of little character. It is harder to look at your own tastes as a contributing factor of these changes. But along with the power of capital and the state, our own tastes have shaped a habitus of lattes, Whole Foods, and designer jeans that has the cultural power to displace chicken shacks and dollar stores. Our tastes for consuming the city unconsciously confirm the official rhetoric of upscale growth.

Jane Jacobs seduced us with her vision of the urban village. Unlike her communitarian vision of social harmony, though, we have to go beyond the block to decide what kind of *city* we want. This should not be the city of Robert Moses, whose dictatorial ability to conceive and carry out big plans stirs nostalgia among today's power brokers. We need small-scale streets and shops, ethnic and working-class residents, and low rents that allow residents to put down roots in the heart of the city. Moses used federal government funds and local government power to give land to the cultural institutions of New York University and Lincoln Center that still provide jobs for artists and creative support staff today. The state failed, though, to provide stable long-term housing for these necessary, low- and middle-income workers. Jacobs didn't talk about housing prices, but affordable housing and low commercial rents are crucial to keeping the kinds of people and stores she liked in her neighborhood. Though she advocated a mix of new and old buildings that would keep rents low, she failed to see how maintaining the physical fabric of the old city, its loft buildings and four- and five-story townhouses, would create a precious commodity that few longtime residents and store owners could afford. This vulnerability to the displacing effects of growth is especially acute in "uncommon spaces" such as the East and West Village, in the heart of the original city.

Though *Time Out New York* applauds the Destination Culture of shopping, food, bar scenes, and arts communities that has developed in Manhattan and downtown Brooklyn, most of the magazine's readers have already moved away to neighborhoods in Queens, where rents are lower. Even there, though, the media buzz of magazines and the self-conscious prose of blogs have begun to celebrate authentic neighborhoods, such as "the REAL Astoria," as a post on Craigslist says. "It still has the family owned markets & delis, mom and pop shops, etc., that are now vanishing in NYC and being overtaken by these glass windowed behemoth condos. True pre-war buildings still exist, contrary to what they're building in Manhattan.... Tree-lined streets. Humility. Soul."[28]

This future was largely unknown when Jane Jacobs wrote about the city. But she lived long enough to see the long arm of redevelopment touch SoHo and Williamsburg and to understand the vulnerable charm of mom-and-pop stores. She didn't believe in government action, though, to save authentic places. To the end of her life she put no faith in zoning or any other plan that was imposed from outside a neighborhood. Her work cannot guide us to devise strategies for protecting residents and businesses that would break the great power of those who own, and those who can zone, the land.

Because authenticity begins as an aesthetic category, it appeals to cultural consumers, especially young people, today. But it also has a lot to do with economics and power. To claim that a neighborhood is authentic suggests that the group that makes the claim knows what to do with, how best to represent, its "authentic" character. Whether members of this group are rappers or gentrifiers, their ability to represent the streets gives them a right to claim power over them. This right, though, is often limited to preserving the *look* and the *experience* of authenticity rather than preserving the community that lives there.

Authenticity must be used to reshape the rights of ownership. Claiming authenticity can suggest a right to the city, a human right, that is cultivated by longtime residence, use, and habit. Just as icons—in the original, religious meaning of the word—derive their meaning from the rituals in which they are embedded, so do neighborhoods, buildings, and streets. If these built forms of culture were torn apart by the state in the 1950s and

1960s in the pursuit of progress or to help real estate developers buy cheap land, they are no longer embedded in the "fabric of tradition" that Walter Benjamin describes. If we appreciate them as authentic, we are speaking from a distance of space and time, where we no longer participate in the routines and rituals of their origins. But to appreciate their authenticity in terms of *social* origins requires respect, as the food blog Porkchop Express says, for the social classes and ethnic groups that have made these spaces authentic—and a politics that enables them, and their spiritual descendants, to stay in place. Zoning, limits on rent increases, government-backed mortgage guarantees for store owners, special privileges for start-up businesses and young apprentices that will maintain crafts and trades, street vending, and even gardening: these are the basic building blocks that can produce the neighborhood self-sufficiency Jane Jacobs prized.

Jacobs was wrong to distrust the capacity of state power to protect the city's authenticity. Neither in her time nor in ours, though, has the state been a good partner of communities, and certainly not of poor and working-class communities. The betrayal of community-based plans and values on the waterfront in Williamsburg and on 125th Street in Harlem does not build trust. Imposing expensive licensing requirements on the Red Hook food vendors and taking the land developed by community gardeners deny men and women with little money but a lot of energy the state's protection. The city government has accepted the use of inclusionary zoning to ensure a share of affordable apartments in new residential projects, where developers are willing to be persuaded by subsidies. But New York's political leaders have made no effort to halt the state legislature's elimination of rent controls, and they are too tightly allied with private developers, and too stymied by New York State's constitution, to try to establish new limits on their own. Neither has the city government supported the use of community benefits agreements, which would guarantee needed jobs and housing. In the few cases where developers have accepted such agreements public officials fail to enforce them. But without the power of state laws neighborhoods have no way to fight market forces that destroy community institutions.

What is required is to build the political will for this from the bottom up, and to build this resistance among a wide public of voters, including many in the middle class, may require a rhetoric that connects the social goal of rootedness and the economic goal of stable rents to the cultural power of authenticity. If mom-and-pop stores are more "authentic" than big-box chains, the state should mandate their inclusion in every new building project and in every shopping block. If the social life of the streets is truly important, the state should make sure that all the men and women who use the streets have affordable rents so they can continue to live in their neighborhood.

It was easier, at the end of the past century, to see the shards of both origins and new beginnings in urban decay. Though few city dwellers want to return to those years of abandoned houses and dangerous streets, reclaiming our origins in the small scale of old buildings, the low rents of working-class neighborhoods, and fewer corporate names would take us a long way toward regaining that era's strong sense of authenticity. But we cannot limit our efforts to buildings; we must reach a new understanding of the authentic city in terms of people. Authenticity is nearly always used as a lever of cultural power for a group to claim space and take it away from others without direct confrontation, with the help of the state and elected officials and the persuasion of the media and consumer culture. We can turn this lever in the direction of democracy, however, by creating new forms of public-private stewardship that give residents, workers, and small business owners, as well as buildings and districts, a right to put down roots and remain in place. This would strike a balance between a city's origins and its new beginnings; this would restore a city's soul.

Introduction. The City That Lost Its Soul

1. I have adapted "origins" and "new beginnings" from the distinction made by Edward Said in *Beginnings* (New York: Columbia University Press, 1985). For public discussions of "soul," see Sewell Chan, http://cityroom.blogs.nytimes.com/2007/10/04/has-new-york-lost-its-soul/, October 4, 2007 and "The Over-Successful City: The Struggle for the Character of New York City," a lecture by Kent Barwick, the president of the Municipal Art Society, at The New School, October 17, 2008.

2. Cover story, *Time,* March 24, 2008, pp. 52–54; James H. Gilmore and B. Joseph Pine II, *Authenticity: What Consumers Really Want* (Cambridge, MA: Harvard Business School Press, 2007); Walter Benjamin, *The Arcades Project,* trans. Howard Eiland and Kevin McLaughlin (Cambridge, MA: Harvard University Press, 1999) ; Jean Baudrillard, *The Consumer Society* (London: Sage, 1998).

3. John Hannigan, *Fantasy City: Pleasure and Profit in the Postmodern Metropolis* (London: Routledge, 1998). I first used "domestication by cappuccino" to describe the upgrading of Bryant Park in midtown Manhattan in *The Cultures of Cities* (Oxford: Blackwell, 1995).

4. I am using *terroir,* a term that usually refers to the specific combination of land, culture, and climate that produces distinctive foods and wines, to suggest that the distinctive character of urban neighborhoods is similarly produced by specific demographic, social, and cultural processes.

5. Miriam Greenberg, *Branding New York: How a City in Crisis Was Sold to the World* (New York: Routledge, 2008); Bernard Frieden and Lynne B. Sagalyn, *Downtown Inc.* (Cambridge, MA: MIT Press, 1989); Sharon Zukin, *Loft Living: Culture and Capital in Urban Change* (Baltimore: Johns Hopkins University Press, 1982); Lynne B. Sagalyn, *Times Square Roulette* (Cambridge, MA: MIT Press, 2001).

6. On the influence of surroundings on an audience's experience of authenticity, see David Grazian, *Blue Chicago: The Search for Authenticity in Urban Blues Clubs* (Chicago: University of Chicago Press, 2003). On the development of the city as a stage set, see M. Christine Boyer, *The City of Collective Memory* (Cambridge, MA: MIT Press, 1993).

7. These are the words of the *New York Times* reporter Clyde Haberman, moderating the panel discussion on "Has New York Lost Its Soul?," http://cityroom.blogs. nytimes.com/2007/10/04/has-new-york-lost-its-soul/, October 4, 2007.

8. E. B. White, *Here Is New York* (New York: Little Bookroom, 1999), p. 36.

9. Pierre Bourdieu, *Distinction: A Social Critique of the Judgement of Taste,* trans. Richard Nice (Cambridge, MA: Harvard University Press, 1984), p. 370; Loretta Lees, "Super-gentrification: The Case of Brooklyn Heights, New York City," *Urban Studies* 40, no. 12 (2003): 2487–509; Neil Smith, "New Globalism, New Urbanism: Gentrification as Global Urban Strategy," *Antipode* 34, no. 3 (2002): 440.

10. Edwin G. Burrows and Mike Wallace, *Gotham: A History of New York City to 1898* (New York: Oxford University Press, 1999), p. 695; Henry James, *The American Scene* (1907; Bloomington: Indiana University Press, 1968), p. 77. James also notes the disappearance of both his parents' house and the original home of the Metropolitan Museum of Art, "stately though scrappy, in a large eccentric house in West Fourteenth Street" (p. 190). Also see Max Page, *The Creative Destruction of Manhattan, 1900–1940* (Chicago: University of Chicago Press, 1999).

11. Robert Beauregard, *Voices of Decline: The Postwar Fate of American Cities* (Oxford: Blackwell, 1993); Robert A. Caro, *The Power Broker: Robert Moses and the Fall of New York* (New York: Vintage, 1974); Samuel Zipp, "Manhattan Projects: Cold War Urbanism in the Age of Urban Renewal (New York)," PhD dissertation, Yale University, 2006.

12. Herbert J. Gans, *The Urban Villagers* (New York: Free Press, 1962); Jane Jacobs, *The Death and Life of Great American Cities* (New York: Random House, 1961).

13. Suleiman Osman, "The Birth of Postmodern New York: Gentrification, Postindustrialization and Race in South Brooklyn, 1950–1980," PhD dissertation, Harvard University, 2006; Walter Firey, "Sentiment and Symbolism as Ecological Variables," *American Sociological Review* 10 (1945): 140–48. Jonathan Lethem's partly autobiographical novel *The Fortress of Solitude* (New York: Doubleday, 2003), based on growing up in Boerum Hill, Brooklyn, during the 1970s, gives a sharp sense of the mutual fear of white gentrifiers and black and Latino longtime residents, whom the gentrifiers gradually overwhelm and replace. Japonica Brown-Saracino finds a small but significant group of "social preservationists" who combine the social characteristics of

gentrifiers and the social goals of community preservationists. "Social Preservationists and the Quest for Authentic Community," *City and Community* 3, no. 2 (2004): 125–56.

14. The aesthetic and political complexity of gentrification in London in the 1970s is beautifully evoked by Patrick Wright in *On Living in an Old Country* (Oxford: Oxford University Press, 2009). Richard Florida, *The Rise of the Creative Class* (New York: Basic Books, 2002).

15. Other public sector administrators: notably, city planners Edward J. Logue in Boston, New Haven, and New York; Edmund Bacon in Philadelphia; and Austin Tobin, head of the Port Authority of New York and New Jersey, builder and owner of the World Trade Center. Villain: Marshall Berman, *All That Is Solid Melts into Air* (New York: Simon and Schuster, 1982), pp. 287–348. For a more favorable view, see Hilary Ballon and Kenneth T. Jackson, eds., *Robert Moses and the Modern City: The Transformation of New York* (New York: Norton, 2007).

16. Robert Fishman, "Revolt of the Urbs: Robert Moses and His Critics," in Ballon and Jackson, *Robert Moses and the Modern City*, pp. 122–29; Zukin, *Loft Living*; Anthony Flint, *Wrestling with Moses: How Jane Jacobs Took on New York's Master Builder and Transformed the American City* (New York: Random House, 2009).

17. White, *This Is New York*, pp. 48, 54.

18. Sam Binkley, *Getting Loose: Lifestyle Consumption in the 1970s* (Durham, NC: Duke University Press, 2007).

19. Brian J. Godfrey, *Neighborhoods in Transition: The Making of San Francisco's Ethnic and Nonconformist Communities* (Berkeley: University of California Press, 1988); Christopher Mele, *Selling the Lower East Side: Culture, Real Estate, and Resistance in New York City* (Minneapolis: University of Minnesota Press, 2000); Marvin J. Taylor, ed., *The Downtown Book: The New York Art Scene, 1974–1984* (Princeton, NJ: Princeton University Press, 2006). On Wicker Park in Chicago in the 1990s, see Richard Lloyd, *Neo-Bohemia: Art and Commerce in the Post-industrial City* (New York: Routledge, 2006).

20. Sharon Zukin, *Point of Purchase: How Shopping Changed American Culture* (New York: Routledge, 2004), pp. 182–86; Greenberg, *Branding New York*, pp. 71–96.

21. Herbert J. Gans, "Urban Vitality and the Fallacy of Physical Determinism," in *People and Plans: Essays on Urban Problems and Solutions* (1962; New York: Basic Books: 1968), pp. 25–33.

22. Hari Kunzru, "Market Forces," *The Guardian*, December 7, 2005, www.guardian.co.uk.

23. Sharon Zukin, Valerie Trujillo, Peter Frase, Danielle Jackson, Tim Recuber, and Abraham Walker, "New Retail Capital and Neighborhood Change: Boutiques and Gentrification in New York City," *City and Community* 8, no. 1 (2009): 47–64.

24. Lloyd, *Neo-Bohemia*; Jason Patch, "Ladies and Gentrification: New Stores, New Residents, and New Relations in Neighborhood Change," in *Gender in an Urban*

World, Research in Urban Sociology, 9, ed. J. DeSena (Amsterdam: Elsevier, JAI Press, 2008), pp. 103–26.

25. Zukin, *Point of Purchase,* p. 14; Mary Douglas, "In Defense of Shopping," and Daniel Miller, "Could Shopping Ever Really Matter?," in *The Shopping Experience,* ed. Pasi Falk and Colin Campbell (London: Sage, 1997), pp. 15–30, 31–55; Grazian, *Blue Chicago,* pp. 240–42.

26. Marshall Berman, *The Politics of Authenticity: Radical Individualism and the Emergence of Modern Society* (New York: Atheneum, 1970); Lionel Trilling, *Sincerity and Authenticity* (Cambridge, MA: Harvard University Press, 1972); Norbert Elias, *The Civilizing Process: The History of Manners* (1939), trans. Edmond Jephcott (New York: Urizen, 1978), pp. 22–29; Bourdieu, *Distinction,* p. 74; Theodor Adorno, *The Jargon of Authenticity* (1964), trans. Knut Tarnowski and Frederic Will (London: Routledge, 2003).

27. Jerrold Seigel, *Bohemian Paris* (New York: Viking, 1986); Robert Darnton, "Finding a Lost Prince of Bohemia," *New York Review of Books,* April 3, 2008, pp. 44–48.

28. Thorstein Veblen, *The Theory of the Leisure Class* (1899; New York: Oxford University Press, 2008); David Brooks, *Bobos in Paradise* (New York: Simon and Schuster, 2000), p. 83, emphasis added. Also see David Ley, "Artists, Aestheticization and the Field of Gentrification," *Urban Studies* 40 (2003): 2527–44; Mike Featherstone, "The Aestheticization of Everyday Life," in *Consumer Culture and Postmodernism* (London: Sage, 1991), pp. 65–82.

29. Gans, "Urban Vitality," p. 30; Mark Crinson, ed., *Urban Memory: History and Amnesia in the Modern City* (London: Routledge, 2005).

30. Kevin Fox Gotham, "The Secondary Circuit of Capital Reconsidered: Globalization and the U.S. Real Estate Sector," *American Journal of Sociology* 112, no. 1 (2006): 231–75.

31. Jacobs, *Death and Life,* p. 313. *Time-Life* and Rockefeller Foundation: Roger Montgomery, "Is There Still Life in *The Death and Life?*," *Journal of the American Planning Association* 64, no. 3 (1998): 1–7.

32. For a critical view of the New York City Planning Commission, see Tom Angotti, *New York for Sale: Community Planning Confronts Global Real Estate* (Cambridge, MA: MIT Press, 2009).

33. Amanda Burden (chairman, New York City Planning Commission), quoted in Janny Scott, "In a Still-Growing City, Some Neighborhoods Say Slow Down," *New York Times,* October 10, 2005; also Amanda Burden, "Jane Jacobs, Robert Moses, and City Planning Today," www.gothamgazette.com, November 6, 2006.

Chapter 1. How Brooklyn Became Cool

1. "Legal or illegal": Andrew Naymark, "The Evolution of North Brooklyn's Art Spaces," *Block,* April 11, 2006; also see Melena Ryzik, "Dark 2BR Loft? That's Code for

a Club," *New York Times*, March 26, 2006; Tom Breihan, "Portable Noise Pollution," *Village Voice*, June 20, 2006; Annie Fischer, "Brooklyn, a Place to Impress Strangers," *Village Voice*, April 29, 2008.

2. Lyle Rexer, "Brooklyn, Borough of Writers," *New York Times*, May 8, 1983; Alfred Kazin, *Walker in the City* (New York: Harcourt Brace, 1951); Benjamin Luke Marcus, "McCarren Pool," in *Robert Moses and the Modern City: The Transformation of New York*, ed. Hilary Ballon and Kenneth T. Jackson (New York: Norton, 2007), p. 146.

3. James Agee, *Brooklyn Is: Southeast of the Island: Travel Notes* (1939; New York: Fordham University Press, 2005); Suleiman Osman, "The Birth of Postmodern New York: Gentrification, Postindustrialization, and Race in South Brooklyn, 1950–1980," PhD dissertation, Harvard University, 2006.

4. Betty Smith, "Why Brooklyn Is That Way," *New York Times*, December 12, 1943.

5. Rexer, "Brooklyn, Borough of Writers." This 1983 interview with Paula Fox suggests a much more settled, optimistic view of gentrification than she depicted in her novel *Desperate Characters* (New York: Norton, 1970). See Osman, "Birth of Postmodern New York." By the 1980s Brooklyn Heights and Park Slope were gentrified and mainly white; Bedford-Stuyvesant and Fort Greene were declining and mainly black. On nearby Clinton Hill, see Lance Freeman, *There Goes the 'Hood: Views of Gentrification from the Ground Up* (Philadelphia: Temple University Press, 2006); on Boerum Hill, Jonathon Lethem, *The Fortress of Solitude* (New York: Doubleday, 2003).

6. Interview with Noah Baumbach by Philip Lopate on DVD of *The Squid and the Whale* (2005). Density of bars: www.freewilliamsburg.com/bars/index.html.

7. Ida Susser, *Norman Street: Poverty and Politics in an Urban Neighborhood* (New York: Oxford University Press, 1982); Winifred Curran, "'From the Frying Pan to the Oven': Gentrification and the Experience of Industrial Displacement in Williamsburg, Brooklyn," *Urban Studies* 44 (2007): 1427–40; also see interviews in *Made in Brooklyn*, a documentary film by Isabel Hill (1993). The city government did, however, support housing programs managed by community-based organizations, mainly Puerto Rican or Hasidic, on the Southside of Williamsburg. Nicole P. Marwell, *Bargaining for Brooklyn: Community Organizations in the Entrepreneurial City* (Chicago: University of Chicago Press, 2007).

8. Josh Barbanel, "Board Acts to Evict Artists Occupying Brooklyn Lofts," *New York Times*, December 21, 1985; Sharon Zukin, *Loft Living: Culture and Capital in Urban Change* (Baltimore: Johns Hopkins University Press, 1982).

9. "NYC's Artists-in-Residence," www.gothamist.com/archives/2006/10/30/nycs_creative_c.php; Mark Rose, "Brooklyn Unbound," *New York Press*, 1991, http://nervepool.net/ebinstro2.html, accessed March 2007; www.nycbloggers.com, August 2006. Because these blogs are self-registered by their proprietors, the numbers and locations are only approximate.

10. Holland Cotter, "Brooklyn-ness, a State of Mind and Artistic Identity in the Un-Chelsea," *New York Times*, April 16, 2004, emphasis added.

11. Marcus, "McCarren Pool"; "McCarren Park Pool Controversy," http://gothamist.com, May 25, 2006; www.mccarrenpark.com; http://thepoolparties.com.

12. Thaddeus Kromelis, "Galapagos," www.11211magazine.com, 1, no. 1 (2000); Rose, "Brooklyn Unbound"; Brad Gooch, "The New Bohemia: Portrait of an Artists' Colony in Brooklyn," *New York,* June 22, 1992, pp. 24–31; Jonathan Fineberg, catalogue essay in *Out of Town: The Williamsburg Paradigm,* Krannert Art Museum, University of Illinois, Urbana-Champaign, 1993.

13. This is the same "industrial district" dynamic that animates all geographical clusters of economic activity, including those based on the arts. See Richard Lloyd, *Neo-Bohemia: Art and Commerce in the Post-industrial City* (New York: Routledge, 2006); Elizabeth Currid, *The Warhol Economy: How Fashion, Art, and Music Drive New York City* (Princeton, NJ: Princeton University Press, 2007).

14. On the gradual growth of the artists' community, see the description of the documentary film *Brooklyn DIY* (2009) directed by Marcin Ramocki, at www.ramocki.net/brooklyndiy.html.

15. For a description of this raw aesthetic, see Kromelis, "Galapagos."

16. http://en.wikipedia.org/wiki/Ebon_Fisher—cite_ref-8; Melissa Rossi, "Where Do We Go after the Rave?," *Newsweek,* July 26, 1993, p. 58; also www.nervepool.net, accessed January 2007.

17. Kromelis, "Galapagos"; John Korduba, "Remembrance of Things Repast," www.11211magazine.com, 4, no. 3 (2004); www.galapagosartspace.com.

18. William Powhida, "Williamsburg Art Scene," http://www.billburg.com (2003).

19. Eric Asimov, "$25 and Under," *New York Times,* September 2, 1994; Jennifer Bleyer, "The Day When Back in the Day Ended," *New York Times,* June 19, 2005; Tara Bahrampour, "The Births of the Cool," *New York Times,* May 19, 2002; Joyce Ketterer, "L Café," www.11211magazine.com, 3, no. 1 (2002).

20. Greg Sargent, "Gentrification's Foamy First Wave," *New York,* May 10, 2006; Steve Hindy, cofounder, Brooklyn Brewery, personal communication, April 2007.

21. www.brooklynindustries.com; Lexy Funk, talk at Science, Industry, and Business Library, New York Public Library, February 2007; Peter Geoghegan, personal communication, June 2006.

22. Jason Patch, "The Embedded Landscape of Gentrification," *Visual Studies* 19 (2004): 169–86; Jay Walljasper and Daniel Kraker, "Hip Hot Spots: The 15 Hippest Places to Live," *Utne Reader,* November–December 1997, www.utne.com/issues/1999_84/view/948–1.html.

23. On film noir as a representation of the changing postwar city, see Edward Dimendberg, *Film Noir and the Spaces of Modernity* (Cambridge, MA: Harvard University Press, 2004).

24. Mary Procter and Bill Matuszeski, *Gritty Cities: A Second Look at Allentown, Bethlehem, Bridgeport, Hoboken, Lancaster, Norwich, Paterson, Reading, Trenton, Troy, Waterbury, Wilmington* (Philadelphia: Temple University Press, 1978), pp. 4–5.

25. Iver Peterson, "Economics and Changing Public Interest Turn Midwest into a Film-Making Center," *New York Times,* November 23, 1980; Ben A. Franklin, "Baltimore Celebrating Its New Leases on City Life," *New York Times,* July 1, 1980.

26. Sharon Conway, "The Urban Verbs: Still Waiting for That Big-Time Contract," *Washington Post,* February 19, 1979; Tom Shales, "Backyard Palms: How L.A. Sees Life," *Washington Post,* August 10, 1977.

27. Martin Gottlieb, "New York Area Has Not Been Left Behind," *New York Times,* March 25, 1984; Andrew L. Yarrow, "Tribeca: A Guide to Its Old Styles and Its New Life," *New York Times,* October 18, 1985; Kirk Johnson, "About Real Estate: A Census for SoHo and NoHo," *New York Times,* May 31, 1985, and "An Artists' Colony Is Emerging in Newark," *New York Times,* February 26, 1985; Michael deCourcy Hinds, "Manhattan's Fringes Getting 'Voguish,'" *New York Times,* June 21, 1987.

28. Catherine Fox, "Gritty West Chelsea Winning Over Art Set," *Atlanta Journal and Constitution,* December 6, 1998; Anna Minton, "London Property," *Financial Times,* September 29, 2000.

29. Shahn: Margarett Loke, "Helen Levitt, Who Froze New York Street Life on Film, Is Dead," *New York Times,* March 30, 2009; Cindy Martin, "From Grit to Glam," *Sunday Telegraph* (Sydney, Australia), October 24, 2004; Jeff Schlegel, "Neighborhood Wears Its Grit Well," *New York Times,* November 27, 2005; Josh Sens, "SoMa, San Francisco," *New York Times,* March 3, 2006; Corey Kilgannon, "In Hell's Basement," *New York Times,* May 20, 2007; Laurents: Ben Brantley, "Our Gangs," *New York Times,* March 20, 2009.

30. Paula J. Massood, *Black City Cinema: African American Urban Experiences in Film* (Philadelphia: Temple University Press, 2003), p. 128.

31. Street movies: James Sanders, *Celluloid Skyline: New York and the Movies* (New York: Knopf, 2003), pp. 161–82; Mos Def: James G. Spady, citing H. Samy Alim, "The Fluoroscope of Brooklyn Hiphop: Talib Kweli in Conversation," *Calaloo* 29, no. 3 (2006): 994. In the independently made movie *Straight Out of Brooklyn* (1991), the writer-director Matty Rich adapts the conventions of the street movie by using Red Hook Houses, a public housing project, as both a location and a metaphor, a strategy used with equally strong effect later in *Clockers* as well as in the first season of the television series *The Wire* (2002–3).

32. Murray Forman, *The 'Hood Comes First: Race, Space, and Place in Rap and Hip-Hop* (Middletown, CT: Wesleyan University Press, 2002), p. 179.

33. Instead of identifying gangsta rap with the authentic rootedness of the 'hood, Davarian L. Baldwin sees it as a desire for escape through upward social mobility. "Black Empires, White Desires: The Spatial Politics of Identity in the Age of Hip-Hop," in *That's the Joint! The Hip-Hop Studies Reader,* ed. Murray Forman and Mark Anthony Neal (New York: Routledge, 2004), p. 170.

34. Massood, *Black City Cinema,* p. 194.

35. Forman, *The 'Hood Comes First,* p. 328; Gooch, "The New Bohemia," p. 28.

36. See U.S. Census, 1970–2000. For a view of tensions caused by the whitening of Brooklyn, see Adam Sternbergh, "The What You Are Afraid Of," *New York,* June 2, 2008, www.nymag.com.

37. Sam Roberts, "New York City Losing Blacks, Census Shows," *New York Times,* April 3, 2006. Until the 1980s inner-city housing patterns throughout the United States showed higher income, native-born whites moving out to better neighborhoods or suburbs, while lower income ethnic minorities and immigrants moved in.

38. Named for Article 197a of the New York City charter, community-based plans may be drawn up by a local community board or a borough board, a borough president, the mayor, the City Planning Commission, or the Department of City Planning. If they are approved by the Planning Commission and adopted by the City Council, the plans do not require construction but are supposed "to guide future actions of city agencies," notably zoning changes, in these areas. New York City Department of City Planning, Community-Based Planning, www.nyc.gov/html/dcp/html/community_planning/197a.shtml. Jane Jacobs's letter, dated April 15, 2005, in www.thebrooklynrail.org/local/april05/jacobs.html. On the demise of Williamsburg's 197a plan and on limits to 197a plans in general, see Tom Angotti, *New York For Sale* (Cambridge, MA: MIT Press, 2008).

39. According to the policy of "inclusionary zoning," which has been used by local governments around the United States since the 1970s, the New York City government offers a bonus to developers, permitting them to build to a larger floor area ratio, if they permanently reserve a certain percentage of the floor space for "affordable" apartments: units that are rent-stabilized (with fixed annual rent increases) and rented to low-income households (who earn 80 percent or less of the "area median income") and moderate-income households (who earn 125 percent or less of the AMI). On the Williamsburg waterfront, in return for including the "affordable" units, developers who began construction before the law expired also receive 421A property tax exemptions for ten to fifteen years. Old Dutch Mustard Factory: "Williamsburg Developer 'Behooved' to Trash the Mustard," www.curbed.com, November 7, 2006; http://80metropolitan.com, April 2009.

40. Helen Klein, "Trader Joe's Bklyn Bound; Beep Touts Trendy Market's Arrival," *Brooklyn Graphic,* March 29, 2007, www.courierlife.net.

Chapter 2. Why Harlem Is Not a Ghetto

1. Gilbert Osofsky, *Harlem: The Making of a Ghetto* (New York: Harper & Row, 1963); "black cultural sublime": Henry Louis Gates Jr., "Harlem on Our Minds," *Critical Inquiry* 24, no. 1 (1997): 10.

2. Sharon Zukin et al., "New Retail Capital and Neighborhood Change: Boutiques and Gentrification in New York City," *City and Community* 8, no. 1 (2009): 47–64;

Joseph P. Fried, "Learning from the Experts, via Bill Clinton," *New York Times,* July 10, 2005; John Leland, "A New Harlem Gentry in Search of Its Latte," *New York Times,* August 7, 2003.

3. Interview with Nino Settepani, August 2006; "We are catalysts": Chester Higgins Jr., "Vision," *New York Times,* May 10, 2006; Trymaine Lee, "Harlem Pas de Deux," *New York Times,* February 17, 2008; "faggoty": John L. Jackson Jr., *Real Black: Adventures in Racial Sincerity* (Chicago: University of Chicago Press, 2005), pp. 53–54.

4. "Harlem Homecoming," www.hgtv.com, December 18, 2006.

5. Janny Scott, "Out of College, but Now Living in Urban Dorms," *New York Times,* July 13, 2006.

6. "Building Green in Harlem," www.dwell.com, February–June 2007; Marc Kristal, "Harlem Renaissance," *Dwell,* December 2004. For more stories like this, see Chris Smith, "Real E$tate 2000: Uptown Boomtown," *New York,* April 10, 2000; Dan Shaw, "Habitats/Harlem: The Path Uptown Was Paved with Pampers," *New York Times,* April 30, 2006; overseas see, Graeme Culliford, "Young, White Professionals Snap Up Harlem's Brownstones," www.telegraph.co.uk, May 20, 2006.

7. *State of New York City's Housing and Neighborhoods 2006,* Furman Center for Real Estate and Urban Policy, New York University Law School, http://furmancenter. nyu.edu/SOC2006.htm; David R. Jones, "Subsidized Housing," www.gothamgazette. com, March 30, 2006.

8. Beth J. Harpaz, "Harlem's Tourist Appeal Remains Strong Despite Change," www.usatoday.com/travel/news, December 20, 2007.

9. Gates, "Harlem on Our Minds," p. 12. In his book *Real Black,* the anthropologist John L. Jackson Jr., who has done ethnographic research in Harlem since the 1980s, contrasts external signs of racial "authenticity," such as dark skin, with a softer, more subjective performance of racial identity, tied to intention, that he calls "sincerity." In her study of gentrification, *Harlem between Heaven and Hell* (Minneapolis: University of Minnesota Press, 2002), the anthropologist Monique Taylor considers how authenticity is represented in Harlem by contrasting "market" (buying a house) and "membership" (being black) as alternative means of identification with the neighborhood.

10. "Crisis of definition": Paula Masood, "African American Aesthetics and the City: Picturing the Black Bourgeoisie in Harlem," draft chapter (2008). Masood argues that in the early 1900s visual images of black urban spaces such as Harlem in photographs and the first moving pictures were few and far between because the black middle class did not want to popularize pictures of the low life. Certainly cheap and borderline criminal amusements were widely available in black neighborhoods—both because they catered to working-class customers and recent urban migrants, especially single men, and because white working-class neighborhoods didn't want a mixed clientele in these sorts of places—very much like the concentration of illegal drug traffic in black neighborhoods in recent times. On halting of construction

projects: Sarah Ryley, "Harlem Is Losing a Bit of Its $oul: 125th St. Boom Goes Bust," www.nypost.com, April 5, 2009.

11. Kenneth B. Clark, *Dark Ghetto: Dilemmas of Social Power* (New York: Harper & Row, 1965), p. 27. Clark's title recalls W. E. B. Du Bois's use of the phrase "dark bodies" as both physical description and metaphor in *The Souls of Black Folk* (1904).

12. Authentically poor and black: The sociologist Mary Pattillo argues that race, that is, black residents, continues to be a defining characteristic of a ghetto, but poverty does not. Along with other researchers, she emphasizes that black middle-class neighborhoods even today are home to poor as well as upper-middle-income blacks and to established criminals as well as high-status politicians and professionals; they also tend to have historical concentrations of poverty, public housing projects, and bad public schools. When middle-class blacks move to a better neighborhood, moreover, white people leave, and the geographical concentration of blacks, including poor blacks, expands to include that area, with the result of enlarging the ghetto rather than permitting some to escape it. Mary Pattillo, "Extending the Boundaries and Definition of the Ghetto," *Ethnic and Racial Studies* 26 (2003): 1046–57.

13. Fred Ferretti, "Mr. Untouchable," *New York Times Magazine,* June 5, 1977, www.nytimes.com. Frank Lucas's career was later turned into the Hollywood film *American Gangster* (2007).

14. M. S. Handler, "75 Artists Urge Closing of Museum's 'Insulting' Harlem Exhibit," *New York Times,* January 23, 1969; Martin Arnold, "Paintings Defaced at Metropolitan; One a Rembrandt," *New York Times,* January 17, 1969.

15. Allon Schoener, "Introduction to the New Edition," in Schoener, ed., *Harlem On My Mind,* 2nd ed. (New York: Dell, 1979). Also see Michael Kimmelman, "Art View; Culture and Race: Still on America's Mind," *New York Times,* November 19, 1995.

16. James Baldwin, "Negroes Are Anti-Semitic Because They're Anti-White," *New York Times Magazine,* April 9, 1967; Jerald E. Podair, *The Strike That Changed New York: Blacks, Whites, and the Ocean Hill–Brownsville Crisis* (New Haven, CT: Yale University Press, 2003).

17. Michael Sterne, "In Last Decade, Leaders Say, Harlem's Dreams Have Died," *New York Times,* March 1, 1978.

18. Mark Jacobson, "The Return of Superfly," *New York,* August 7, 2000, www.nymag.com; Sterne, "In Last Decade."

19. For different views, focusing on the landlords' rationale, on the one hand, and the Federal Housing Administration's and city government agencies' responsibility, on the other, see George Sternlieb and Robert W. Burchell's study of Newark, *Residential Abandonment: The Tenement Landlord Revisited* (New Brunswick, NJ: Rutgers University, Center for Urban Policy Research, 1973) and Walter Thabit, *How East New York Became a Ghetto* (New York: New York University Press, 2003). Spike Lee's movie *Jungle Fever* (1991) features a powerful scene in which the main character, an

African American architect who lives in a brownstone on Strivers' Row, visits his brother, a crack addict, in a hellish den of drug users in an abandoned building.

20. See Richard Schaeffer and Neil Smith, "The Gentrification of Harlem?," *Annals of the Association of American Geographers* 76 (1986): 347–65. By contrast, whites did gentrify Manhattan's Upper West Side and Park Slope in Brooklyn, where Puerto Ricans and Italians lived, despite a riot between youth of both groups in Park Slope in 1973. At the same time, new Caribbean and Asian immigrants settled in lower-middle-class white and poor black neighborhoods, buying homes and anchoring stores and some public institutions. But immigrants were not as symbolically visible a group as white gentrifiers—at least, to members of the media, who often live in gentrifying neighborhoods. For interesting views of immigrant diversity in East Harlem at this time, see Russell Leigh Sharman, *The Tenants of East Harlem* (Berkeley: University of California Press, 2006).

21. Maggie Garb, "If You're Thinking of Living in West Central Harlem; Abandonment Down, Refurbishment Up," *New York Times*, June 21, 1998; Ronald Smothers, "On 125th Street, New Hopes for Harlem's Renewal," *New York Times*, June 11, 1986.

22. Bart Landry, *The New Black Middle Class* (Berkeley: University of California Press, 1987); Gates, "Harlem on My Mind," pp. 5–7; Maggie Garb, "If You're Thinking of Living in West Harlem; Brownstones in Manhattan, at a Discount," *New York Times*, February 25, 2001.

23. Gates, "Harlem on My Mind," p. 11.

24. Kareem Abdul-Jabbar with Raymond Obstfeld, *On the Shoulders of Giants: My Journey through the Harlem Renaissance* (New York: Simon and Schuster, 2007), pp. 28–42; Claude McKay, *Harlem: Negro Metropolis* (New York: E. P. Dutton, 1940); Lizabeth Cohen, *A Consumers' Republic: The Politics of Mass Consumption in Postwar America* (New York: Knopf, 2003), pp. 41–53. The internal stratification of African American neighborhoods—and of all ghettos—in the face of racial segregation is, of course, widely noted, from such classic studies as W. E. B. Du Bois's *The Philadelphia Negro* (1899), E. Franklin Frazier's *The Negro Family in Chicago* (1932), and St. Clair Drake and Horace Cayton's *Black Metropolis* (1945), to Mary Pattillo's *Black Picket Fences* (Chicago: University of Chicago Press, 1999) and *Black on the Block* (Chicago: University of Chicago Press, 2007).

25. Sterne, "In Last Decade"; Sharon Zukin, *The Cultures of Cities* (Oxford: Blackwell, 1995), pp. 230–47.

26. Paul Stoller, *Money Has No Smell: The Africanization of New York City* (Chicago: University of Chicago Press, 2002); Lily M. Hoffman, "Revalorizing the Inner City: Tourism and Regulation in Harlem," in *Cities and Visitors*, ed. Lily M. Hoffman, Susan S. Fainstein, and Dennis R. Judd (Malden, MA: Blackwell, 2003), pp. 91–112.

27. Zukin, *Cultures of Cities*, pp. 234, 235; Jennifer Lee, "From Civil Relations to Racial Conflict: Merchant-Customer Interaction in Urban America," *American*

Sociological Review 67 (2002): 77–98; Philip Kasinitz and Bruce Haynes, "The Fire at Freddy's," *Common Quest* 1 (1996): 24–34.

28. Michael Porter, ""The Competitive Advantage of the Inner City," *Harvard Business Review* 73, no. 3 (1995): 55–71; U.S. Department of Housing and Urban Development, *New Markets: The Untapped Retail Buying Power in America's Inner Cities* (Washington, DC, 1999). Joseph H. Holland's career is an outstanding example of the new generation of black entrepreneurs. The developer of The Lenox, a luxury apartment house at 129th Street and Lenox Avenue, Holland is a graduate of Cornell and Harvard Law School, ran for New York State attorney general in 1994, held the position of cochair of Governor Pataki's election campaign in that year, and was appointed New York State housing commissioner. One of his first entrepreneurial efforts in Harlem was to set up a shelter for homeless men whose residents were employed in a Ben & Jerry's ice cream store on 125th Street; he also lived in the shelter: "Despite a comfortable suburban upbringing in Hampton, Va., and Bronxville, N.Y., Mr. Holland has focused his energies on Harlem because he feels a 'spiritual calling' to live and work there" (*Crain's New York Business*, "Rising Stars under 40," 1991, www.newyorkbusiness-risingstars.com). Republicans: Curtis L. Taylor, "A Return to Harlem: GOP Club Will Reopen at Hotel Theresa," *Newsday*, August 28, 2002.

29. Steven Malanga, "Making Markets in Harlem: New York Shifts Harlem's Redevelopment Plan," *Crain's New York Business*, November 15, 1999.

30. Compstats from the 25th and 28th precincts, which include East and West 125th Street, show a 70 percent decrease in major crimes from murder and rape to grand larceny between 1990 and 2006; the Business Improvement District that was established in the early 1990s also employs security guards. "So to me": quoted in Lee, "From Civil Relations to Racial Conflict," p. 89.

31. Terry Pristin, "Harlem's Pathmark Anchors a Commercial Revival on 125th Street," *New York Times*, November 13, 1999; "nearly impossible": Sasha M. Pardy, "Updated: Flocking Downtown: Developers Increasingly Taking on Urban Infill," CoStar Group, www.costar.com/news, August 20, 2007.

32. President Clinton: Andrea Bernstein, "McCall and the Harlem International Trade Center Corp.," WNYC-FM News, October 15, 2002.

33. Rivka Gewirtz Little, "The New Harlem: Who's behind the Real Estate Gold Rush and Who's Fighting It?," *Village Voice*, September 18–24, 2002.

34. Zukin et al., "New Retail Capital and Neighborhood Change." These numbers come from a research project that I carried out with a group of PhD students at the City University Graduate Center and reflect an analysis of entries in Cole's Reverse Telephone Directories for 1990, 1995, and 2005 and first-hand observations by my coauthors in 2006. We defined "corporate" retail capital as publicly traded, franchised, or large local or translocal chains with considerable market share in New York City (e.g., Old Navy, HMV, Popeye's, Sleepy's). "Entrepreneurial" retail capital refers to small local chains or individually owned stores such as Settepani, with a recognizably

hip, chic, or trendy atmosphere, offering innovative or value-added products (e.g., designer furniture or clothing, gourmet food) and enjoying a buzz factor in promotion, including heavy press coverage and online presence. "Old-style" local capital refers to individually owned small businesses that served long-term residents prior to recent redevelopment (e.g., 8th Avenue Deli, African Hair Braiding). These changes hit Korean merchants as well as other store owners, dramatically reducing the number of Korean-owned stores in Central Harlem. Pyong Gap Min, *Ethnic Solidarity for Economic Survival: Korean Greengrocers in New York City* (New York: Russell Sage Foundation, 2008).

35. Nonetheless, Harlem's City Council members voted together as a bloc to approve the final plans in order to avoid political payback to any who voted differently. "The Main Street": in 2007 the American Planning Association named 125th Street one of ten "great streets" in the country, the only New York City street to make this list (www.planning.org/greatplaces/streets).

36. Frankie Edozien, Melissa Jane Kronfeld, and Andy Geller, "New-look Harlem Clears a Big Hurdle," *New York Post*, March 11, 2008.

37. www.harlemrecordshack.com; Timothy Williams, "Longtime Harlem Fixture Now Sells CDs on Street," *New York Times*, October 9, 2008; Kathianne Boniello and Catherine Nance, "Harlem Shuffle," *New York Post*, August 12, 2007; John Eligon, "An Old Record Shop May Fall Victim to Harlem's Success," *New York Times*, August 21, 2007.

38. "Change is inevitable": Gabriela Jara and Stephanie Shih, "Sale of Chunk of Harlem Land May Oust Businesses," *Columbia Daily Spectator*, September 21, 2007; hurled shouts: Edozien et al., "New-look Harlem."

39. Photos by Camilo José Vergara, 1977–2007, Harlem database, http://invinciblecities.camden.rutgers.edu. "Last cheap leases": Tommy Fernandez, "Harlem Land Grab Leaves Little Room for Bargains; Expecting Upscale Residential Growth, Businesses Rush to Set Up Shop," *Crain's New York Business*, February 2004.

40. Zukin et al., "New Retail Capital and Neighborhood Change." We chose fifteen restaurants, shops, cafés, and art galleries that had opened in Central Harlem since 2000 and got a lot of attention in major media, from *O* magazine and *Vogue* to *Black Enterprise*, the *New York Times*, and *New York* magazine, as well as on New York City television news programs and various lifestyle websites. My coauthors carried out interviews with nine owners and managers in spring and summer 2006 and researched six other businesses through the media. To protect our respondents' anonymity, I have changed their names and the identifying characteristics of their businesses, except where I use information published in the media or on websites.

41. "Empowerment Zone Lends $1 Million to National African Themed Internet and Catalog Retailer," http://beta.asoundstrategy.com/umez/?itemCategory=26087&siteid=26&priorId=0&CFID=351296&CFTOKEN=38922963, August 22, 2005.

42. Zukin et al., "New Retail Capital and Neighborhood Change."

43. Corina Zappia, "Liquid City: Wines to Welcome," www.villagevoice.com, February 18, 2005. The owners emphasize that wines from minority-owned vineyards are not the major part of the business.

44. For example, www.loft124.com, the website for a converted loft building, built in 1906 and renovated in 2007, on 124th Street, features photos of aesthetically impressive brownstone house façades, the Studio Museum gift shop, and an upscale shoe store display, to a jazz soundtrack; www.ellisoncondos.com, named for the author Ralph Ellison, mentions the Studio Museum alongside visual images of the signs from the Apollo and Sylvia's.

45. "Children's Express: Harlem Gets Its Groove Back, but at What Expense?," *New York Amsterdam News,* May 10, 2001; J. Zamgba Browne, "Harlem Housing Crunch Addressed at the Schomberg," *New York Amsterdam News,* July 11, 2002; Jamal E. Watson, "Gentrification: Black and White," *New York Amsterdam News,* July 17, 2003; Jamal E. Watson, "'Magic' Gentrification Squeezes Harlem Small Business," *New York Amsterdam News,* August 14, 2003; Laura McCandlish, "Selling a Deferred Strivers Row Dream," *New York Amsterdam News,* January 13–19, 2005; Curtis Sherrod, "Harlem Property Taxes through the Roof," *New York Amsterdam News,* November 24–30, 2005. Mainstream media, especially those with a sizable black readership, also occasionally covered residential displacement; see, for example, Michael Powell, "Harlem's New Rush: Booming Real Estate; Historic District Is Undergoing Transformation," *Washington Post,* March 13, 2005.

46. On an especially fraught discussion thread on www.brownstoner.com, about the gentrification of mixed-income black neighborhoods in Brooklyn, see Adam Sternbergh, "The What You Are Afraid Of: A Mischievous Online Bogeyman Is Haunting the Dreams of New Brooklyn," *New York,* May 25, 2008.

47. Thread about Harlem: http://curbed.com/archives/2007/03/30/harlem_heat_twofer_ellington_loft_124.php, March 30, 2007. All quotes and aliases are exactly as posted, and I have no idea who the writers of these posts really are, or even if some of them are real estate agents who want to excite interest in Harlem.

48. "Thinking of relocating": www.city-data.com/forum/new-york/80966-upper-middle-class-african-american-communities.html, May 12, 2007. All quotes and aliases are exactly as posted.

49. The drummers perform from afternoon to late at night in the summer, and several posts on Curbed.com complain about the noise; also see Margot Adler, "Drumming Up a Protest in a Harlem Park," *Weekend Edition Sunday,* National Public Radio, September 2, 2007; Timothy Williams, "An Old Sound in Harlem Draws New Neighbors' Ire," *New York Times,* July 6, 2008. "Status over convenience": Herbert J. Gans, "Urban Vitality and the Fallacy of Physical Determinism," in *People and Plans* (1962; New York: Basic Books, 1968), p. 30. In Harlem today "quality and convenience are, according to new [black] gentrifiers, inferior and inadequate" (Taylor, *Harlem between Heaven and Hell,* p. 123). For first-hand accounts of conflicts of interest

between new, middle-class, black residents and poorer, black, longtime residents in Harlem, see Taylor, *Harlem between Heaven and Hell*; Derek S. Hyra, *The New Urban Renewal: The Economic Transformation of Harlem and Bronzeville* (Chicago: University of Chicago Press, 2008). For similar conflicts in a black, gentrifying neighborhood in Chicago, see Pattillo, *Black on the Block*.

50. *Blacks See Growing Values Gap between Poor and Middle Class,* Pew Research Center, November 2007.

51. Charles B. Rangel, Foreword to *Harlem on My Mind,* ed. Allon Schoener, 3rd ed. (New York: New Press, 2007). For another view that Harlem's culinary history is not limited to southern soul food, see Damian M. Mosley, "Cooking Up Heritage in Harlem," in *Gastropolis: Food and New York City,* ed. Annie Hauck-Lawson and Jonathan Deutsch (New York: Columbia University Press, 2009), pp. 274–92.

Chapter 3. Living Local in the East Village

1. "Talk of the Town," *The New Yorker,* October 14, 1967, p. 49, on www.diggers.org/free_store.html; Paul Berger, "Witness to What Was, Skeptic of What's New," *New York Times,* October 28, 2007.

2. Hilly Kristal, "The History of CBGB and OMFUG," www.cbgb.com/history/history13.htm; Marvin J. Taylor, ed., *The Downtown Book: The New York Art Scene, 1974–1984* (Princeton, NJ: Princeton University Press, 2006).

3. Personal communication, February 2006.

4. Ian Altveer and Jennifer Sudul, "An Interview with Carlo McCormick," *The Downtown Show: The New York Art Scene, 1974–1984, Grey Gazette* 9, no. 1 (2006); gay artist: personal communication, February 2006.

5. Altveer and Sudul, "An Interview with Carlo McCormick."

6. Kevin Hetherington, "The Time of the Entrepreneurial City: Museum, Heritage and Kairos," in *Consuming the Entrepreneurial City: Image, Memory, Spectacle,* ed. Anne M. Cronin and Kevin Hetherington (New York: Routledge, 2007).

7. James H. Gilmore and B. Joe Pine II, *Authenticity: What Consumers Really Want* (Cambridge, MA: Harvard Business School Press, 2007).

8. Edwin G. Burrows and Mike Wallace, *Gotham* (New York: Oxford University Press, 1999), p. 762.

9. For an excellent history of the transformation of the East Village from the early 1900s to the 1980s, see Christopher Mele, *Selling the Lower East Side: Culture, Real Estate, and Resistance in New York City* (Minneapolis: University of Minnesota Press, 2000).

10. "Mobile awareness": Sam Binkley, *Getting Loose: Lifestyle Consumption in the 1970s* (Durham, NC: Duke University Press, 2007), p. 51.

11. Limits on residential rents were first imposed during the housing shortage of World War II, when many landlords were accused of raising rents to unaffordable levels. Rent control, the more severe system, prohibits landlords from raising rents without making improvements, and all rent rises must be approved by the New York State Division of Housing and Community Renewal; tenants in rent-controlled apartments cannot be removed. Rent stabilization, begun in the late 1960s, subjects rent increases to the decisions of a citywide, publicly and privately appointed board representing landlords and tenants; in practice, a stabilized rent is subject to increase every year or every other year when the lease is renewed, and, unlike tenants in rent-controlled apartments, tenants in rent-stabilized units can be removed under certain circumstances. Both types of tenants have the right to pass on their apartment to their companion or a family member. When a rent-regulated apartment is vacated, however, the rent is either "decontrolled" or "destabilized." Under constant attack by the real estate industry, rent regulation has been gradually phased out by the state legislature since the 1970s.

12. "Ukrainian soul food": www.veselka.com; history of the stores and of the block comes from interviews with store owners carried out by Ervin Kosta and published in Sharon Zukin and Ervin Kosta, "Bourdieu Off-Broadway: Managing Distinction on a Shopping Block in the East Village," *City and Community* 3, no. 2 (2004): 101–14. Although I use the stores' real names, I have given the owners pseudonyms.

13. For different views, see Neil Smith, *The New Urban Frontier: Gentrification and the Revanchist City* (New York: Routledge, 1996); Q. Sakamaki, *Tompkins Square Park* (New York: Powerhouse Books, 2008).

14. Maureen Dowd, "Youth, Art, Hype: A Different Bohemia," *New York Times Magazine,* November 17, 1985.

15. Claudia Strasser, *The Paris Apartment: Romantic Décor on a Flea Market Budget* (New York: HarperCollins, 1997); www.theparisapartment.com.

16. Residential rents listed in www.prudentialelliman.com, October 2007, February 2009. In addition to the difference between rent controlled and decontrolled apartments, rents for the rent-stabilized units in the building run from $535 to $1,500, but destabilized rents vary from $1,900 a month for a one-bedroom apartment on a low floor to $2,500 for the same size apartment higher up.

17. Commercial rents on this block run between $35 and $100 a square foot, or $3,500 to $10,000 a month; recent rises: Eric Marx, "East Village Store Rents Go North," http://ny.therealdeal.com, January 2007; CBGB: http://vanishingnewyork.blogspot.com, August 29, 2007; St. Marks Place: Lisa Chamberlain, "Square Feet/Manhattan; For the East Village, a New Retail Face," *New York Times,* January 30, 2005.

18. David Kamp, *The United States of Arugula: How We Became a Gourmet Nation* (New York: Broadway Books, 2006), p. 202; Priscilla Ferguson and Sharon Zukin, "The Careers of Chefs," in *Eating Culture,* ed. Ron Scapp and Brian Seitz (Albany: State University of New York Press, 1998), pp. 92–111.

19. "What Dean & Deluca did was give the food market a clean artistry that made it very now, very tied to the moment when SoHo was being noticed": Florence Fabricant, food journalist, *New York Times,* quoted in Kamp, *United States of Arugula,* p. 208. "Authenticity" defined in terms of European food: Shyon Baumann and Josée Johnston, *Foodies: Democracy and Distinction in the Gourmet Foodscape* (New York: Routledge, forthcoming), and in terms of freshness: Susanne Friedberg, *Fresh: A Perishable History* (Cambridge, MA: Harvard University Press, 2009).

20. "About saving a way of life": Peter Steinbreuk, the son of the "preservationist and architect" Victor Steinbreuk, who fought to save Pike Place Market, quoted in Kamp, *United States of Arugula,* p. 277; Starbucks: James Lyons, "'Think Seattle, Act Globally': Specialty Coffee, Commodity Biographies, and the Promotion of Place," *Cultural Studies* 19, no. 1 (2005): 14–34.

21. Suzanne Wasserman, "The Good Old Days of Poverty: Merchants and the Battle over Pushcart Peddling on the Lower East Side," www.h-net.org/ business/bhcweb/ publications/BEHprint/v027n2/p0330-p0339.pdf; "Mayor Bloomberg Presents Doris C. Freedman Award to Barry Benepe and Robert Lewis—Founders of the Greenmarket—on Its 30th Anniversary," http://home.nyc.gov, May 24, 2006.

22. Under the Greenmarket's rules, the principal farmers (who own the farms and grow or make the products that are sold at their stand) must come to each market where they sell at least once a month. In practice, many of the larger stands hire day workers from either the city or the country.

23. "Fresh means that it was still milk inside the goat just a few days ago. With vacuum packed, you don't know how old it is or where it has been. The label may tell you where a product originated—but how far did it travel? Not vacuum-packed means for us in the Catskill Region, *that it was produced just down the road, just over the river.*" Sally Fairbairn, "An Island of Optimism, A Real Farmscape," www. catskillmtn.org/publications/articles/2002–01-coach-farm.html, emphasis added. Also see Florence Fabricant, "Coach Farm Goats Have a New Cheesemaker," *New York Times,* March 14, 2007.

24. Michèle de la Pradelle, *Market Day in Provence,* trans. Amy Jacobs (Chicago: University of Chicago Press, 2006).

25. Hari Kunzru, "Market Forces," *The Guardian,* December 7, 2005, www.guardian. co.uk.

Chapter 4. Union Square and the Paradox of Public Space

1. The difference between the two organizations that manage Union Square is their geographical jurisdiction: the BID is responsible for Fourteenth Street between First and Sixth Avenues and the area around Union Square Park; the LDC is responsible

for the park-centered Union Square area, including Seventeenth and Eighteenth Streets, to the north of the park.

2. Developed under this name in New York City and State, BIDs are a special form of the tax-increment financing (TIF) districts that local governments in Canada and the United States began to use in the 1960s as a way of funding specific areas, especially in troubled downtown business districts, without raising taxes or devoting a disproportionate share of overall revenue. Similar self-financed districts have been put in place in several European countries as well as in Australia, South Africa, and Japan. See, for example, Kevin Ward, "'Policies in Motion,' Urban Restructuring and State Management: The Trans-local Expansion of Business Improvement Districts," *International Journal of Urban and Regional Research* 30, no. 1 (2006): 54–75; Malcolm Tait and Ole B. Jensen, "Travelling Ideas, Power and Place: The Cases of Urban Villages and Business Improvement Districts," *International Planning Studies* 12, no. 2 (2007): 107–28. Because of their high visibility, use of the media to promote their cause, inevitable association with the quality-of-life policing strategies publicized by the Giuliani administration, and deliberate international outreach, New York City BIDs have become the preeminent model of this form of organization in a period of worldwide pressure for privatization.

3. See Setha Low and Neil Smith, eds., *The Politics of Public Space* (New York: Routledge, 2006); Don Mitchell, *The Right to the City: Social Justice and the Fight for Public Space* (New York: Guilford, 2003); and Sharon Zukin, *The Cultures of Cities* (Oxford: Blackwell, 1995); also see Rosalyn Deutsche's aptly titled *Eviction: Art and Spatial Politics* (Cambridge, MA: MIT Press, 1996). Judges' rulings in various states from the 1940s on have tried to limit private owners' control over political demonstrations, boycotts, handing out of political leaflets, and other expressions of free speech in shopping malls, but there is neither a federal law nor a consistent state standard that determines whether shopping malls are, in this sense, public space.

4. This is a different genealogy of public space than we get from Jürgen Habermas, who traces the modern public sphere back to the gatherings of more elite groups (educated middle-class men) in a paid consumption space, the café. See Kevin Hetherington, *The Badlands of Modernity* (London: Routledge, 1997), pp. 1–19; Tony Bennett, *The Birth of the Museum* (London: Routledge, 1995); Roy Rosenzweig and Elizabeth Blackmar, *The Park and the People: A History of Central Park* (Ithaca, NY: Cornell University Press, 1992). Though today attention often focuses on racial and religious differences, struggles have been waged over every social group's right of access to "public" space, including, if we can imagine it, granting permission to use public libraries to children under the age of fourteen or sixteen a century ago.

5. Broken windows, turnstile jumpers: this refers to the theory, developed by the criminologist George Kelling in New Jersey around 1980 and made famous by New York City Mayor Rudolph Giuliani and Police Commissioner William Bratton in the 1990s, that the smallest signs of disorder and misbehavior will, if left uncorrected, lead

to widespread perceptions of decline and to worse behavior. "Distasteful...encounters": George L. Kelling and James Q. Wilson, "The Police and Neighborhood Safety: Broken Windows," *Atlantic Monthly,* March 1982, www.theatlantic.com/doc/198203/broken-windows. "Eyes on the street": Jane Jacobs, *The Death and Life of Great American Cities* (New York: Random House, 1961).

6. "Image crisis": Miriam Greenberg, *Branding New York: How a City in Crisis Was Sold to the World* (New York: Routledge, 2008).

7. Edwin G. Burrows and Mike Wallace, *Gotham: A History of New York City to 1898* (New York: Oxford University Press, 1999), pp. 577–78.

8. "Mass meetings": Union Square, New York City Department of Parks and Recreation, www.nycgovparks.org; "people's forum": "Recreation for All Planned by Stover," *New York Times,* February 15, 1910.

9. Burrows and Wallace, *Gotham,* p. 1120; M. Christine Boyer, *Manhattan Manners: Architecture and Style, 1850–1900* (New York: Rizzoli, 1985), p. 87; Donna Haverty-Stacke, *America's Forgotten Holiday: May Day and Nationalism, 1867–1960* (New York: New York University Press, 2008).

10. Ladies Mile:Boyer, *Manhattan Manners,* pp. 43–129; James Thurber, "Talk of the Town: Mob Scene," *The New Yorker,* October 26, 1929, p. 21.

11. Robert A. M. Stern, Thomas Mellins, and David Fishman, *New York 1960* (New York: Monacelli Press, 1995), pp. 245, 247.

12. Fourteenth Street's reputation: Robert W. Walsh, "Union Square Park: From Blight to Bloom," *Economic Development Journal,* spring 2006, pp. 39–46; Walsh was the Union Square Partnership's executive director in the 1990s.

13. Headlines: Walsh, "Union Square Park," p. 41.

14. Reinforcing the idea that the geographical divide between uptown and downtown also signals a cultural difference, many of these artistic downtown residents still claim they never travel "above Fourteenth Street." See Marvin J. Taylor, ed., *The Downtown Book: The New York Art Scene, 1974–1984* (Princeton, NJ: Princeton University Press, 2006).

15. Walsh, "Union Square Park," p. 39; farmers: personal communications, 2007–8; police officer: personal communication, July 2008; "coffee and a bagel": Iver Peterson, "Union Square: Gritty Past, Bright Future," *New York Times,* November 26, 1989.

16. Stern, Mellins, and Fishman, *New York 1960,* p. 247; steel gates: personal communication, December 2007.

17. Fragmented geography, "bringing...resources together": Walsh, "Union Square Park," p. 40.

18. Walsh, "Union Square Park," p. 41.

19. William H. Whyte, *The Social Life of Small Urban Spaces* (Washington, DC: Conservation Foundation, 1980).

20. Janet Allon, "Neighborhood Report: Union Square; New Manager Hits Pavement on 14th," *New York Times,* January 11, 1998.

21. Douglas Martin, "This Time, Parks Mean Business," *New York Times*, February 16, 1996.

22. "Imploding": personal communication, December 2005.

23. Eliot Brown, "Judge on Union Square Park: Renovations OK, but Hold Off on Restaurant," *New York Observer*, May 7, 2008; Anemona Hartocollis, "A Street Performer Crusades for the First Amendment," *New York Times*, September 26, 2007; http://washingtonsquarepark.wordpress.com/2008/06/05; "Union Square Pavilion Restaurant Gets Green Light from Judge," http://gothamist.com, March 31, 2009; also www.revbilly.com/ and video of his May 1 appearance in the park on www.youtube.com/watch?v=HUbUyDnxJQM.

24. Shadi Rahimi, "An Antiwar Speech in Union Square Is Stopped by Police Citing Paperwork Rules," *New York Times*, September 20, 2005; Ethan Wilensky-Lanford, "A Pretend Preacher, a Real Arrest and a Debate about Free Speech," *New York Times*, July 1, 2007; James Barron, "Police and a Cyclists' Group, and Four Years of Clashes," *New York Times*, August 4, 2008.

25. Maarten Hajer and Arnold Reijndorp, *In Search of New Public Domain* (Rotterdam: NAI, 2001), p. 53; "aliens": Lyn H. Lofland, *The Public Realm* (New York: De Gruyter, 1998), p. 167.

26. "Manicured spaces": Ole B. Jensen, "The BID's of New York: Power, Place, and the Role of Business Improvement Districts," paper presented at the eighteenth AESOP Congress, Grenoble, July 1–3, 2004, p. 10; "an earlier set of values": Heather MacDonald, "Why Business Improvement Districts Work," *Civic Bulletin*, no. 4, May 1996, www.manhattan-institute.org/html/cb_4.htm; Bennett, *Birth of the Museum*, p. 24. Certainly the use of surveillance for social control takes many modern forms, beginning with Jeremy Bentham's panopticon and leading up to today's closed-circuit TV and biometric screening.

27. Darren Walker quoted in Sewell Chan, http://cityroom.blogs.nytimes.com/2007/10/04/has-new-york-lost-its-soul/, October 4, 2007.

28. Thomas J. Lueck, "Public Needs, Private Answers—A Special Report; Business Districts Grow, at Price of Accountability," *New York Times*, November 20, 1994; Dan Barry and Thomas J. Lueck, "Control Sought on Districts for Businesses," *New York Times*, April 2, 1998; Thomas J. Lueck, "Business Improvement District at Grand Central Is Dissolved," *New York Times*, July 30, 1998; Terry Pristin, "Annual Budgets— Increases Refused by Giuliani Administration," *New York Times*, July 27, 1999.

29. Terry Pristin, "Mayor Sees Bigger Public Private Partnerships," *New York Times*, May 15, 2002; Rich Calder, "Fiscal Crisis Guts City Park Plans," www.nypost.com, May 26, 2009.

30. Bruce Lambert, "Neighborhood Report: Union Square; Confronted by the Homeless Domino Effect, Another Park Cracks Down," *New York Times*, June 12, 1994. For a contrasting, highly critical view, see Neil Smith, *The New Urban Frontier: Gentrification and the Revanchist City* (New York: Routledge, 1996).

31. Gregory Squires, ed., *Unequal Partnerships: The Political Economy of Urban Redevelopment in Postwar America* (New Brunswick, NJ: Rutgers University Press, 1989); MacDonald, "Why Business Improvement Districts Work."

32. Ingrid Gould Ellen, Amy Ellen Schwartz, and Ioan Voicu, "The Impact of Business Improvement Districts on Property Values: Evidence from New York City," *Brookings-Wharton Papers on Urban Affairs* 8 (2007): 1–31; New York City Department of Small Business Services, *Introduction to Business Improvement Districts*, www.nyc.gov/html/sbs/downloads/pdf/bid_brochure.pdf, accessed July 2008.

33. Cara Buckley, "Ah, the Heat, the Crowd, the Park, and the Booze," *New York Times*, July 16, 2008.

34. Ellen, Schwartz, and Voicu, "The Impact of Business Improvement Districts."

35. Glenn Collins, "Bryant Park, Towers Rising All Around, Braces for a Tidal Wave of Traffic," *New York Times*, June 5, 2008; Lysandra Ohrstrom, "Fashion Week in Bryant Park May Go Out of Style," *New York Observer*, www.observer.com, February 5, 2009. The operations budgets of the elite parks managed by BIDs and private conservancies are many times greater than the average budgets financed by the Parks Department. At Bryant Park, for example, the BID spends *more than a half-million dollars per acre,* but the Parks Department's average expenditure per acre citywide is less than ten thousand dollars. This difference in financial resources guarantees a vastly different level of services: 110 of 239 "parks enforcement officers" listed by the Parks Department as employees work in the elite parks, where they are privately funded by the BIDs. Rich Calder, "Raiders of the 'Lost' Parks," *New York Post*, July 6, 2008, and "City's Park 'Row,'" *New York Post*, July 7, 2008.

36. That the Twin Towers became a preeminent image of the city—an image, as people say, that was iconic—also reflects the concerted public relations campaign financed for many years by public agencies. Miriam Greenberg, "The Limits of Branding: The World Trade Center, Fiscal Crisis and the Marketing of Recovery," *International Journal of Urban and Regional Research* 27, no. 2 (2003): 386–418. For an excellent history of the building of the World Trade Center, see Eric Darton, *Divided We Stand: A Biography of New York's World Trade Center* (New York: Basic Books, 1999); also Michael Sorkin and Sharon Zukin, eds., *After the World Trade Center* (New York: Routledge, 2002).

37. Fragmentation made it hard to construct a harmonious resolution of differences. Each element of this brief description has been subject to extensive controversy, litigation, and negotiation, beginning with the amount of the insurance payments, Silverstein's role in relation to the Port Authority's, the Port Authority's role in relation to the city government's, and the mayor's role in relation to the governor's. As Paul Goldberger notes, the public would surely have approved the state's and city's purchase of the developer's lease, but the governor was not inclined to pursue this issue. See Paul Goldberger, *Up From Zero: Politics, Architecture, and the Rebuilding of New York* (New York: Random House, 2004).

38. Thirty percent: Theresa Agovino, www.crainsnewyork.com, September 11, 2008. Security plans: Carrick Mollenkamp and Christine Haughney, "'Ring of Steel' for New York? To Protect Lower Manhattan, Police Study London's Effort: Cameras, Controlling Access," *Wall Street Journal*, January 25, 2006; Cara Buckley, "NY Plans Surveillance Veil for Downtown," *New York Times*, July 9, 2007. "Army of cops": Alison Gendar and Douglas Feiden, "Security Plan for WTC Means Army of Cops, Barriers and Traffic Hell," *New York Daily News*, April 6, 2008; Charles V. Bagli, "Police Want Tight Security Zone at Ground Zero," *New York Times*, August 12, 2008; Al Baker, "Police Seek a Second Zone of High Security in the City," *New York Times*, March 31, 2009.

39. Within days, a sixteen-year-old boy was arrested and charged with second-degree murder, gang assault, and weapons possession. Emily Vasquez, "Trouble Found Them: Two Groups of Restless Teenagers," *New York Times*, December 8, 2006; also "Teen Dead after Stabbing in Union Square," www.wnbc.com, December 7, 2006; www.NY1.com, December 13, 2006.

Chapter 5. A Tale of Two Globals

1. *The WPA Guide to New York City: The Federal Writers' Project Guide to 1930s New York* (1939; New York: Pantheon, 1982); H. P. Lovecraft, "The Horror at Red Hook," and Thomas Wolfe, "Only the Dead Know Brooklyn," in *Brooklyn Noir 2: The Classics,* ed. Tim McLoughlin (Brooklyn: Akashic Books, 2005) pp. 17–45, 46–52.

2. Though Red Hook Houses was built to very high standards for its time, especially in contrast to public housing in other U.S. cities, its reputation by the 1990s was mired in the tragic murder of Patrick Daly, a local elementary school principal, who was caught in the crossfire of a gun battle between rival gangs while looking for a student. After witnesses came forward despite threats against them, three teenagers were convicted of the murder; one lived in Red Hook Houses at the time, and another had lived there earlier. See Nicholas Dagen Bloom, *Public Housing That Worked: New York in the Twentieth Century* (Philadelphia: University of Pennsylvania Press, 2008), pp. 56–57, 66–67; Joseph P. Fried, "Youths Guilty in the Slaying of a Principal," *New York Times*, June 16, 1993.

3. On Red Hook's economic decline and the lack of social interaction between the small number of elderly white homeowners who worked on the docks and the much larger number of black and Puerto Rican residents who lived mainly in the public housing project and were not hired for those jobs, see Philip Kasinitz and David Hillyard, "The Old-Timers' Tale: The Politics of Nostalgia on the Waterfront," *Journal of Contemporary Ethnography* 24, no. 2 (1995): 139–64; Philip Kasinitz and Jan Rosenberg, "Missing the Connection: Social Isolation and Employment on the Brooklyn Waterfront," *Social Problems* 43, no. 2 (1996): 180–94.

4. Jennifer 8. Lee, "City Room: Hoping the Swedish Meatballs Hold Out in Red Hook," *New York Times,* May 16, 2008; "Three Die in Saudi Shop Stampede," BBC News-World, September 1, 2004, http://news.bbc.co.uk/1/hi/world/middle_east/3618190.stm.

5. "Hundreds Pack Hearing to Oppose Ikea Plan in New Rochelle," *New York Times,* November 17, 2000; "New Rochelle Residents Turn Out in Force to Block Ikea," www.newrules.org/retail, January 1, 2001.

6. Gowanus Canal: Amy Waldman, "Ikea Scrapping Plans for Store amid Resistance by Neighbors," *New York Times,* June 17, 2001.

7. In addition, during the four years that passed between the City Council's approval of the sale of the warehouse and Fairway's opening its doors, the developer faced a lawsuit filed by community groups, criticism of his use of nonunion construction workers, and a bribery scandal involving the local City Council member, who was charged with selling his vote on the project. Monica Drake, "Neighborhood Report: South Brooklyn; Is There a Fairway in Red Hook's Future?," *New York Times,* April 23, 2000; Nichole M. Christian, "In Red Hook, Worries on the Waterfront," *New York Times,* March 11, 2002; William K. Rashbaum, "Brooklyn Councilman Is Charged in an Extortion Scheme," *New York Times,* March 29, 2002; Corey Kilgannon, "Brooklyn Groups Sue to Keep Supermarket out of Red Hook," *New York Times,* May 31, 2002; Jotham Sederstrom, "Red Hook Foodies Ask: So, Where Is Fairway?," www.brooklynpaper.com, May 14, 2005; Jonathan Bowles, "Outside the Box: Developer Greg O'Connell Seeks Balanced Building for Red Hook," *City Limits,* May/June 2005, www.citylimits.org; Florence Fabricant, "Food Stuff: Fairway Opens Its Brooklyn Doors," *New York Times,* May 17, 2006. 197a plan: Tom Angotti, *New York For Sale* (Cambridge, MA: MIT Press, 2008), pp. 161–66.

8. As on the Williamsburg waterfront, construction and development projects that involved changing the use of this site, which also required zoning exemptions and public subsidies, had to pass through a Uniform Land Use Review Procedure. This procedure allows for public input (comments, lobbying, a 197a plan) and legally mandates public hearings and public testimony at each level of city government, from local community boards (which have an advisory voice in the matter) to the City Planning Commission and City Council (which has the determining vote). "Investment of this size": Diane Cardwell, "Panel Approves Plan by Ikea to Open Store in Red Hook," *New York Times,* October 6, 2004. Also see Luis Perez and Eric Herman, "An Ikea Grows in B'klyn; 50M Store Set for Red Hook," *New York Daily News,* October 26, 2002; Melissa Grace, "Squaring Off on Ikea; Red Hook Welcomes Jobs but Fears Pollution," *New York Daily News,* December 2, 2002; Hugh Son, "Wrench in Red Hook; Civic Leader Says Ikea's Racially Divisive," *New York Daily News,* April 25, 2004; Hugh Son, "Ikea Plan Winning Backers," *New York Daily News,* July 29, 2004; Hugh Son, "Wary in Red Hook; Superstore Traffic Feared," *New York Daily News,* August 2, 2004; Nicholas LoVecchio, "Mike's Hedge Furnishes Anti-Ikea Lot with

Hope," *New York Daily News,* October 8, 2004; Joyce Shelby, "Comptroller Hits Ikea Parking Plan," *New York Daily News,* May 5, 2006.

9. "Swedephilia": Ursula Lindqvist, "The Cultural Archive of the IKEA Store," *Space and Culture* 12, no. 1 (2009): 43–62.

10. Except where noted, all information about the Red Hook food vendors comes from interviews carried out by Kathleen Dunn from June through September 2008. I have given all the vendors pseudonyms unless the information comes from published sources, including online sources; Cesar Fuentes, the executive director of the Food Vendors Committee of Red Hook Park, Inc., appears, with his permission, under his real name.

11. Liga Mexicana: Kevin McCoy and Carolina Gonzalez, "Soccer Is the Game of Newcomers," *New York Daily News,* June 22, 1998.

12. Latinos in general make up 28 percent of the city's population. Immigration data from U.S. Census, 1970, 1980, 1990, 2000 and Public Use Microdata Sample files, with thanks to Joseph Salvo and Adam Willett, Population Division, New York City Department of City Planning; 2007 population data from Laura Limonic, *The Latino Population of New York City, 2007,* Center for Latin American, Caribbean, and Latino Studies, City University of New York Graduate Center, December 2008. "Tortilla triangle": Seth Kugel, "New Yorkers & Co.; How Brooklyn Became New York's Tortilla Basket," *New York Times,* February 25, 2001.

13. "This was dumpy": Bowles, "Outside the Box."

14. Eric Asimov, "$25 and Under," *New York Times,* May 13, 1994.

15. First-world reviewers: Shyon Baumann and Josée Johnston, *Foodies: Democracy and Distinction in the Gourmet Landscape* (New York: Routledge, forthcoming).

16. Certainly immigrants from different regions of Italy and China run businesses side by side in Little Italy and Chinatown, and Chinese from Hong Kong, Taiwan, Vietnam, and Singapore, as well as from the Republic of China, join together in Lunar New Year parades. But West Indian Carnival and the Red Hook food vendors collapse *national* differences into a larger regional identity, a difference of scale that stretches the idea of authenticity beyond the borders of the nation-state.

17. Because Brooklyn Flea is held on private property—the schoolyard of a Catholic school—food vendors are not required to pass health code inspections. Several Red Hook food vendors began to rent space at Brooklyn Flea in 2008 while they tried to pass their inspections and get a license to sell food at the ball fields, in a public park.

18. Allison Bojarski, "Soccer, Swimming, y Salsa: The Red Hook Latino Food Stalls," http://gothamist.com, August 25, 2004.

19. "Everything you always wanted to know about Red Hook, but were afraid to ask," http://porkchop-express.blogspot.com, August 22, 2006.

20. According to Parks Department: Peter Meehan, "Red Hook Vendors Pressed to Get New Permit," *New York Times,* June 6, 2007.

21. "Total support": Andy Newman, "The Food's Still Great, but Success Divides the Vendors," *New York Times,* September 28, 2007. Speaking about this dispute in 2008, Cesar said he is paid $150 per day, or $5,000 for the year, a daily rate that he compared to that of a laborer and much less than the salary of a full-time executive director of any small nonprofit organization.

22. From 2000 through 2007 twelve vendors belonged to the food vendors' association. In 2008 two members were not able to conform to the Health Department's requirements and decided not to return to the ball fields. Cesar says that he found one of these vendors another location in Brooklyn where she could prepare and sell huaraches; the other family owns a restaurant. In addition to the vendors who formed the association, other Latino vendors, who sold their food on the baseball fields near IKEA and were unable or unwilling to form an association, did not bid for concession permits and were not allowed to continue selling food at this location. The Parks Department also banned a vendor who sold toys near the food vendors; according to Cesar, "We were able to talk and get some things worked out," and that vendor got a temporary use permit.

23. Mike McLaughlin, "The Red Hook Vendors Are Back!," *Brooklyn Paper,* www. brooklynpaper.com, March 15, 2008; "Red Hook'd: The Interview," http://porkchop-express.blogspot.com, June 3, 2008; "Brian Lehrer Live" (video), WNYC, http:// blblog.org, June 18, 2008.

24. No negative comments about the Red Hook vendors appeared on Chowhound. com, and only a few were posted among the five-star rave reviews on Yelp.com, but it is noteworthy that a Chowhound post, anticipating the next new trend, told readers to hurry to the Chinese food stands in the Roosevelt shopping mall in Queens "before CH anoints it the next Red Hook ballfields" (Steve R., http://chowhound. chow.com, Outer Boroughs Board, December 22, 2008).

25. "Madhouse," "less remote": Kareem Fahim, "Brooklyn Neighbors Admit a Big Box Isn't All Bad," *New York Times,* August 11, 2008; "transformative," "to other places": Philip Nobel, "Far Corner: Welcome, Ikea Shoppers!," *Metropolis,* October 2008, p. 100.

26. Daniel Meyer in Mark Bittman, "Which Food Is Really Safe?," http://bitten. blogs.nytimes.com, August 22, 2008, and in Mark Bittman, "The Meatball of the Matter," http://bitten.blogs.nytimes.com, September 5, 2008; comment posted by John Z., September 6, 2008.

27. "2008 Vendy Awards Finalists!," http://streetvendor.org, October 18, 2008; Patrick Huguenin, "3 Brothers behind Calexico Are Improving the a la Cart Menu," www. nydailynews.com, April 26, 2008. The cross-ethnic cooking and selling of ethnic foods is not a new story. In *The Cultures of Cities* (Oxford: Blackwell, 1995), I wrote about the Chinese owners and staff of a fast-food tortilla restaurant on Forty-second Street. Since then, with transnational migration of many groups across multiple national borders, increased selling of cultural identities through cuisine, and predominant

hiring of Mexican workers in all of New York's restaurant kitchens regardless of cuisine, the cross-ethnic selling of ethnic foods has become more common.

28. Jonathan Bowles, *A World of Opportunity,* Center for an Urban Future, New York, February 2007; Colin Moynihan and Sewell Chan, "Hearing on Street Vendors Gets Heated," http://cityroom.blogs.nytimes.com, November 14, 2008. Even in the Brooklyn neighborhood of Sunset Park, where many Latino immigrants own shops and restaurants, the Business Improvement District has been working with the City Council to clear vendors from Fifth Avenue, the main Latino shopping street (Jessica Lee, "Sunset Park Sidewalk Clash," http://www.indypendent.org, May 15, 2009).

29. Charles V. Bagli, "Lease Ends Uncertainty for Red Hook Cargo Docks," *New York Times,* April 25, 2008; Rich Calder, "Ikea Berth Pangs," *New York Post,* June 23, 2008; Charles V. Bagli, "For Reinvention, Red Hook Follows Its Roots," *New York Times,* November 23, 2008. By the same token, some elected officials, notably U.S. Representative Jerrold Nadler, have for years pressed the state and the federal governments to build new infrastructure to support manufacturing and port activities on the waterfront. Also, as I have already pointed out, the city comptroller suggested in 2006 that paving over the graving dock would be premature (Shelby, "Comptroller Hits Ikea Parking Plan").

30. "Architecture for Humanity New York and the Red Hook Vendors Announce Results of Design Competition," http://afhny.org/news, December 17, 2008.

Chapter 6. The Billboard and the Garden

1. All personal information about community gardeners comes from interviews carried out by Dmitri Chitov and Sharon Zukin from 2005 to 2008; to protect their anonymity, gardeners are identified by pseudonyms, and identifying information is generalized.

2. Staten Island and Queens, less densely built and with somewhat higher household incomes, have very few community gardens. Data from Efrat Eizenberg, "From the Ground Up: Community Gardens in New York and the Politics of Spatial Transformation," PhD dissertation, City University of New York Graduate Center, 2008.

3. Joseph P. Fried, "City's Housing Administrator Proposes 'Planned Shrinkage' of Some Slums," *New York Times,* February 3, 1976. The city's police and fire departments had already begun reducing essential services in East New York and Williamsburg a few years earlier, as did the public school and public hospital systems. See Walter Thabit, *How East New York Became a Ghetto* (New York: New York University Press, 2003); Ida Susser, *Norman Street: Poverty and Politics in an Urban Neighborhood* (New York: Oxford University Press, 1982), and Deborah Wallace and Rodrick Wallace, *A Plague on Your Houses: How New York Was Burned* (London: Verso, 1998).

4. Luc Santé, "My Lost City," *New York Review of Books,* November 6, 2003, www. nybooks.com.

5. On the confluence of social, ethnic, and environmental activism in the 1970s, see Matthew Gandy, *Concrete and Clay: Reworking Nature in New York City* (Cambridge, MA: MIT Press, 2002).

6. See the websites www.lizchristygarden.org and www.greenguerillas.org. "A more unlikely place": quoted in Sarah Ferguson, "A Brief History of Grassroots Greening in NYC," *New Village Journal* 1 (2001), www.newvillage.net.

7. Photos: www.lizchristygarden.org; squatters: Janet Abu-Lughod, ed., *From Urban Village to East Village: The Battle for New York's Lower East Side* (Oxford: Blackwell, 1994); Dennis Hevesi, "East New York: A Neighborhood Reborn," *New York Times,* June 10, 2001.

8. Ferguson, "A Brief History."

9. Jesse McKinley, "Adam Purple's Last Stand," *New York Times,* February 22, 1998; Abu-Lughod, *From Urban Village to East Village.* Also see chapter 3.

10. Though the lots were "city owned," their management, and control of the gardens, was distributed among different agencies, from the Parks Department and HPD to the Department of Education and the transit authority. A centralized inventory was a step toward more rational use of any kind. Twenty-five thousand vacant lots: Mark Francis, Lisa Cashdan, and Lynn Paxon, *Community Open Spaces* (Washington, DC: Island Press, 1984), p. 43; eleven thousand: Anne Raver, "Hundreds Gather to Protest City's Auction of Garden Lots," *New York Times,* April 11, 1999. Amount of land: according to Francis, Cashdan, and Paxon, citing a study by the New York City Open Space Coalition, about two thousand acres throughout the city in the early 1980s. Without informing: Anne Raver, "Is This City Big Enough for Gardens and Houses?," *New York Times,* March 27, 1997. Five years to sell off: Neighborhood Open Space Coalition–Friends of Gateway, www.treebranch.com/community_gardens. htm; justified the loss: Anne Raver, "Houses before Gardens, the City Decides," *New York Times,* January 9, 1997.

11. Raver, "Is This City Big Enough"; Anne Raver, "City Rejects $2 Million Offer for Gardens," *New York Times,* April 23, 1999.

12. Raver, "Is This City Big Enough"; Amy Waldman, "Cricket Invaders Turn an Auction into 'Madness,'" *New York Times,* July 21, 1998; Anne Raver, "Hundreds Gather to Protest City's Auction of Garden Lots," *New York Times,* April 11, 1999.

13. "Spaces of engagement": Christopher M. Smith and Hilda E. Kurtz, "Community Gardens and Politics of Scale in New York City," *Geographical Review,* 93, no. 2 (2003): 193–212. "Era after communism": though this was widely reported, and repeated for years, I have not found a direct source for the quotation. One website says the mayor uttered these words during his weekly radio broadcast in January 1999: www.notbored.org/gardens.html. Months later the phrase was repeated,

without citing a source, by John Kifner, "Giuliani's Hunt for Red Menaces," *New York Times*, December 20, 1999.

14. Anne Schwartz, "Community Gardens," www.gothamgazette.com, July 2006; Andrew C. Revkin, "Spitzer and Pataki Dueling over Environmental Mantle," *New York Times*, October 19, 1999; "Metro News Briefs: New York; Spitzer Sues to Block Auction of Garden Sites," *New York Times*, May 11, 1999.

15. Richard Stapleton, "Bringing Peace to the Garden of Tranquility," *Land&People* magazine, Trust for Public Land, fall 1999, www.tpl.org; C. J. Chivers, "After Uprooting Gardeners, City Razes a Garden," *New York Times*, February 16, 2000; "Death of a Garden" (editorial), *New York Times*, February 17, 2000.

16. Jennifer Steinhauer, "Ending a Long Battle, New York Lets Housing and Gardens Grow," *New York Times*, September 19, 2002. The Parks Department controls 28 percent of nearly seven hundred community gardens; 18 percent are held by HPD; 17 percent by the city's Department of Education; 10 percent are in private hands; 9 percent are owned by the Trust for Public Land; 6 percent by the New York Restoration Project. Smaller numbers of community gardens are distributed among a few other city agencies (Eizenberg, *From the Ground Up*).

17. Legislation was required because ownership of parkland would be transferred from the state (i.e., the city government) to a "private" group, raising the same issue as in Union Square Park (see chapter 4). Increase in value: Ioan Voicu and Vicki Been, "The Effect of Community Gardens on Neighboring Property Values," *Real Estate Economics* 36, no. 2 (2008): 241–83; lack of control, displacement: Daisy Hernandez, "A Bitter Harvest for the Losers; Some Ask Why Compromise Doesn't Protect Their Gardens," *New York Times*, October 12, 2002; foundations' influence: Anne Raver, "Healthy Spaces, for People and the Earth," *New York Times*, November 6, 2008; expire in 2010: Brigid Bergin, "Toward a Garden Truce, Fertile and Long-Lasting," *City Limits*, June 18, 2007, www.citylimits.org.

18. Alex Schmidt, "Community Gardeners Now Covered by City Insurance," *Downtown Express*, April 21–27, 2006; especially in Harlem: Schwartz, "Community Gardens," and see chapter 2; urban farming: Jim Dwyer, "Sweat Equity Put to Use within Sight of Wall St.," *New York Times*, October 8, 2008; Mark Winston Griffith, "The 'Food Justice' Movement: Trying to Break the Food Chains," www.gothamgazette.com, December 2003; www.agmkt.state.ny.us/cg/CGHome.html; http://www.justfood.org/jf/. These farmers' markets are not connected to the Greenmarket network of farmers' markets described in chapters 3 and 4. Also see Manhattan Borough President, *Food in the Public Interest: How New York City's Food Policy Holds the Key to Hunger, Health, Jobs and the Environment*, February 2009, http://mbpo.org.

19. See Amy B. Trubek, *The Taste of Place: A Cultural Journey into Terroir* (Berkeley: University of California Press, 2008); Pierre Boisard, *Camembert: A National Myth*, trans. Richard Miller (Berkeley: University of California Press, 2003).

20. Members, dues: Eisenberg, *From the Ground Up;* Added Value: Dwyer, "Sweat Equity Put to Use."

21. Miranda J. Martinez, "The Struggle for the Gardens: Puerto Ricans, Redevelopment, and the Negotiation of Difference in a Changing Community," PhD dissertation, New York University, 2002; Joseph Sciorra, "Return to the Future: Puerto Rican Vernacular Architecture in New York City," in *Re-Presenting the City: Ethnicity, Capital and Culture in the 21st Century Metropolis,* ed. Anthony D. King (Hampshire, UK: Macmillan, 1996), pp. 60–92.

22. Martinez, "Struggle for the Gardens"; Smith and Kurtz, "Community Gardens and Politics of Scale," pp. 205–6.

23. Martinez, "Struggle for the Gardens"; Dmitri Chitov, "Cultivating Social Capital on Urban Plots: An Ethnographic Study of Community Gardens in New York City," senior honors paper, Brooklyn College, fall 2005; Efrat, "From the Ground Up."

24. By the same token, the social construction of rural agricultural *terroirs* also involves disputes over farming and certainly marketing practices, although outsiders do not usually hear about them unless state regulations are involved. See, for example, Boisard, *Camembert;* Jillian Cavanaugh, "Making Salami, Producing Bergamo: The Production and Transformation of Value in a Northern Italian Town," *Ethnos* 72, no. 2 (2007): 114–39.

25. A long-running controversy at the 6th and B Garden in the East Village concerned the Tower of Toys erected by Eddie Boros, a local resident who for more than twenty years collected various objects from the streets, including toys, which he used to erect a sixty-five-foot tower in the garden. Other garden members complained that the tower was dangerous, that rainwater that remained in bottles and other open vessels on the tower attracted mosquitoes, and that Boros exceeded the size limits of his plot, but he refused to take down the structure, and it proved impossible to evict him or the tower, which became a local landmark. The gardeners finally dismantled it after Boros died. At a meeting to discuss what to do with the remaining objects, one of the gardeners sighed that outsiders might be more sentimental about them than the gardeners were. Colin Moynihan, "Artist Is Gone, but 65 Feet of Protest Still Stands," *New York Times,* April 30, 2007.

26. Chitov, "Cultivating Social Capital on Urban Plots."

27. By 2008 Friends of Hudson River Park, a private conservancy that supports a state park on the West Side of Manhattan, was preparing a proposal to create the first residential BID, arguing that the park increased property values by such a substantial amount that developers, landlords, and residents should be glad to pay the additional tax a BID requires. Anne Schwartz, "A Property Tax for Parks?," www.gothamgazette.com, October 2008. For a general critique of the public sector's entrepreneurial approach, see David Harvey, "From Managerialism to Entrepreneurialism: The Transformation of Urban Governance in Late Capitalism," in *Spaces of Capital* (New York: Routledge, 2001), pp. 345–68.

28. See Georg Simmel, "The Metropolis and Mental Life," in *The Sociology of Georg Simmel*, ed. and trans. Kurt Wolff (New York: Free Press, 1950), pp. 409–24; Walter Benjamin, *The Arcades Project*, trans. Howard Eiland and Kevin McLaughlin (Cambridge, MA: Harvard University Press, 1999); Peter Fritzsche, *Reading Berlin 1900* (Cambridge, MA: Harvard University Press, 1996); David M. Henkin, *City Reading: Written Words and Public Spaces in Antebellum New York* (New York: Columbia University Press, 1998).

29. Henry James, *The American Scene* (1906; Bloomington: Indiana University Press, 1968), pp. 81, 130–33, 185.

30. Gregory F. Gilmartin, *Shaping the City: New York and the Municipal Art Society* (New York: Clarkson Potter, 1995), pp. 139–48, 236–37.

31. Tama Starr and Edward Hayman, *Signs and Wonders* (New York: Doubleday, 1998); William R. Taylor, ed., *Inventing Times Square: Commerce and Culture at the Crossroads of the World* (New York: Russell Sage Foundation, 1991).

32. Kathleen Hulser, "Visual Browsing: Auto-flâneurs and Roadside Ads in the 1950s," in *Suburban Discipline*, ed. Peter Lang and Tam Miller (New York: Princeton Architectural Press, 1997), pp. 8–19; on the early 1900s: Catherine Gudis, *Buyways: Billboards, Automobiles, and the American Landscape* (New York: Routledge, 2004).

33. For criticism of billboards, see Peter Blake, *God's Own Junkyard: The Planned Deterioration of America's Landscape* (New York: Holt, Rinehart & Winston, 1964). On the flight from traditional urban amusement and shopping centers, see John Hannigan, *Fantasy City* (New York: Routledge, 1998); Lizabeth Cohen, *A Consumers' Republic: The Politics of Mass Consumption in Postwar America* (New York: Knopf, 2003).

34. Gilmartin, *Shaping the City*, pp. 443–61; Lynne B. Sagalyn, *Times Square Roulette* (Cambridge, MA: MIT Press, 2001); Sharon Zukin, *Point of Purchase: How Shopping Changed American Culture* (New York: Routledge, 2004); *Style Wars* (film, 1982); Miriam Greenberg, *Branding New York: How a City in Crisis Was Sold to the World* (New York: Routledge, 2008).

35. MTA's revenue: Jennifer 8. Lee, "A 'Full-Body Wrap' for Times Square Shuttle," *New York Times*, http://cityroom.blogs.nytimes.com, October 2, 2008.

36. Douglas Martin, "Bazaars Set Off Debate over Role of Parks," *New York Times*, December 1, 1998; Nicolai Ouroussoff, "Art and Commerce Canoodling in Central Park," *New York Times*, October 21, 2008.

37. "Advertising extravaganza": Thomas Duane, quoted in David W. Dunlap, "Your Ad Here," *New York Times*, April 16, 2000.

38. Environmental stewards: Andrew Light, "Elegy for a Garden," www.terrain.org, 15 (fall–winter 2004); Eizenberg, referring to the French social theorist Henri Lefebvre in "From the Ground Up," calls these politically active citizens *citadins*. Also see Marshall Berman, *The Politics of Authenticity: Radical Individualism and the Emergence of Modern Society* (New York: Atheneum, 1970); Sam Binkley, *Getting Loose: Lifestyle Consumption in the 1970s* (Durham, NC: Duke University Press, 2007).

Conclusion. Destination Culture

1. Jane Jacobs, *The Death and Life of Great American Cities* (New York: Random House, 1961).

2. Walter Benjamin, "The Work of Art in the Age of Mechanical Reproduction," in *Illuminations*, ed. Hannah Arendt, trans. Harry Zohn (New York: Schocken, 1968), pp. 217–42.

3. Adam Moss, "In Conversation: Woody Allen," *New York*, October 6, 2008, http://nymag.com.

4. Herbert Muschamp, "Architecture: Remodeling New York for the Bourgeoisie," *New York Times*, September 24, 1995.

5. The "urban village" is Herbert Gans's great contribution to our understanding of the postwar city and is based on his in-depth study of the Italian West End of Boston in the 1950s: Herbert J. Gans, *The Urban Villagers: Group and Class in the Life of Italian-Americans* (New York: Free Press, 1962). On the Italian working-class North End in the 1930s, see William F. Whyte, *Street Corner Society: The Social Structure of an Italian Slum* (Chicago: University of Chicago Press, 1943), quote from p. 273.

6. Gans, *Urban Villagers*, pp. 317–19, 328. On the slow attrition of downtowns between the two World Wars, see Duncan W. Rae, *City: Urbanism and Its End* (New Haven, CT: Yale University Press, 2004); Alison Isenberg, *Downtown America* (Chicago: University of Chicago Press, 2004).

7. By the middle of the first decade of the twenty-first century the proportion of self-declared white residents of New York City had gradually increased, especially in Manhattan and Brooklyn, for the first time in fifty years, while the share of Latino immigrants had declined. Sam Roberts, "'White Flight' Has Reversed," *New York Times*, September 23, 2008. On the nationwide "demographic inversion" that has moved poor minority group members and immigrants to inner suburbs and exurbs and attracted more affluent, mostly white residents to urban centers throughout the United States, see Alan Ehrenhalt, "Trading Places," *The New Republic*, August 13, 2008, www.tnr.com/politics.

8. "Our Ideal 'Hood," *Time Out New York*, September 19–25, 2008, www.timeout.com/newyork/articles/features/60501/new-yorks-best-neighborhoods-now.

9. John Logan and Harvey Molotch, *Urban Fortunes: The Political Economy of Place* (Berkeley: University of California Press, 1986).

10. Amnesia: Mark Crinson, *Urban Memory: History and Amnesia in the Modern City* (London: Routledge, 2005).

11. Leslie Sklair, *Sociology of the Global System* (Baltimore: Johns Hopkins University Press, 1995), p. 63.

12. Doctoroff: Transcript of conference "Creative New York," April 2006, www.nyc-future.org, accessed June 2006. Parades: see www.cowparade.com. Fashion weeks:

Eric Wilson, "The Sun Never Sets on the Runway," *New York Times*, September 8, 2008; design festivals: Monica Khemsurov, "Design on Tour," *T: The New York Times Style Magazine*, September 21, 2008.

13. Jacobs, *Death and Life*. David Harvey has developed the theory of the "geopolitics of capitalism" or "the spatial fix" throughout his career, for example, in *Spaces of Capital: Towards a Critical Geography* (New York: Routledge, 2001). On globalization of real estate investment, see Kevin Fox Gotham, "The Secondary Circuit of Capital Reconsidered: Globalization and the U.S. Real Estate Sector," *American Journal of Sociology* 112, no. 1 (2006): 231–75. Private equity funds, affordable housing: Tom Waters and Victor Bach, *Closing the Door 2008: Subsidized Housing Losses in a Weakened Market*, Community Service Society, New York, October 2008; Kira Bindrim, "'Predatory Equity' Smothering Affordable Housing," *Crain's New York Business*, October 2, 2008, www.crainsnewyork.com.

14. Malcolm Tait and Ole B. Jensen, "Travelling Ideas, Power and Place: The Cases of Urban Villages and Business Improvement Districts," *International Planning Studies* 12, no. 2 (2007): 107–27; Donald McNeill, "McGuggenisation? National Identity and Globalisation in the Basque Country," *Political Geography* 19 (2000): 473–94; "copies what others are doing": Paul J. DiMaggio and Walter Powell, "The Iron Cage Revisited: Institutional Isomorphism and Collective Rationality in Organizational Fields," *American Sociological Review* 48 (1983): 147–60. Real estate developer Forest City Ratner commissioned Frank Gehry to design a professional sports arena in Central Brooklyn, which was to be the central attraction in a mammoth development of new housing, offices, and stores that Gehry also designed, but when the economic recession of 2008 made financing difficult, the developer first requested reductions in and then scuttled Gehry's design for the stadium, replacing it with a cheaper, generic model, and delayed construction plans on the mixed-use district. Nicolai Ouroussoff, "Battle Between Budget and Beauty, Which Budget Won," *New York Times*, June 9, 2009.

15. "'Waterfalls' Brought in $69 Million for NYC," Associated Press, October 22, 2008. *Waterfalls* was considered a success despite spewing salt-water mist on plants on the terrace of a waterfront café and in a waterfront green space and killing them—an ironic environmental byproduct of this promotion.

16. Jean Baudrillard, "The Beaubourg-Effect: Implosion and Deterrence," *October* 20 (spring 1982): 8. Careful examination shows that what we think are absolute values, such as tradition and authenticity, are *always* conscious creations, often for political or economic gain. See Eric Hobsbawm and Terence Ranger, *The Invention of Tradition* (Cambridge: Cambridge University Press, 1992); Richard A. Peterson, *Creating Country Music: Fabricating Authenticity* (Chicago: University of Chicago Press, 1997).

17. *Blue Wings* (in-flight magazine of Finnair), September 2004, p. 15; *Wallpaper*, November 2001.

18. Vesterbro tours at www.visitcopenhagen.com/tourist/what_to_see_and_do/tours_&_excursions; festival at www.vesterbrofestival.dk, accessed June 2006.

19. On the production role of new industrial Bohemias, see Laura Bovone, "Fashionable Quarters in the Postindustrial City: The Ticinese of Milan," *City and Community* 4, no. 4 (2005): 359–80; Richard Lloyd, *Neo-Bohemia: Art and Commerce in the Post-industrial City* (New York: Routledge, 2006); Elizabeth Currid, *The Warhol Economy: How Fashion, Art, and Music Drive New York City* (Princeton, NJ: Princeton University Press, 2007); Andy C. Pratt, "Urban Regeneration: From the Arts 'Feel Good' Factor to the Cultural Economy: A Case Study of Hoxton, London," *Urban Studies,* forthcoming.

20. Staged authenticity: Dean MacCannell, *The Tourist: A New Theory of the Leisure Class,* 3rd ed. (Berkeley: University of California Press, 1999).

21. "Daniel J. Wakin, "A Clothing Shop Moves Up, and a Dance Company Must Move Out," *New York Times,* October 7, 2008. Changes in storefronts: data for a sample of three streets in SoHo adapted from Helene Zucker Seeman and Alanna Siegfried, *SoHo: A Guide* (New York: Neal-Schuman, 1978) and *Cole's Reverse Telephone Directory for Manhattan,* 1990, 2000, and 2005. The zoning resolution that established the artists' district in the mid-1970s required all residents to be artists and required all building owners, including co-ops whose owners were artists, to reserve storefronts for rental by manufacturers; the only buildings that could be exempted from these requirements were required to show "financial hardship." In practice, though, as the data on storefronts show, building owners were able to circumvent the law or to charge high rents that artists and manufacturers could not pay. On SoHo's development as an artists' district, see Sharon Zukin, *Loft Living: Culture and Capital in Urban Change,* 2nd ed. (New Brunswick, NJ: Rutgers University Press, 1989).

22. Lorna Blackwood, "Deptford's Cultural Development," *The Times,* November 9, 2007, http://property.timesonline.co.uk.

23. On cultural ambition and competition among Asian cities, see Lily Kong, "Cultural Icons and Urban Development in Asia: Economic Imperative, National Identity, and Global City Status," *Political Geography* 26 (2007): 383–404. On Xintiandi, see Xuefei Ren, "Forward to the Past: Historical Preservation in Globalizing Shanghai," *City and Community* 7, no. 1 (2008): 23–43. The London Development Agency has sponsored cultural hubs, workspaces for artists and artisans in unused factories and warehouses, since 2004.

24. Wang Jie, "Shanghai SoHo—50 Moganshan Road," www.chinadaily.com.cn/citylife, August 29, 2006; www.shangtex.biz/en/, emphasis added.

25. Website of 50 Moganshan Lu art industrial park, www.m50.com.cn.

26. "Money…for someone": Douglas Martin, "Margot Gayle, Urban Preservationist and Crusader with Style, Dies at 100," *New York Times,* September 30, 2008. In Beijing high rents and real estate development have had a similar effect on Factory 798. Henri Benaim, "Rendering Modernity: 798, an Avant-garde Art District in Beijing,"

senior thesis, Department of East Asian Studies, Yale College, 2006. On Shanghainese artists and the international art market, see Charlotte Higgins, "Is Chinese Art Kicking Butt... Or Kissing It?," *The Guardian,* November 9, 2004. Aside from 50 Moganshan Lu, other districts in Shanghai follow different versions of Destination Culture, with more commercial space for architects' and graphic artists' offices (such as Bridge 8) or more space for artists' studios (such as Tianzifang), while still others (such as Yifei Originality Street in Pudong) offer a Disney-like entertainment zone that combines creative production and various sorts of cultural consumption: "Theme pubs, restaurants, art shops and nightclubs have also been set up along the street, which features landscape lighting on trees and walls, with a central plaza." Yang Li Fei, "Chen's Creative Cluster Opens," *Shanghai Daily,* October 10, 2007. Learning from Hoxton, though, a borough in Docklands plans "to create a new cultural destination: along with 257 one, two and three-bedroom residential apartments, the plans include space for bars, cafés, restaurants and a 11,000 sq ft gallery for performances and exhibitions. There will also be live-work units for designers and artists." Blackwood, "Deptford's Cultural Development."

27. Amy Sedaris quoted in Elisabeth Vincentelli, "Amy Sedaris: First Lady of Comedy," *Time Out New York,* September 25–October 1, 2008.

28. Alison Tocci, editor, *Time Out New York,* in panel discussion "Has New York Lost Its Soul?," October 3, 2007 (notes taken at the discussion); http://newyork.craigslist .org, April 2008.

INDEX

HPD. *See* New York City Department of Housing Preservation and Development

Hudson Street, 12, 17–18, 24–25, 40
    See also Jacobs, Jane; West Village

Hue-Man Books, 80, 85

Hughes, Langston, 65, 76

Hunt, Michael, 70

IKEA, *38*, 159–60, *161*, 165–70, 184, 189, 190, 191

immigrants
    1980s-, 60, 77, 133, 171, 196, 197, 217, 222, 257n.20
    in 19th century, 98, 106
    in East Village, 98, 99, 106, 107, 114
    as entrepreneurs, 20, 77
    second generation, 176–77
    See also Red Hook food vendors; *specific nationalities*

inclusionary zoning, 245, 254n.39

indie music, 38, 41, 44

Internet, 37, 87–88
    See also blogs and wikis

Irish immigrants, 25, 98

Italian neighborhoods, 11, 23, 25, 42, 43

Jacobs, Jane
    and authenticity, 11, 12–13, 16–18, 122, 131, 217, 219–20
    on ballet of street, 12, 17, 131, 226
    defeat of Robert Moses, 13–14, 15, 225
    distrust of state power, 13, 219–20, 244, 245
    eyes on street, 17, 129, 226
    and historic preservation, 116, 220
    Hudson Street, 12, 17–18, 24–25, 40
    on low rents, 38
    on neighborhood self-sufficiency, 245
    on public housing projects, 14, 54, 220, 227
    The Death and Life of Great American Cities, 11, 12–13, 16–17, 219, 225
    on Williamsburg rezoning, 59

James, Henry, 9–10, 11, 14–15, 213

Jay-Z, 54, 56, 85

Jeanne-Claude, 233

Jensen, Ole, 233

Jews, 10, 73, 76, 98, 99

Joe's Bed-Stuy Barbershop: We Cut Heads (film), 54

Johnson, Lady Bird, 214

Johnson, Magic, 80

Jordan, June, 40

J. Slab, 170, 177, 192

kairos, 101–2, 104, 105–6, 122

Kansas City, 51

Kazin, Alfred, 39, 40

Klein, S. *See* S. Klein

Knuckles, Kenneth J., 77

Koch, Edward I., 74, 101, 108, 137, 201, 202, 203, 204

Koko's (store), 78

Kristal, Hilly, 99

Kunzru, Hari, 18–19, 121

landlords, abandonment of buildings by, 5, 74, 99, 199
    See also rent control; rent stabilization

landmarks. *See* historic preservation; New York City Landmarks Preservation Commission

Latino immigrants, 11, 48, 49, 53, 54, 58, 60, 161, 165, 171, 197
    See also Red Hook food vendors; *specific nationalities*

Laurents, Arthur, 53

L Café, 49, 76

LedisFlam, 45

Lees, Loretta, 9

Lee, Spike, 17, 54–55, 57, 224, 253n.31, 256n.19

Levine, Ed, 183

Levinson, Aaron, 87

lifestyle journalism, 16, 111, 222

Liz Christy Community Garden, 200

LMDC. *See* Lower Manhattan Development Corporation

Local Development Corporations, 127

local character, East Village, 107, 121

loft living, 5, 12, 16, 24, 42, 103–4, 115, 116, 200, 238
    See also SoHo

public-private partnerships, 221
public spaces
    behavior control in, 129–30, 139,
        142–43, 146
    collective stewardship of, 158, 217, 246
    as democratic, 129
    as diverse, 128
    parks as, 122
    privatized, 122, 127–31, 139, 142–43, 146,
        154, 157–58
    surveillance in, 156–57
    See also billboards; Business
        Improvement Districts;
        community gardens; parks
Puerto Ricans, 42, 43, 44, 50, 98, 99, 100,
    165, 199, 205, 208–10, 217, 257n.20
punk scene, 96, 99, 101, 135
pupusas, 20, 162, 164, 172, 175, 178, 181, 182
    See also Red Hook food vendors

Queens, 16, 55, 58, 91, 146, 272n.2
Quinn, Christine, 211

race, and gentrification, 29, 61
racial tensions, 11, 43–44, 55, 65, 72–74, 76,
    94, 174, 254n.36, 260n.46
Rangel, Charles B., 79, 93
rap music, 55, 56, 57
Reagan administration, 78–79, 154, 204
real estate industry
    blogs and wikis, 88–92
    and homogenization of cities, 7,
        232–33, 242–43
    See also upscale growth; urban
        redevelopment
Record Shack, 69, 78, 83
redevelopment. See urban redevelopment
Red Hook
    community farm, 160, 208
    consumer culture's effect on, 189–90
    film depictions of, 253n.31
    gentrification of, 178, 184, 189, 191
    and globalization, 191
    industrial roots, 165, 168, 169, 191
    pool renovation, 173–74
    public housing, 165, 168, 253n.31

racial tensions, 174
soccer fields, 171, 174
waterfront, 160, 161, 164–65, 168–69, 174,
    189, 191
See also IKEA; Red Hook food vendors
Red Hook food vendors
    as authentic, 164, 165, 175, 176,
        181–83, 188
    blogs and wikis about, 162, 164, 170, 177,
        178, 180–82, 186–87, 188, 190
    competition, 179, 190
    customers (Anglo), 161, 163, 164, 177,
        178, 180–82, 188–89, 190
    customers (Latino), 179–80, 188
    early years, 170–72, 179
    families, 163, 172, 174, 175–76
    future plans, 191–92
    and gentrification, 188, 190, 191
    photo, 163
    licensing and permit requirements, 162,
        175, 176, 178, 183–88, 191, 245
    media coverage, 174–75, 176, 178,
        186, 188
    nationalities of, 161, 177, 179
    opening day, 162–63
    as soccer fans, 161, 170–72, 173, 179,
        180, 184
    stewardship by, 158
Red Hook Food Vendors Association,
    162, 182, 185–86
Reijndorp, Arnold, 142
rent control, 17, 99, 106, 113–14, 227, 245,
    262n.11
rents, 38, 239
    See also affordable housing
rent stabilization, 106, 254n.39, 262.11
retail entrepreneurs
    mom-and-pop stores, 9, 17, 69, 243,
        245–46
    in upscale growth, 7, 9, 19–20, 222
    See also chain stores; IKEA; specific
        neighborhoods
Reverend Billy, 141, 142
Rich, Matty, 165, 253n.31
Richmond, Fred, 200
Robinson, Jackie, 43, 60
Rockefeller, David, 150
Rockefeller, Nelson, 150

roots
  community gardens as expression of,
    197, 216
  role of origins in, 6, 14
  yearning for, 2, 216, 242
Rousseau, Jean-Jacques, 21, 217
Rubulad, 35–38, 60
Ruggles, Samuel Bulkley, 131–32

San Francisco, 15, 51, 53
Santé, Luc, 193, 199
Saturday Night Fever (film), 43
Schaefer brewery, 42, 59
Schoener, Allon, 72, 73
Schumer, Charles, 155, 162
Seattle, 51, 116
Sedaris, Amy, 242–43
September 11 terrorist attacks, 2001, 23,
    84, 147–49
  gatherings in Union Square after, 131,
    147–48
  See also World Trade Center site
Seriouseats.com, 162, 183
Settepani Bakery, 63–64, 64, 65, 66–67, 68
Settepani, Nino, 66
Shaft (film), 71–72
Shange, Sikhulu, 69, 78, 83, 93
Shanghai, 1, 239–42
She's Gotta Have It (film), 54, 57
Shopping
  malls, 128, 134
  See also chain stores; consumption;
    retail entrepreneurs
Siegler, Dan, 49
Silverstein, Larry, 150–51, 155
Simmel, Georg, 127, 212
Sklair, Leslie, 229
S. Klein (department store), 133, 136, 137
Smith, Betty, 40
Smith, Neil, 9
SoHo
  artists in, 16, 42, 45, 52, 200, 238
  cities emulating, 231
  as Destination Culture, 221, 229,
    238–39, 242
  gentrification of, 8
  and giant vinyl billboards, 215

highway proposal by Robert Moses, 14
historic preservation in, 12, 242
industrial roots, 42, 52, 115
loft living in, 12, 24, 42, 115, 200, 238
media coverage of, 5, 52, 238
photo, 238
retail stores, 114, 238–39
Williamsburg exhibition in, 48
SoHo Weekly News, 16, 100, 103
South Bronx, 42, 196, 199, 201, 219
Spiegel, Julius, 184
Spitzer, Eliot, 148, 156, 204–5
The Squid and the Whale (film), 41, 55
Starbucks, 4, 7, 19, 19, 19, 51, 80, 82, 96, 97,
    102, 116, 121, 131
Starr, Roger, 196
state power 10, 11, 13, 158
  in upscale growth, 2, 10, 37, 60, 66,
    227–28, 229, 243
  See also specific government agencies;
    Upper Manhattan Empowerment
    Zone
stewardship
  of public spaces, 158, 217, 246
  See also community gardens; Red
    Hook food vendors; Union
    Square
St. Marks Place, 99, 102, 105, 114, 116
Stone, Edie, 207, 218
Stoute, Steve, 85, 86
Straight Out of Brooklyn (film), 165, 253n.31
street vendors
  on 125th Street, 77, 79, 83
  opposition to, 79, 190–91, 272n.28
  Vendy Award, 179, 190
  See also Red Hook food vendors
Studio Museum, 75
suburbs, 5, 16, 37, 90–91, 92, 116, 134, 219
Sunset Park, 164, 173, 272n.28
super-gentrification, 9, 23
sustainability
  of community gardens, 210, 217–18
  as development model, 197, 207, 210,
    217, 218
  of urban villages, 218, 243–46
sweat equity, 201, 216
Sydney, Australia, 231, 234
Sylvia's (restaurant), 65, 77

Tait, Malcolm, 233
Tammany Hall, 131, 213
terroir
  for artists, 100, 236–37
  community gardens as, 197, 207–8, 210
  defined, 4, 216, 247n.4
  East Village as, 100
  of ghetto, 70
  new urban, 4, 236–37
  Williamsburg as, 38
Thurber, James, 133
Time, 3
TimeOut New York, 226, 244
Times Square, 4, 5, 130, 132, 213–15
Todd Shipyards, 173
Tompkins Square Park, 98, 100–101, 104,
    107–8, 121, 145, 202
Townsend, Alair A., 42
A Tree Grows in Brooklyn, 40, 55
Trust for Public Land, 205
Tubman, Nyema, 85

Ukrainian immigrants, 98, 110
UMEZ. *See* Upper Manhattan
    Empowerment Zone
Uniform Land Use Review Procedure
    (ULURP), 203, 269n.8
Union Square Café, 138, 141
Union Square Local Development
    Corporation, 127, 131, 263n.1
  See also Union Square Partnership
Union Square neighborhood, 116, 121,
    132–39
Union Square Park
  after September 11 attacks, 131, 147–48
  authenticity of, 122, 130–31, 147–48
  behavior control in, 139, 142–43, 146
  crime in, 134–35
  description, 125–27
  drugs in, 130, 135–36
  Greenmarket in, 116, 117–18, 119, 121,
    128, 135–36, 138, 139, 140, 141, 211
  history of, 131–33, 134–42
  pavilion dispute, 139–41
  photos, *126, 130*
  privatization of, 122, 127, 141–42
  protests, 131, 132, 141–42

redevelopment, 137–39
  See also Union Square neighborhood;
    Union Square Partnership
Union Square Partnership, 117, 125, 127,
    128, 135–42, 144, 147, 263n.1
  See also Union Square Park
United House of Prayer for All, 78, 83
Upper Manhattan Empowerment Zone
    (UMEZ), 66, 77, 79, 80, 81–82, 84,
    85, 86, 87
upscale growth
  consumer tastes in, 2, 4, 5, 60, 88,
    229–31, 242–43
  displacing effects of, 243–44
  economic capital in, 2, 17, 18, 23, 25, 37,
    59–60, 66, 87, 88, 229, 243
  media power in, 2, 60, 66, 87, 88,
    228–29
  origins vs. new beginnings in, 2, 4, 8–9,
    18, 222, 223, 226, 230, 234–35, 246
  process of, 2, 4, 8–11
  state power in, 2, 10, 37, 60, 66, 227–28,
    229, 243
  See also gentrification; retail
    entrepreneurs
urban redevelopment, 10–18, 222, 242–43
  See also upscale growth; *specific*
    neighborhoods
urban *terroir. See terroir*
The Urban Villagers (Gans), 22–23
urban village
  coining of phrase, 11, 277n.5
  vs. corporate city, 222–23
  gentrification of, 4, 7, 230, 243–44
  industrial roots of, 222, 223
  and Jane Jacobs, 225, 230, 243
  loss of affordable housing in, 227,
    243–44, 245, 246
  media images of, 223–24
  photo, *2*
  postwar decline of, 223, 225, 226–27
  postwar redevelopment of, 224–27,
    243–45
  Red Hook food vendors as, 191–92
  social relationships in, 11, 224, 226–27
  See also authenticity; Brooklyn; East
    Village; North End; West End;
    Williamsburg